MW01625646

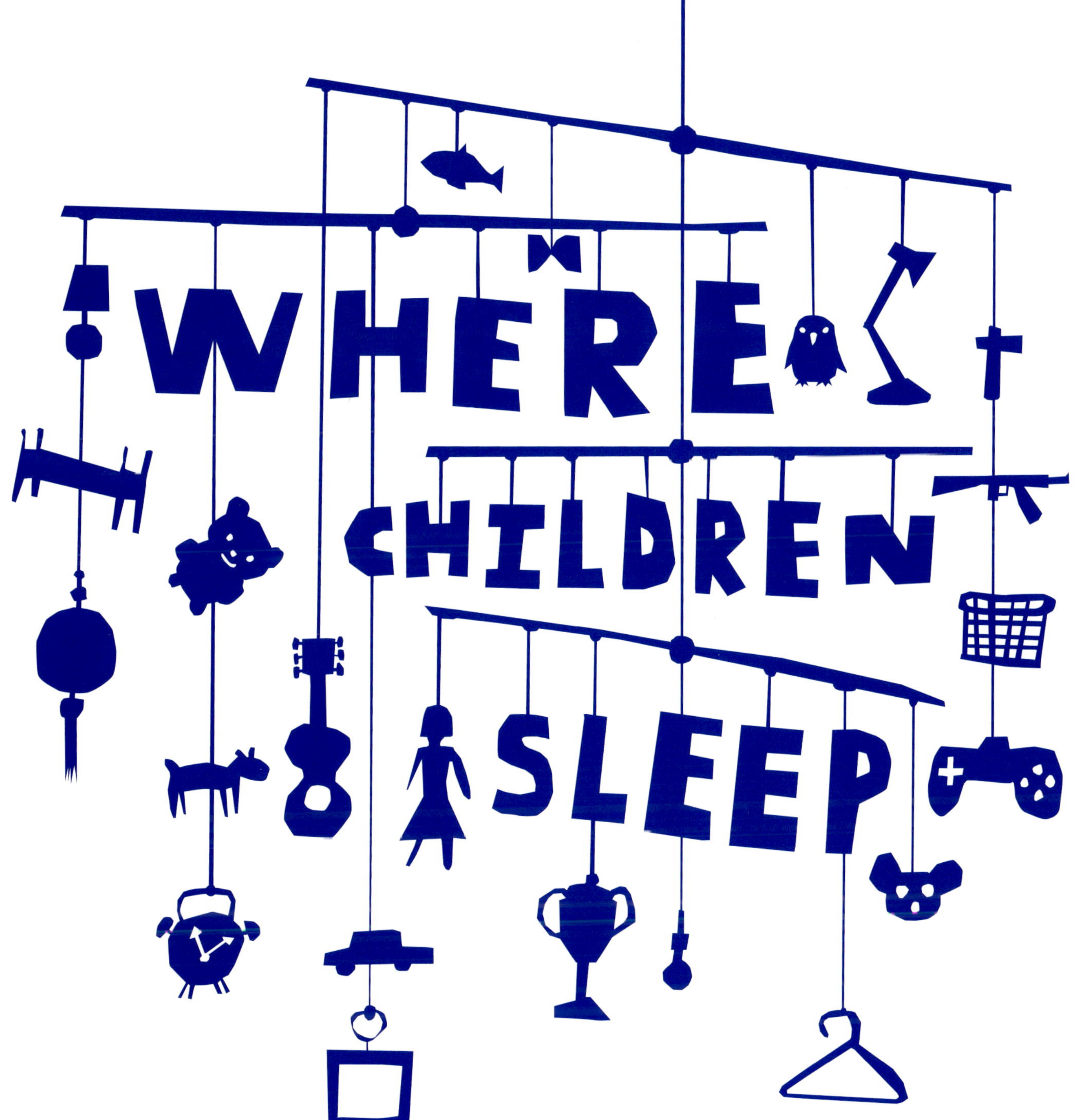
WHERE
CHILDREN
SLEEP

Where Children Sleep
by James Mollison

First published 2010
by Chris Boot

Chris Boot Ltd
79 Arbuthnot Road
London SE14 5NP
United Kingdom
Tel +44 (0)20 7639 2908
info@chrisboot.com
www.chrisboot.com

Interviews & photography production: Amber Mollison
Cover design, drawings & map: Patrick Waterhouse (Fabrica)
Graphic design: Walter Hutton & Guillermo Brotons (Fabrica)
Retouching: Valerio Fanfoni & Andrea Lecardi, ABC Srl, Milan
Text editing: Margaret Anderson & Katie Boot
Project manager: Maxwell Anderson

Distribution (except USA & Canada) by
Thames & Hudson Ltd
181 High Holborn
London WC1V 7QX
Tel +44 (0)20 7845 5000

Distribution in USA & Canada by
D.A.P./Distributed Art Publishers
155 Sixth Avenue, 2nd Floor
New York
NY 10013
Tel +1 212 627 1999

A CIP catalogue record for this book is available from the British Library.

ISBN 978-1-905712-16-8

Printed and bound in China

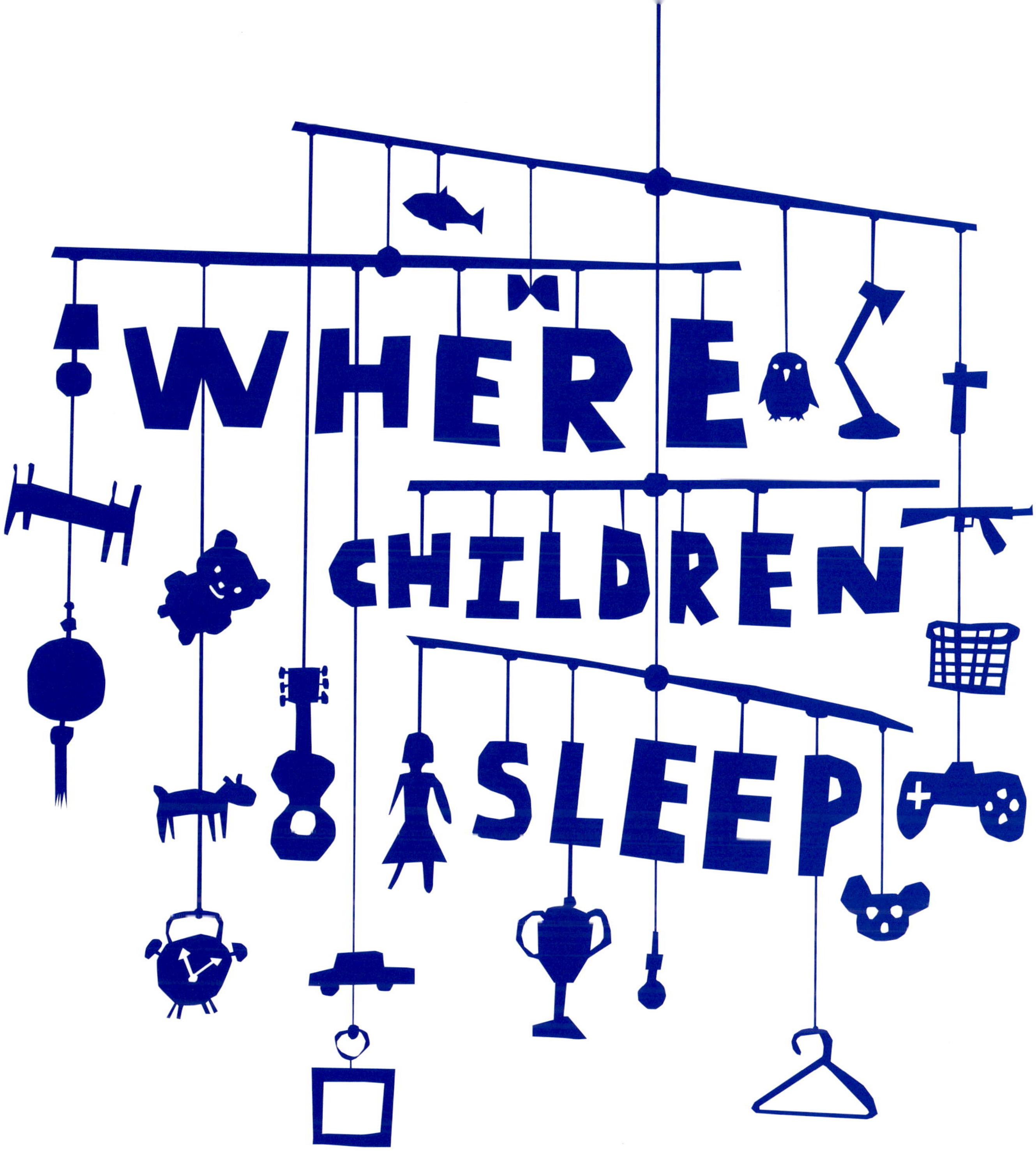

WHERE CHILDREN SLEEP

JAMES MOLLISON

INTRODUCTION

The bedroom of my childhood memories is a small room with sloping eaves in the attic of the family home, a tall semi-detached house in Oxford. It's where I slept between the ages of five and nineteen. First decorated with wooden animals from Kenya (where I was born) and a teddy bear made by Mum, I progressively made the room my own, its changing contents reflecting my identity, interests and aspirations as they evolved through childhood. Important characters in its history included some Action Man figures I bought in a jumble sale (ten pence each, I remember), a Batman car begged from a visiting friend of my parents, and Mumsie and Diddle-Dash, two mice for whom I built a multistorey play area from wooden fruit boxes. Aged nine, I was given responsibility for choosing a new carpet. I chose one in bright red nylon with dominant black and white stripes, which I was very proud of at the time but found highly embarrassing as a style-conscious teenager. When I reached ten, obsessed with Top of the Pops, I used the pages of Smash Hits magazine to decorate the room, one wall initially dedicated to Duran Duran and another to Madonna. These were in turn replaced with army posters, then surfer posters, then Jimi Hendrix and The Rolling Stones, and finally – before I moved out to go to college – posters from the rave scene. My bedroom was my personal kingdom.

When, in 2004, Fabrica (Benetton's creative research centre) asked me to come up with an idea for engaging with children's rights, I found myself thinking about my bedroom: how significant it was during my childhood, and how it reflected what I had and who I was. It occurred to me that a way to address some of the complex situations and social issues affecting children would be to look at the bedrooms of children in all kinds of different circumstances. From the start, I didn't want it just to be about 'needy children' in the developing world, but rather something more inclusive, about children from all types of situations. It seemed to make sense to photograph the children themselves, too, but separately from their bedrooms, using a neutral background.

My thinking was that the bedroom pictures would be inscribed with the children's material and cultural circumstances – the details that inevitably mark people apart from each other – while the children themselves would appear in the set of portraits as individuals, as equals ... just as children.

To begin with, I called the project 'Bedrooms', but I soon realized that my own experience of having a 'bedroom' simply doesn't apply to so many kids. Millions of families around the world sleep together in one room, and millions of children sleep in a space of convenience, rather than a place they can in any sense call their room. I came to appreciate just how privileged I am to have had a personal kingdom to sleep in and grow.

For me, the project became a vehicle to think about issues of poverty and wealth, about the relationship of children to personal possessions, and the power of children – or lack of it – to make decisions about their lives. But this book is not a campaign. There's nothing scientific about the selection of children featured: I travelled where I could, often alongside other projects, and many of the pictures result from chance encounters, following my photographer's nose. I am not qualified to give anyone a lecture on the state of childhood today, or the future of children's rights. Although I have relied on the help of Save the Children, Italy, there is no agenda to the book other than my own journey and curiosity, and wanting to share in pictures and words the stories that I found interesting, or that moved me.

In the end, I hope the pictures and the stories in this book speak to children. Yes, so that lucky children (like I was) may better appreciate what they have. But more than that, I hope this book will help children think about inequality, within and between societies around the world, and perhaps start to figure out how, in their own lives, they may respond.

James Mollison
Venice, May 2010

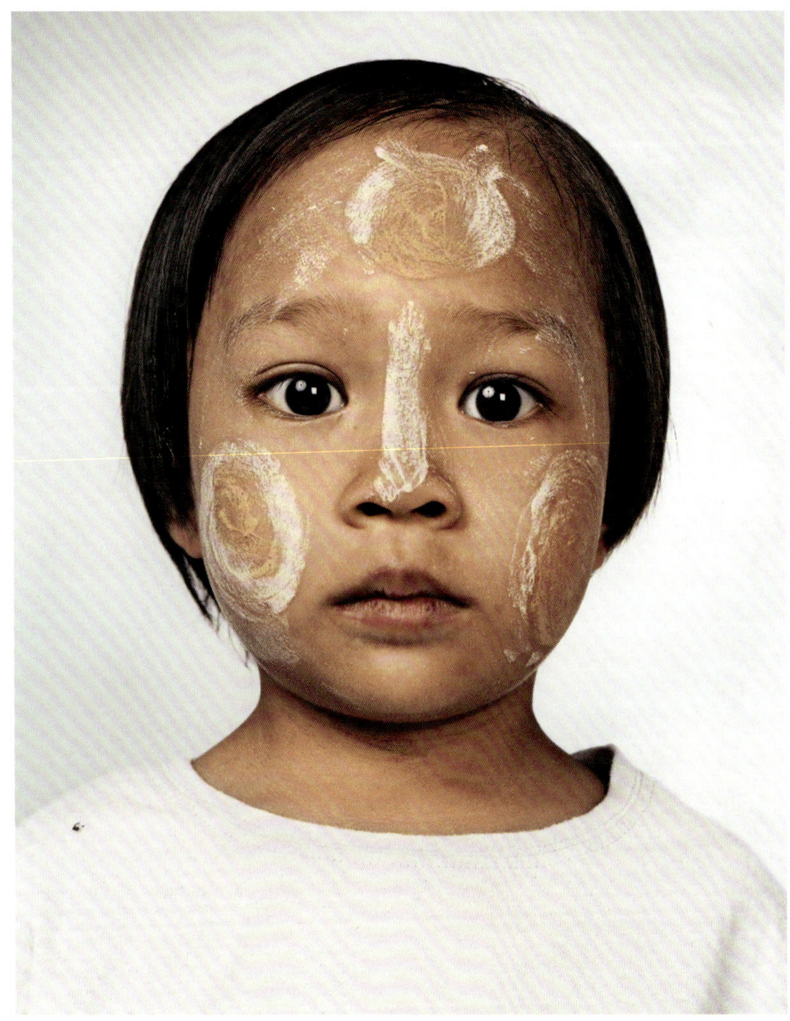

Lay Lay is four years old. The cream she has on her face is made from the bark of the thanaka tree, used to condition and protect the skin. Lay Lay lives in Mae Sot, Thailand, close to the border with Burma. When her mother died, no other members of her family came to claim her, so she was placed in an orphanage. She shares this home with twenty-one other nursery-aged children. The orphanage consists of two rooms. During the day, one room is the classroom and the other is a dining room. At night, these rooms become bedrooms. The tables are pushed to one side and mats are rolled out for the children to sleep on. Each child has one drawer in which to keep their belongings. Lay Lay does not have many belongings - just a few clothes. All that is known of her background is that she is from an ethnic group of people called the Karen, one of the persecuted minority ethnic groups which make up about forty per cent of the Burmese population. Lay Lay and her mother fled from the brutal Burmese military dictatorship and arrived in Thailand as refugees.

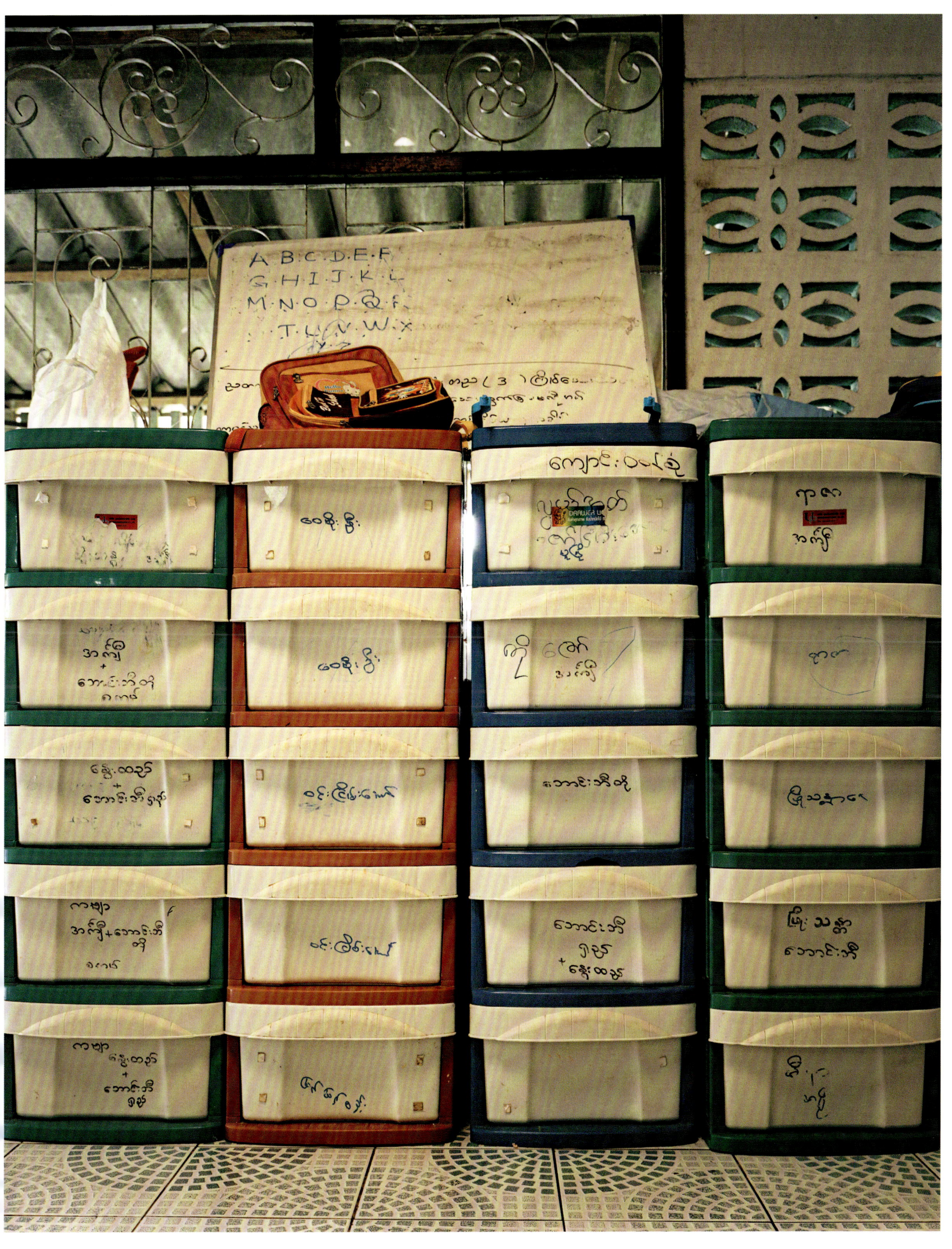
A B C D E F
G H I J K L

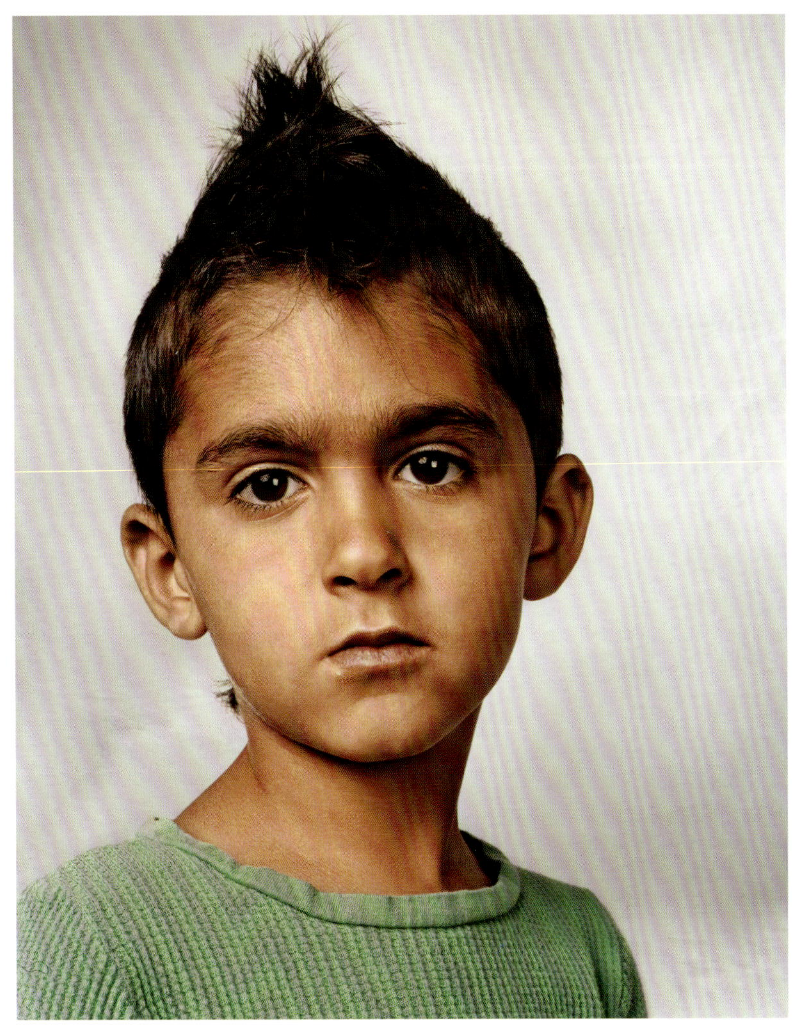

Jivan is four years old. He lives with his parents in a skyscraper in Brooklyn, New York. From his bedroom window, he can see across the East River to New York's Manhattan Island and the Williamsburg Suspension Bridge which connects it to Brooklyn. Jivan has his own bedroom with an en-suite bathroom and a toy cupboard. The room was designed by Jivan's mother, who is an interior designer. His father is a DJ and music producer. Jivan's school is only ten minutes' walk away. To gain a place at this school, Jivan had to take a test to prove that he can mix socially with other children. He found this quite stressful as he is a very shy boy. His parents were also interviewed before he was accepted by the school. Jivan's favourite foods are steak and chocolate. He would like to be a fireman when he grows up.

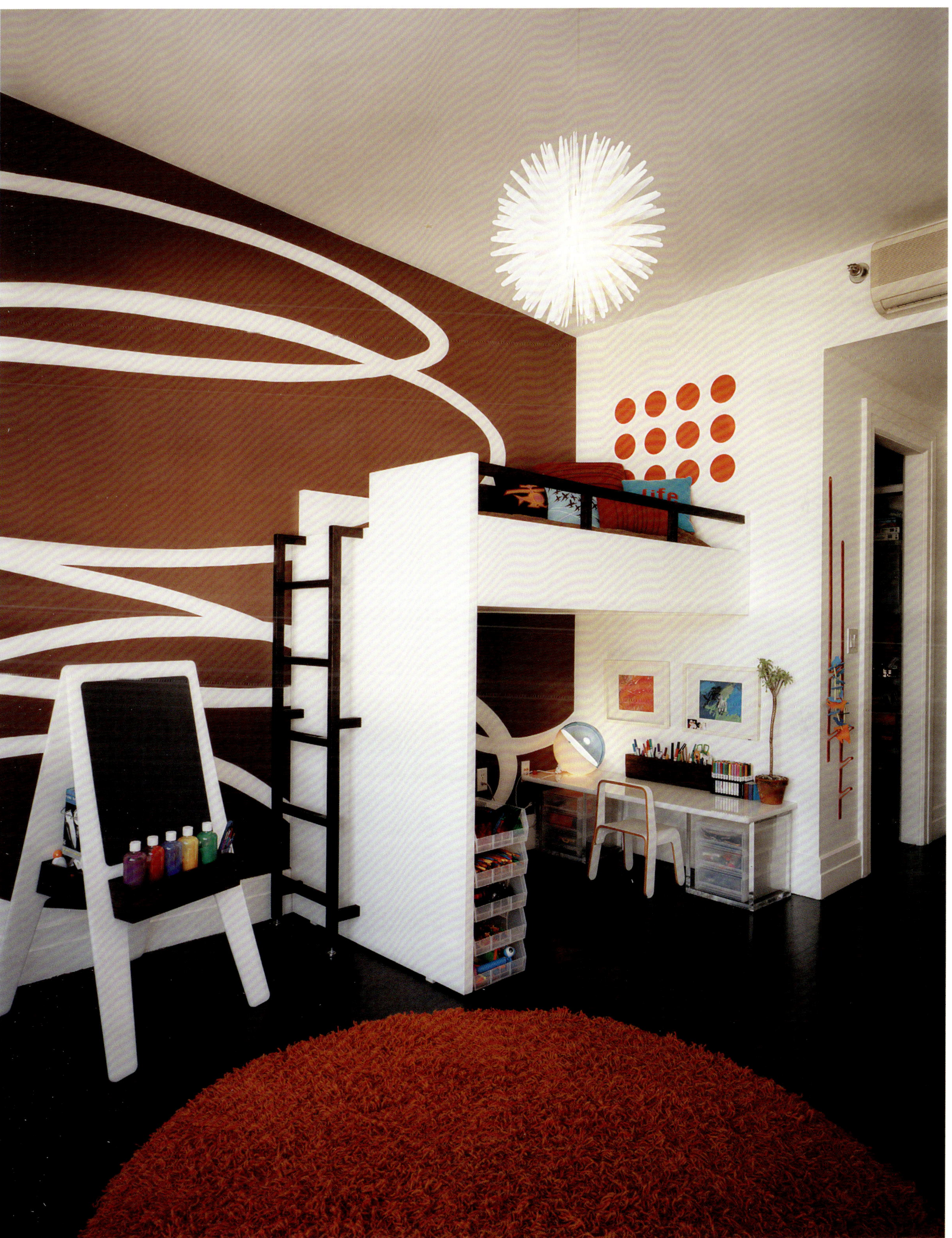
Life

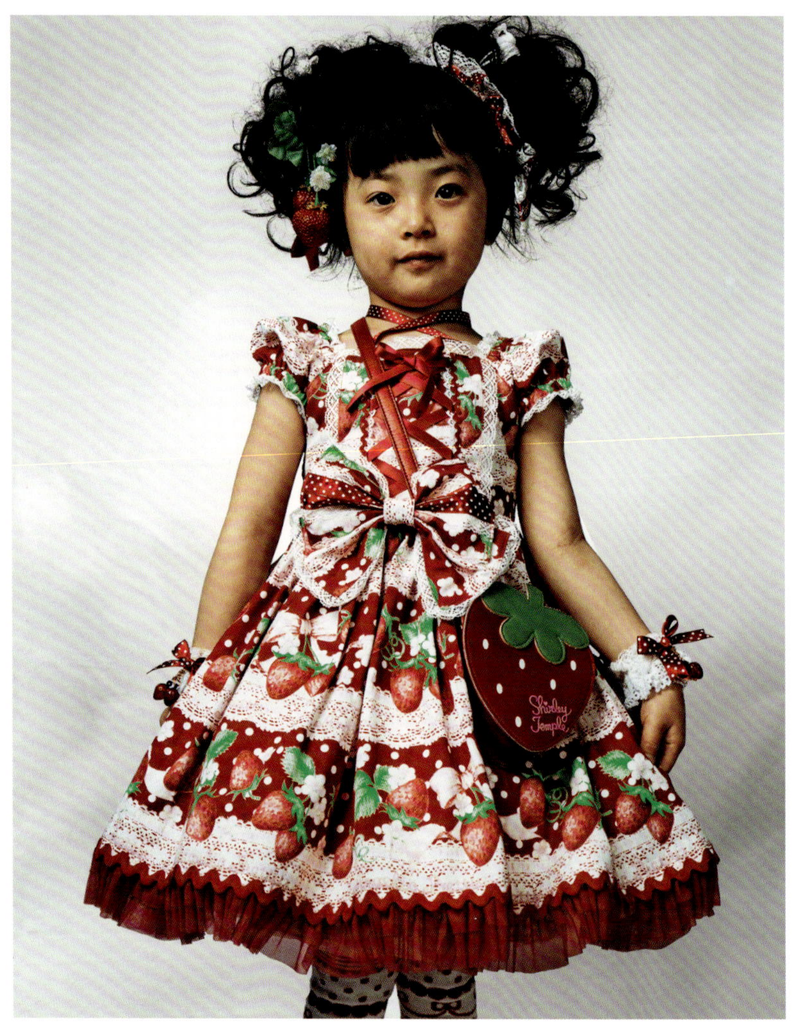

Kaya is four years old. She lives with her parents in a small apartment in Tokyo, Japan. Most apartments in Japan are small because land is very expensive to buy and there is such a large population to accommodate. Kaya's bedroom is every little girl's dream. It is lined from floor to ceiling with clothes and dolls. Kaya's mother makes all Kaya's dresses – up to three a month, usually. Now Kaya has thirty dresses and coats, thirty pairs of shoes, sandals and boots, and numerous wigs. (The pigtails in the picture are made from hairpieces.) Her friends love to come round to try on her clothes. When she goes to school, however, she has to wear a school uniform. Her favourite foods are meat, potatoes, strawberries and peaches. She wants to be a cartoonist when she grows up, drawing Japanese 'anime' cartoons.

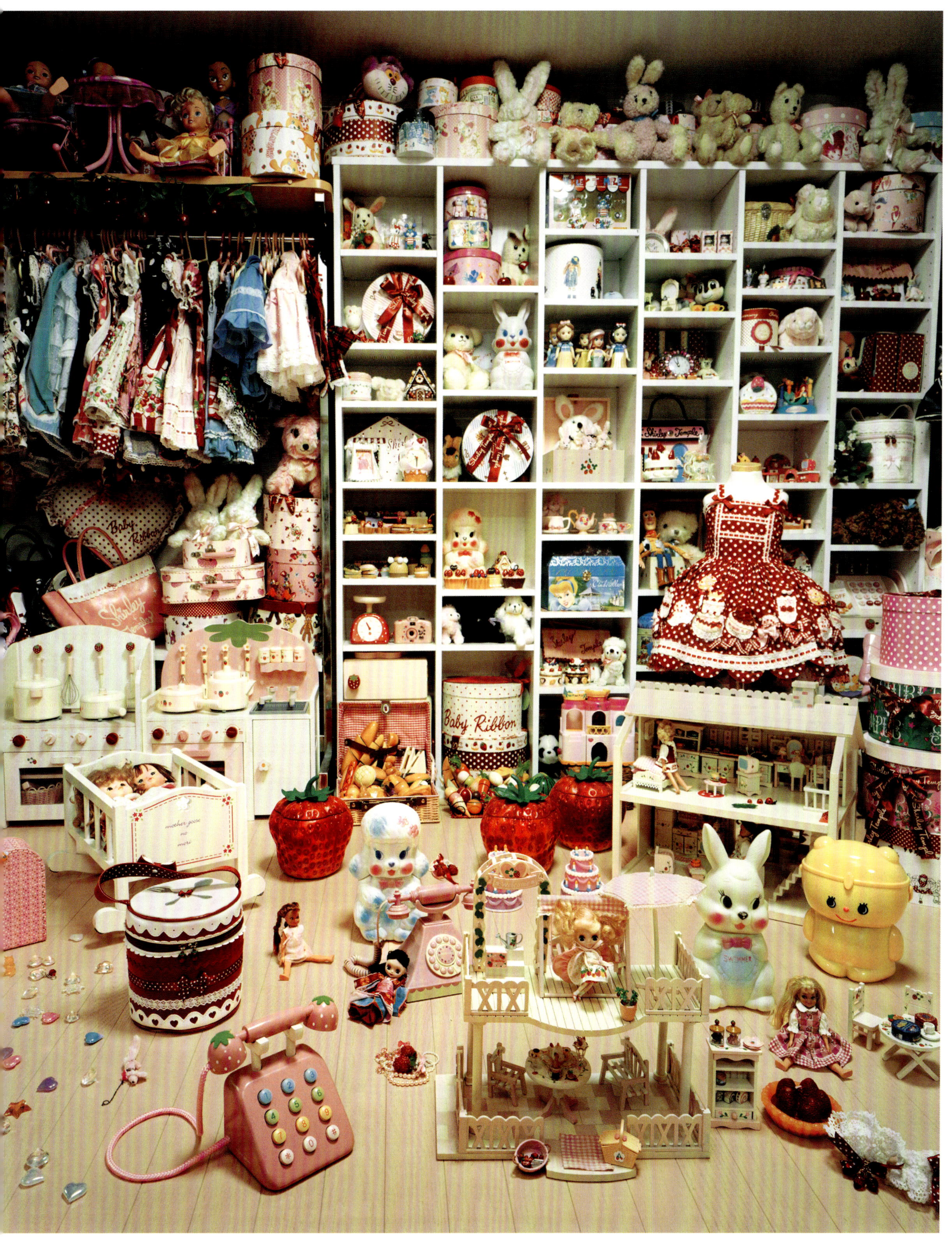
Baby Ribbon
Shirley Temple

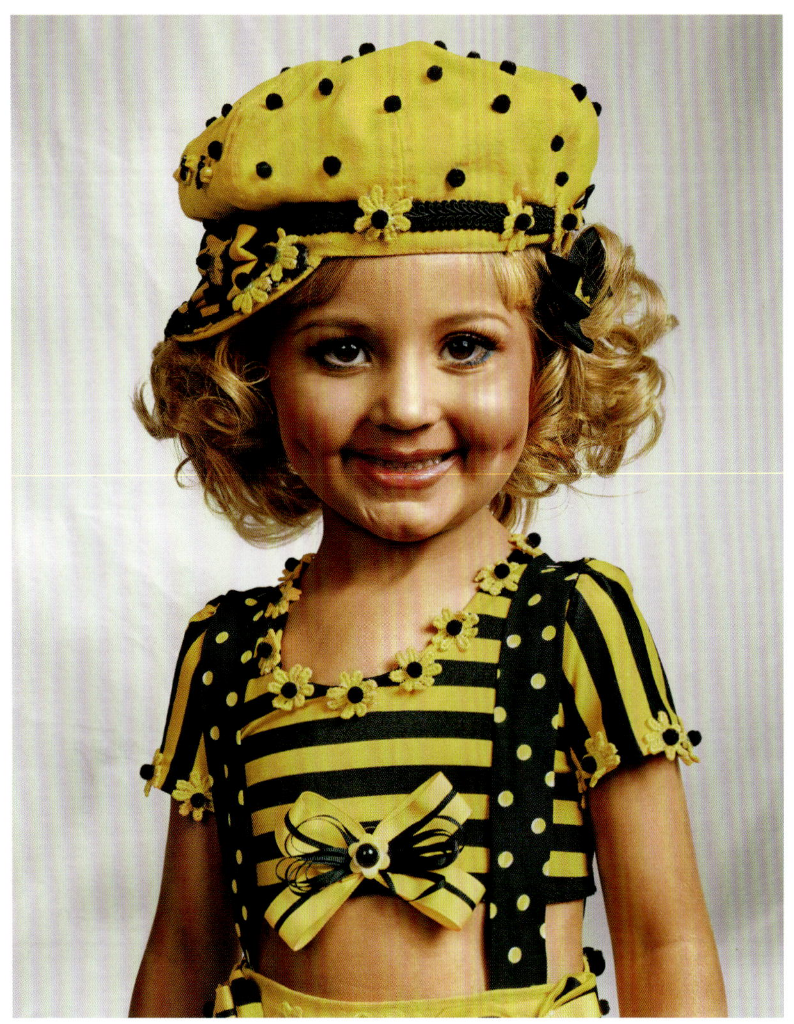

Jasmine prefers to be called by her nickname, Jazzy. She lives in a big house in Kentucky, USA, with her parents and three brothers. Her house is in the countryside, surrounded by farmland. Her bedroom is full of crowns and sashes which she has won in 'child pageants'. She is only four years old and has already entered over a hundred of these competitions. Her spare time is completely taken up with preparation and rehearsal. She practises her stage routines every day with a trainer who teaches her new steps. Each weekend, she participates in a different pageant, arriving on Friday afternoon, performing on Saturday, and attending the crowning ceremony on Sunday. By the end of the show, she is quite exhausted. Jazzy enjoys being pampered and treated like a princess – having her hair done and wearing pretty clothes and make-up, with false nails and a fake tan. It is a very expensive hobby and can cost her parents a thousand dollars for each pageant she takes part in. Jazzy would like to be a rock star when she grows up.

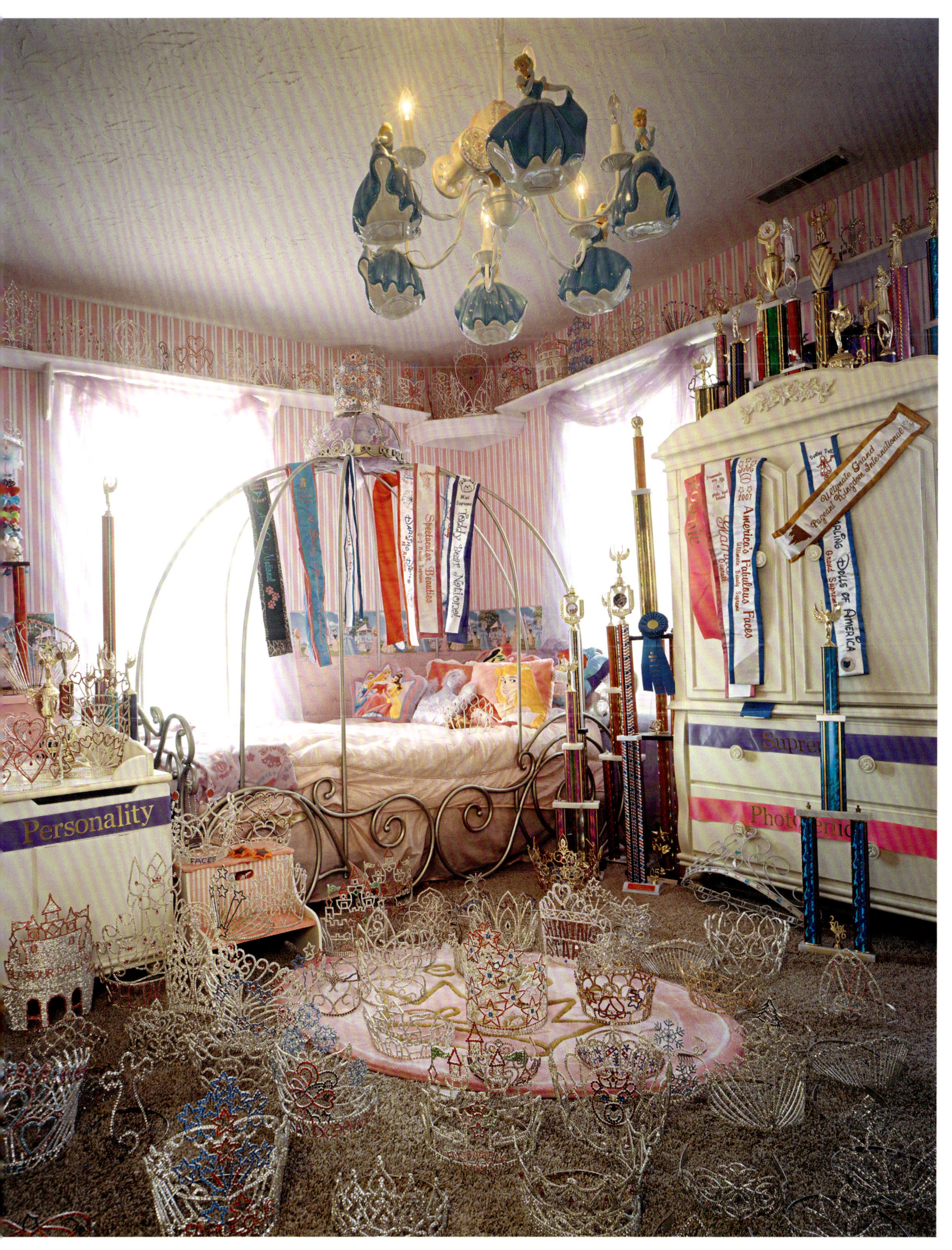

Personality
America's Fabulous Faces
2007
Spectacular Beauties
Teddy Bear National
Ultimate Grand
Pageant Kingdom International
Dolls of America

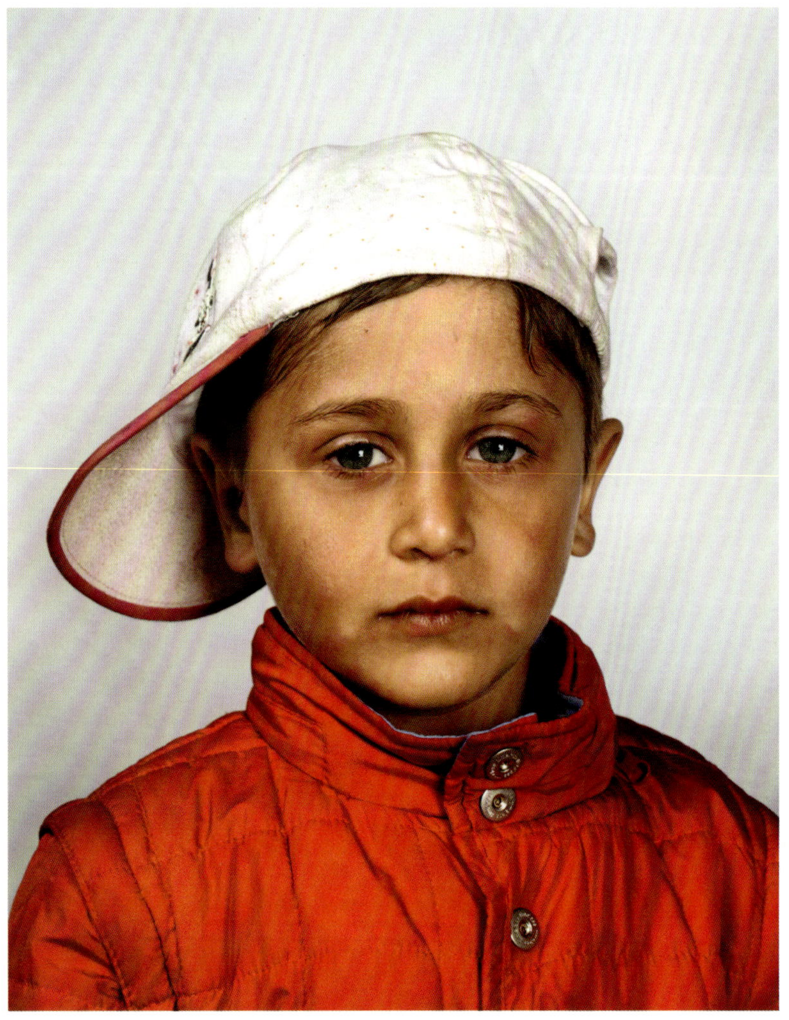

Home for this four-year-old boy and his family is a mattress in a field on the outskirts of Rome, Italy. The family came from Romania by bus, after begging on the streets for enough money to pay for their tickets (€100 per adult and €80 per child). When they first arrived in Rome, they camped in a tent, but the police threw them off the site because they were trespassing on private land and did not have the correct documents. Now the family sleep together on the mattress in the open. When it rains, they hastily erect a tent and use umbrellas for shelter, hoping they will not be spotted by the police. They left Romania without identity documents or work papers and so are unable to obtain legal employment. This boy sits by the kerbside while his parents clean car windscreens at traffic lights, to earn thirty to fifty cents a time. No one from the boy's family has ever been to school. His parents cannot read or write.

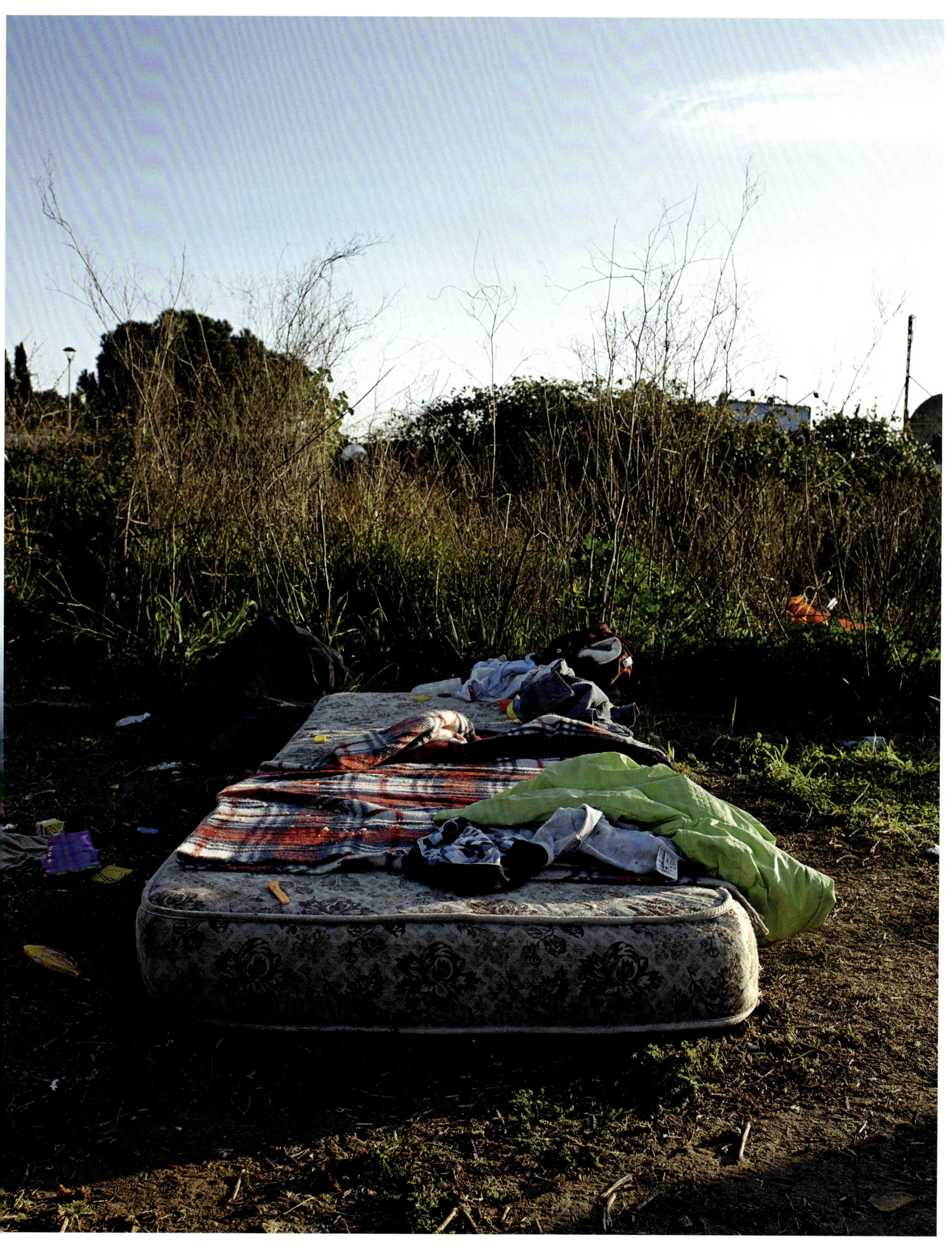

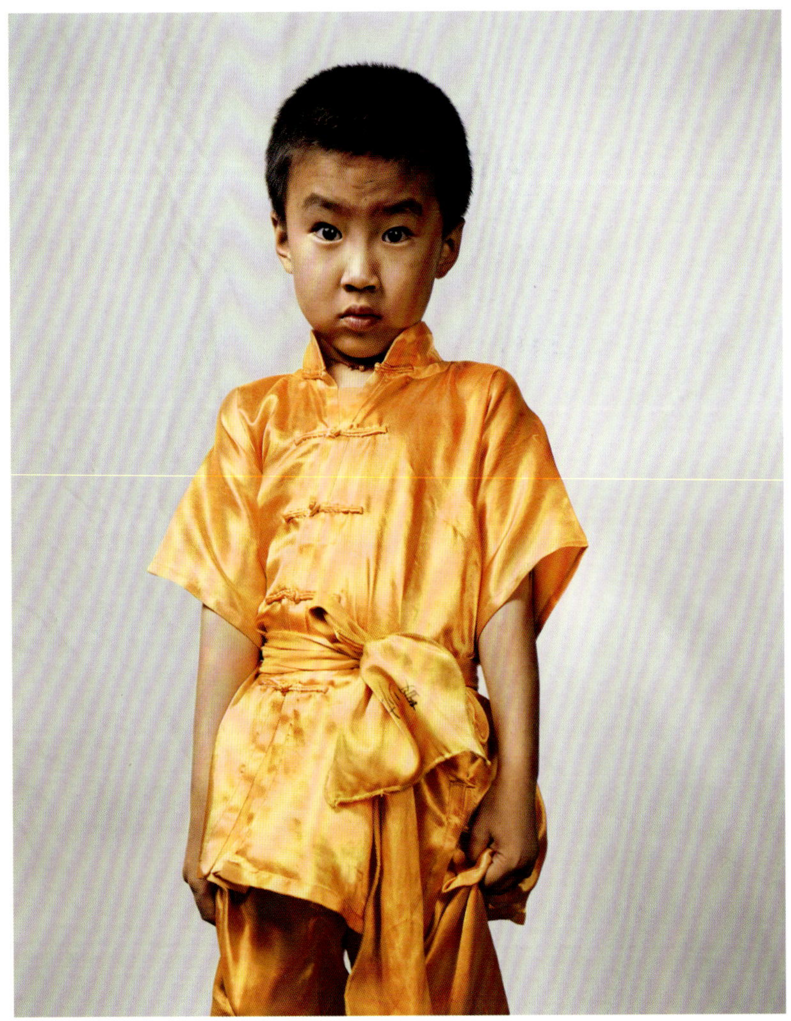

Hang is five years old. He attends a boarding school in Beijing, China, and shares a dormitory with twenty other children. He does not see his parents very often. Hang's school specializes in teaching the Shaolin form of martial arts, which involves fighting bare-handed or using swords, wooden poles, a cutlass or a 'sai' (a three-pronged spear). Some parents send their children to martial arts schools to toughen them up. When Hang first arrived at the school, he was very scared and cried a lot. He had to get used to waking up at 5.40 am every day, running six laps of the field, followed by some basic kung fu practice before breakfast. After breakfast, Hang has to attend four lessons – Chinese, maths, art and English. For four hours every afternoon, he is taught martial art skills. Many of the children go on to join the police force or the armed forces. Some become stuntmen. Hang would like to be a scientist or a car designer when he is older.

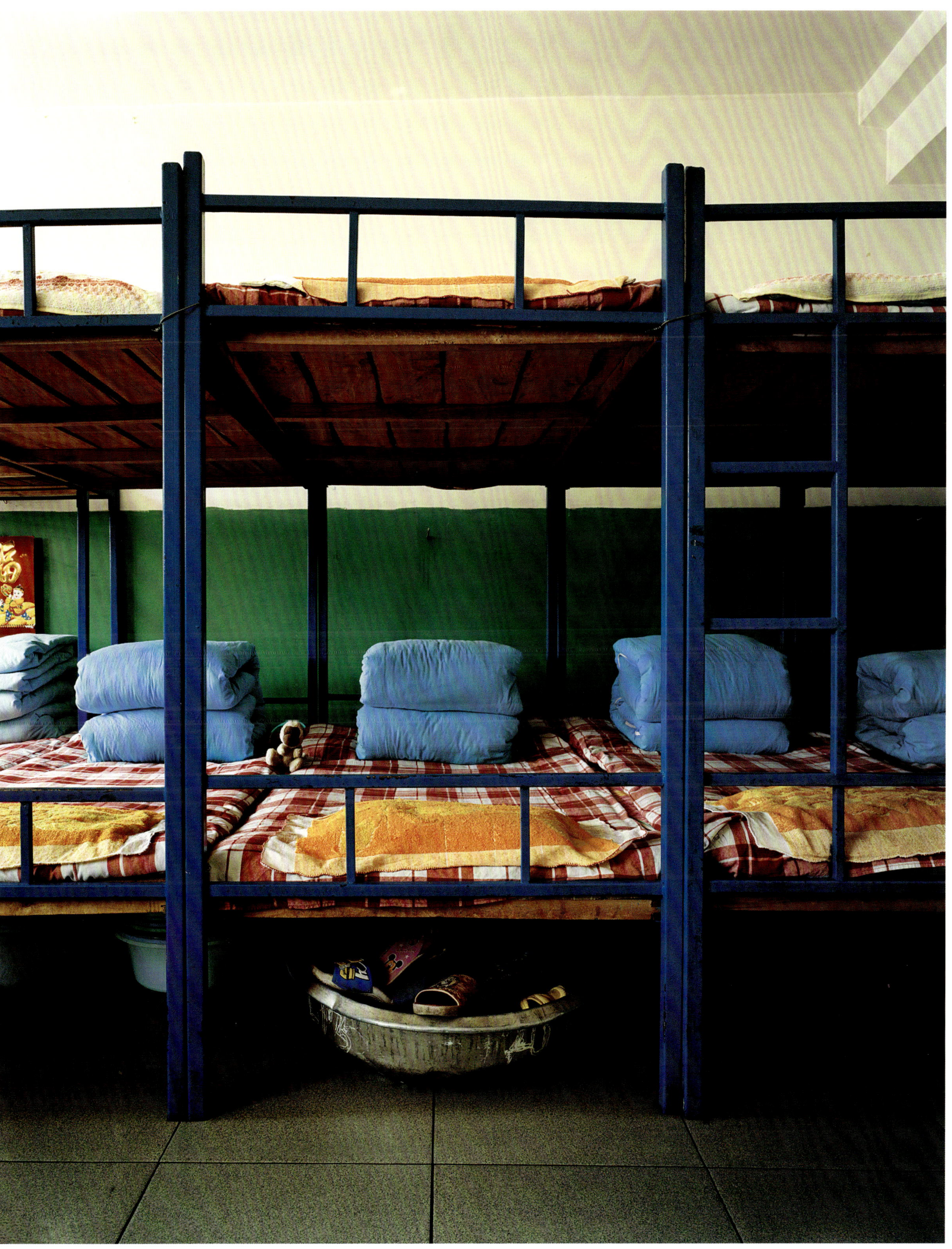

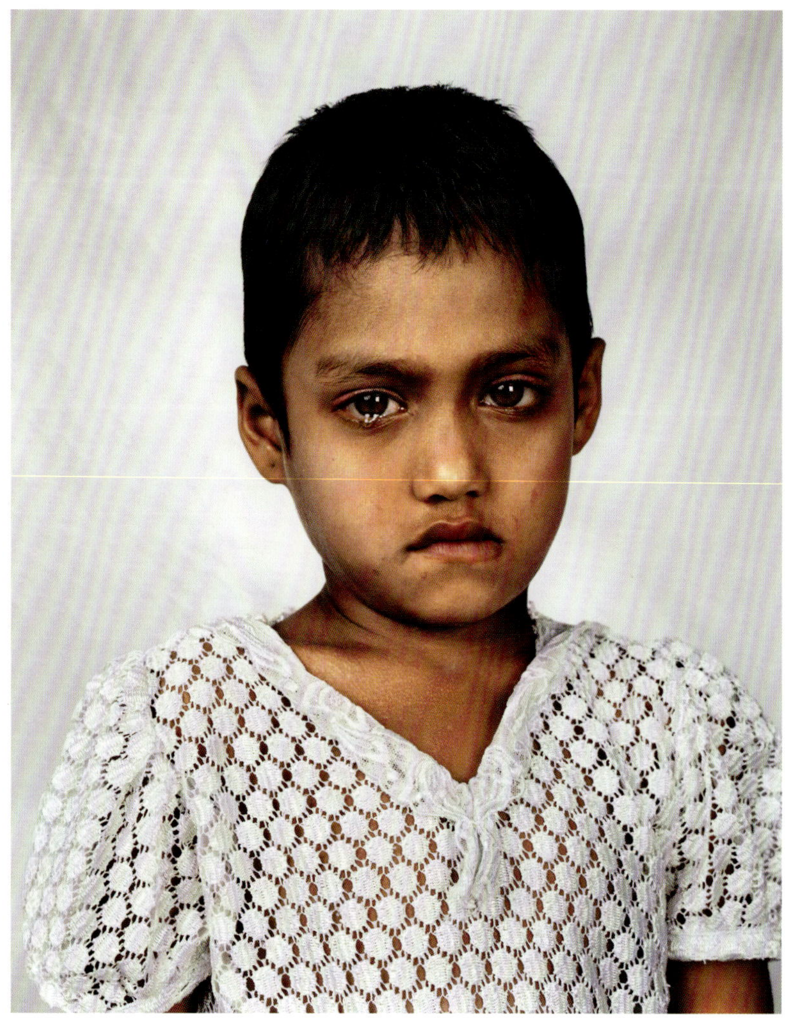

Five-year-old Shameela lives in Mae Sot, Thailand, with her mother and three older siblings. Their home is a leaky one-roomed shack built alongside other huts in the middle of a swamp in the jungle. They share a toilet with about one hundred other people in the village. Shameela's mother fled to Thailand from Burma to escape the harsh military regime. She cannot get a permit to work so she does any odd jobs she can to support her family. They cannot afford to eat meat but have fish twice a week. Shameela was born in Thailand but as the daughter of an asylum seeker, she is not considered to be a Thai citizen. Nor is she considered to be a Burmese citizen as she was not born in Burma. Children like Shameela are therefore stateless, with no official nationality. She is the only one in her family to go to school. She would like to be a nurse when she grows up.

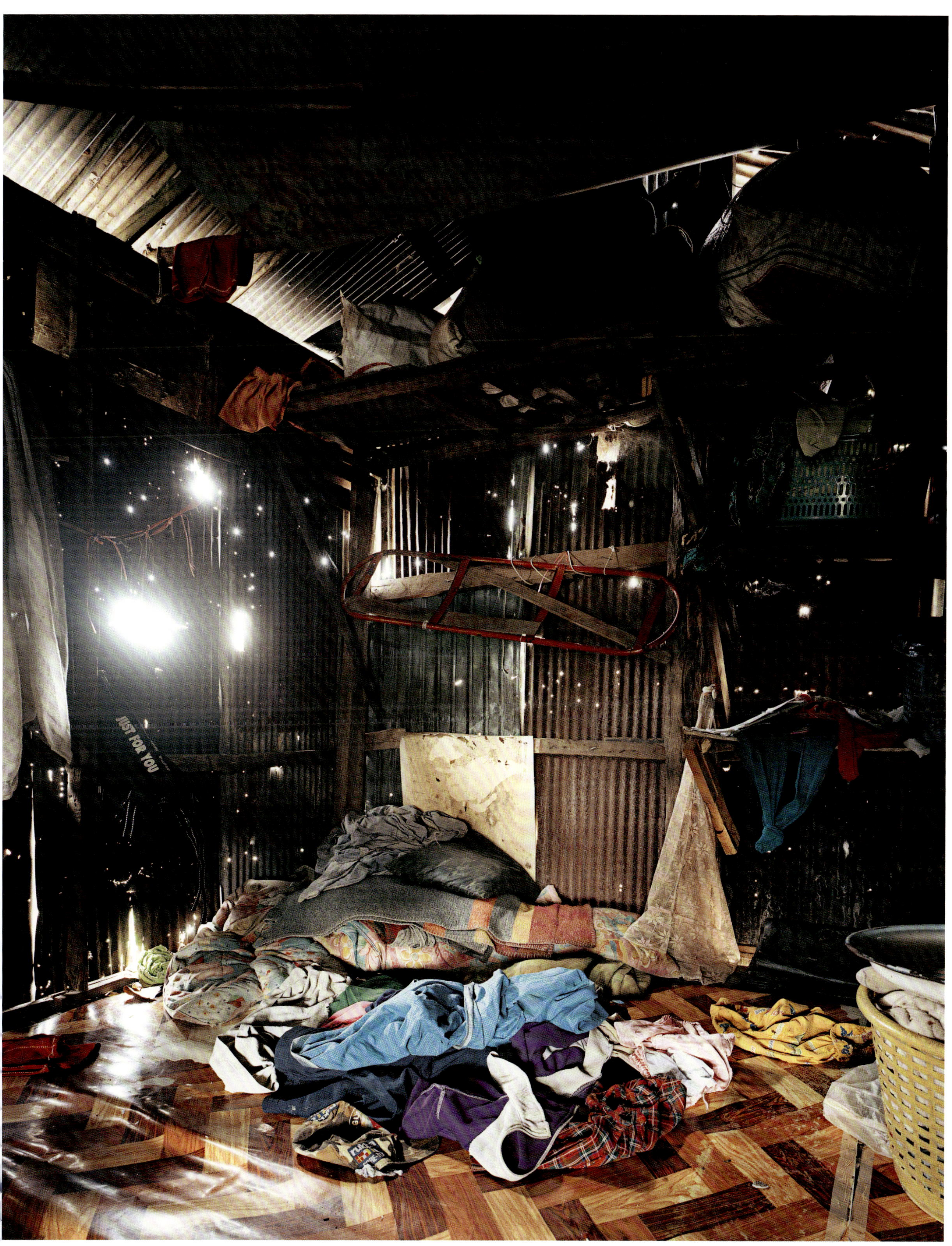
JUST FOR YOU

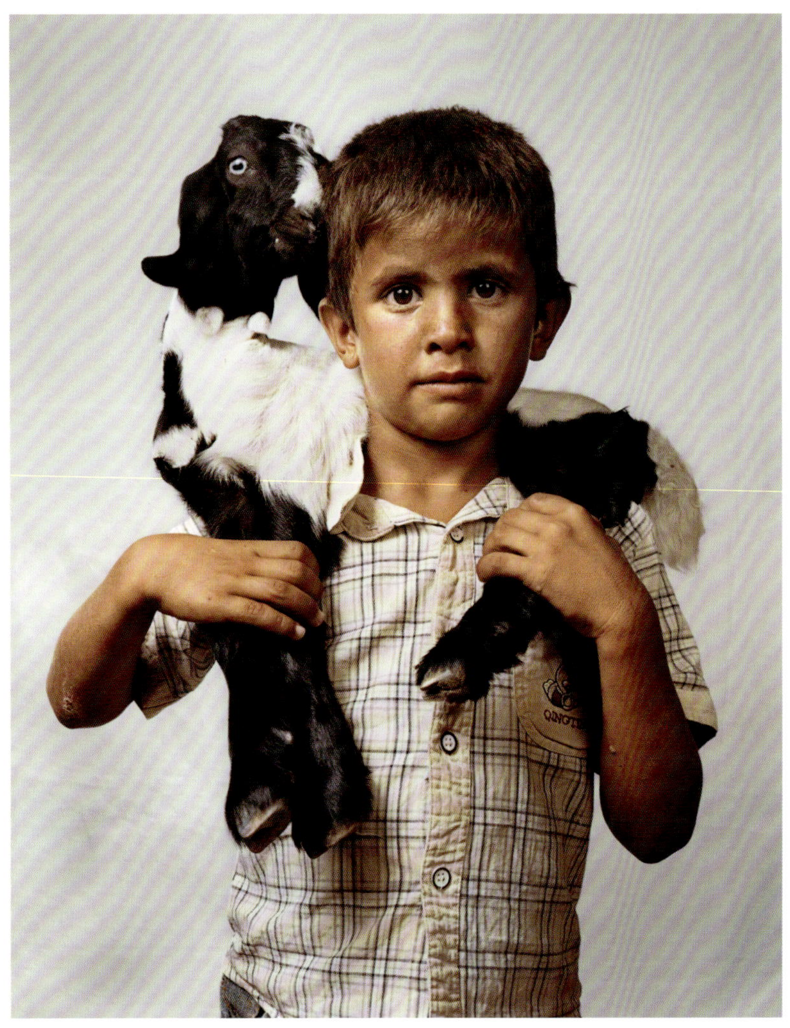

Bilal is six years old. His family are Bedouin Arabs living beside an Israeli settlement at Wadi Abu Hindi, in the West Bank. Their home is a one-roomed shack which they built themselves. The government of Israel has control in this area and has already knocked down their first home because they did not have permission to build it. They are fearful that this will happen to their new home. During the summer, the family sleep outside on a carpet but in winter they sleep inside. Traditionally, the Bedouin people are nomads, but many have been forced to settle because Israeli restrictions prevent their nomadic travels. Their diet consists mostly of rice and yoghurt. Bilal's family own fifteen goats, whose milk is used to make the yoghurt. Once a week they might also eat meat with their rice. Water is delivered in a water truck from which they are allowed to take two litres a day. Bilal does not go to school yet, but helps to look after the goats.

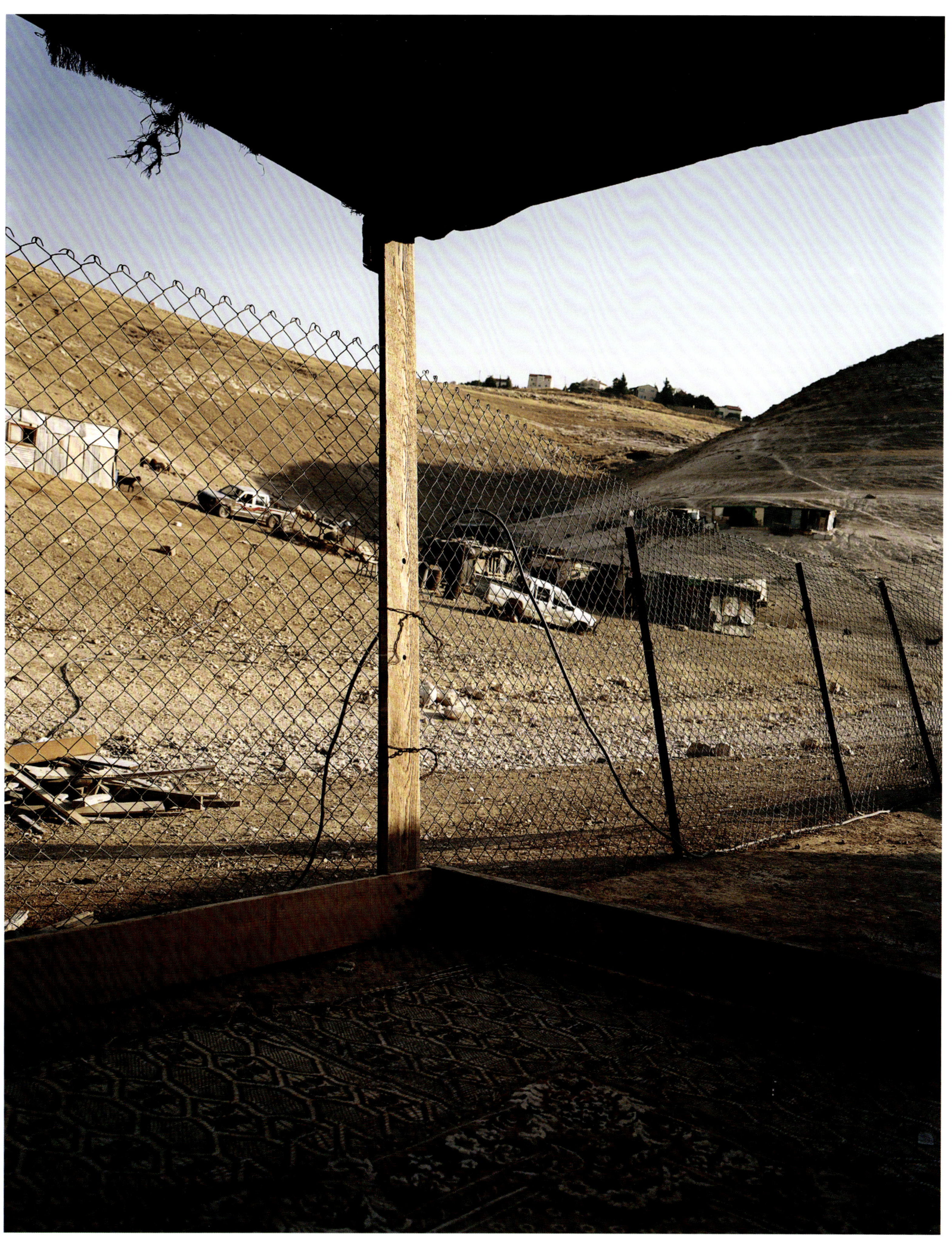

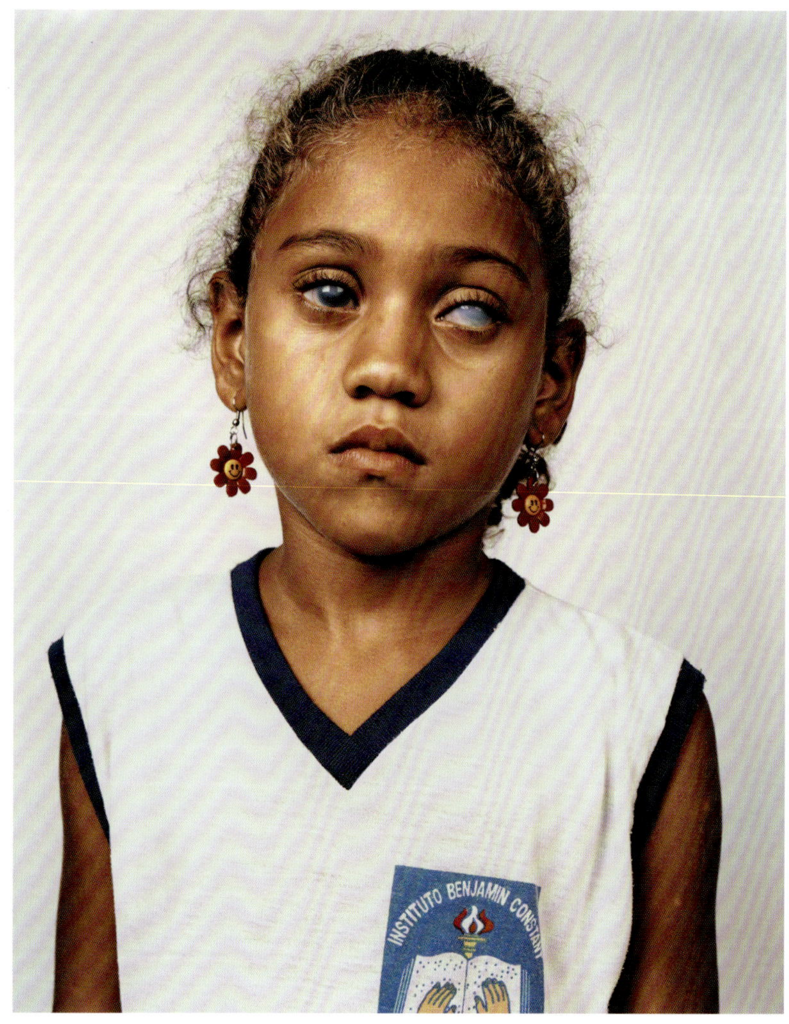

Camila is six years old. She lives in Rochina, the largest shanty town, or 'favela', in Brazil. Her home is a one-roomed shack which doubles as a kitchen and living room by day and a bedroom by night. The sofa becomes Camila's bed. She is totally blind, and only just able to tell the difference between light and dark. She attends a school in Rio de Janeiro for visually impaired children, where she is learning Braille. The bus journey to the school takes one hour each way. Camila's blindness makes her quite vulnerable in the dangerous neighbourhood where she lives. However, she does not complain, and feels that most people treat her kindly, helping her get around when she needs to. Her favourite hobby is playing drums in a band which specializes in a Brazilian samba-style music called 'pagode'. When she grows up, Camila would like to teach computing.

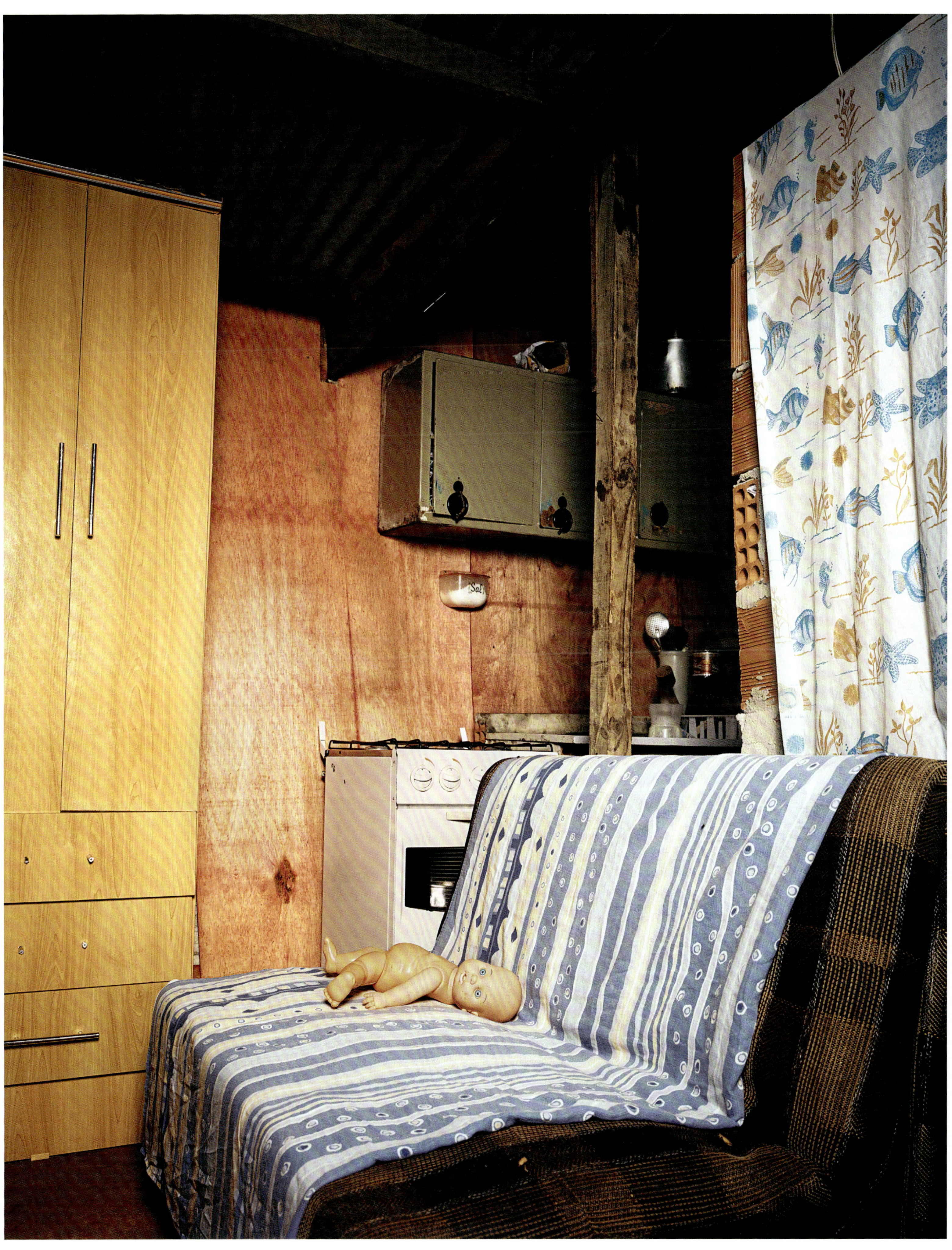
Sal

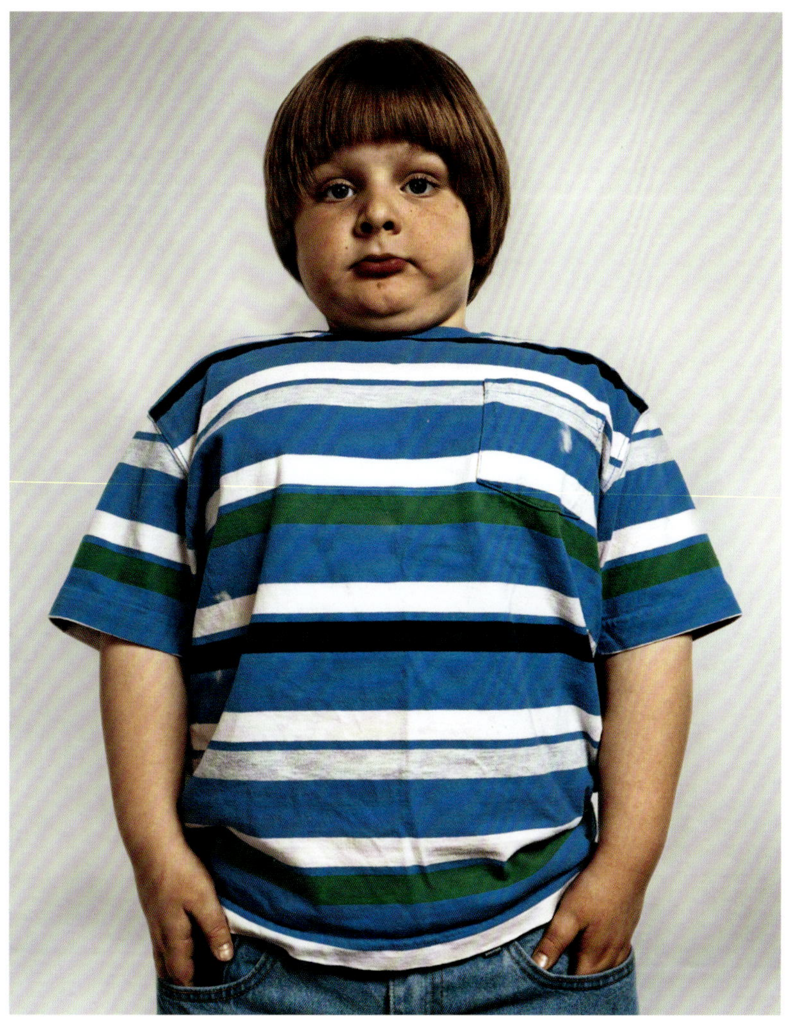

Schuyler is six years old and lives with his parents in an apartment in the Bowery district of Manhattan, New York. The flat is badly in need of repair but the landlord will not make any improvements, because he wants the family to move out so that he can increase the rent. There are five bedrooms, mostly full of toys and other discarded items. Schuyler has recently lost two kilos in weight by cutting down his visits to McDonald's from three times a week to just once a month. He attends a local school and walks the short distance with his mother every day. There are four televisions in Schuyler's home, and he likes to watch his favourite programmes and play video games at the same time. He was first introduced to computers at the age of six months, and by the time he was three years old, he could operate his PlayStation by himself. He would like to be a photographer, a comedian and a racing car driver when he is older.

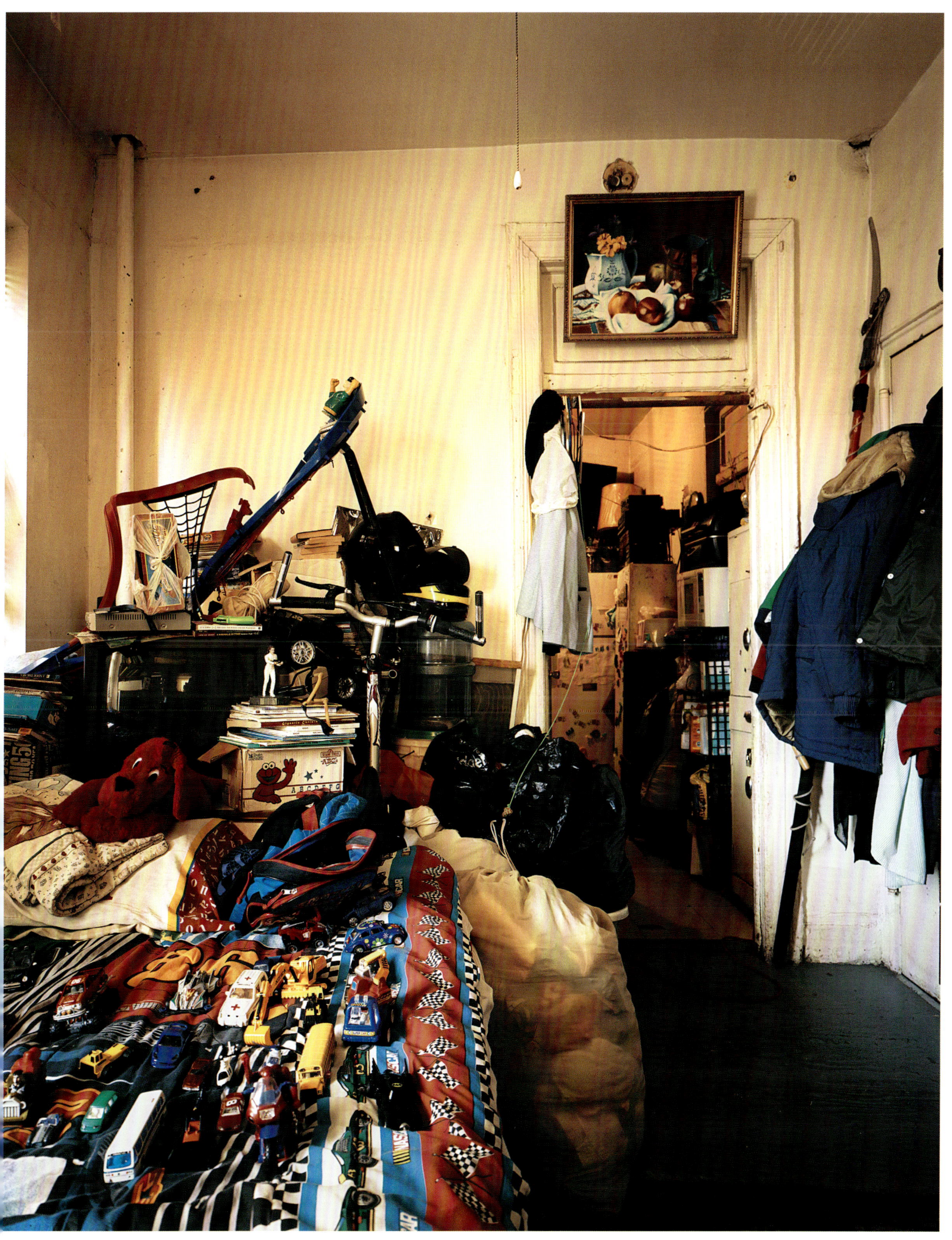
NASCAR

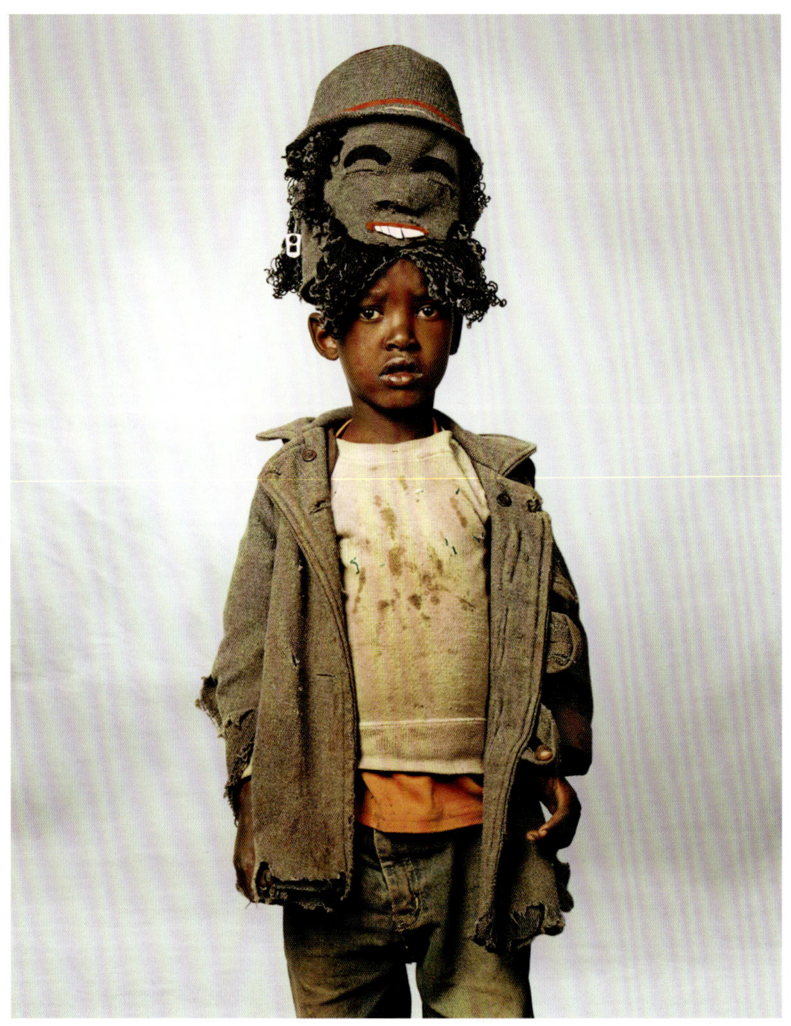

Lehlohonolo is six years old. He and his three brothers live in Lesotho, in southern Africa. The boys are orphans – their father died from AIDS some years ago and they have not heard from their mother since she went away in search of work. It is likely that she also died from an AIDS-related illness. It is quite common in Lesotho for mothers and fathers to die as a result of AIDS, and there are growing numbers of orphans. Lehlohonolo's sixteen-year-old brother is responsible for looking after the family. The boys live in a mud hut where the younger brothers sleep together on the floor, cuddling up to each other for warmth during the freezing cold nights. Two of Lehlohonolo's brothers go to a school eight kilometres away where they are also given monthly rations of food – cereal, pulses and oil. They cannot remember the last time they ate meat. Sadly, they will probably live in poverty for the rest of their lives because crops are difficult to grow on the infertile land and there are no prospects of employment.

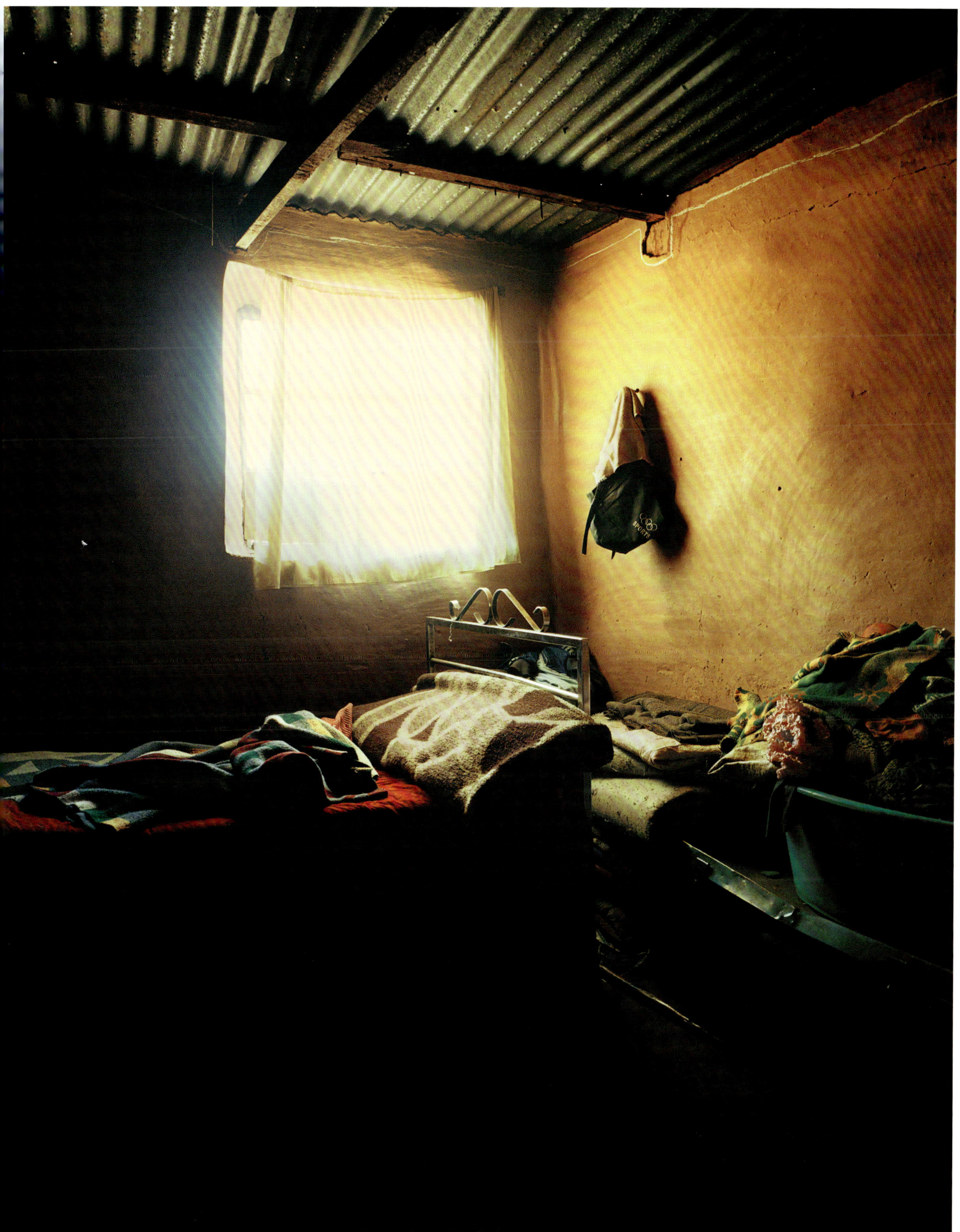
SPORTS

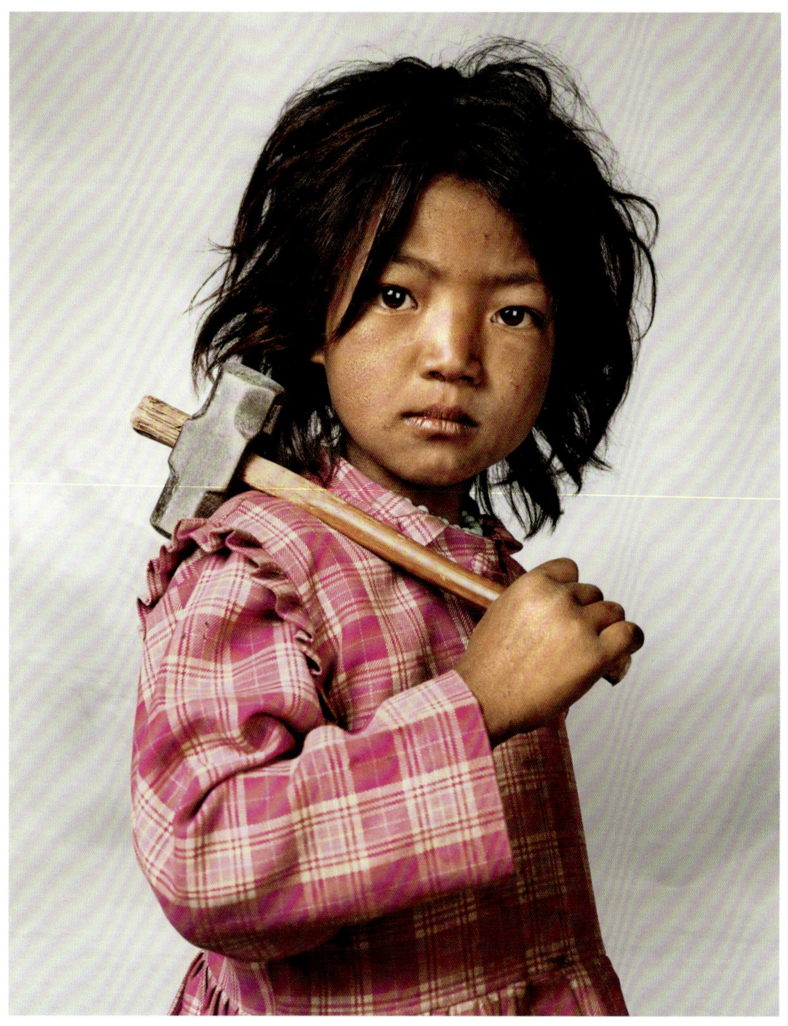

Indira lives with her parents, brother and sister near Kathmandu in Nepal. Her house has only one room, with one bed and one mattress. At bedtime, the children share the mattress on the floor. Indira is seven years old and has worked at the local granite quarry since she was three. The family is very poor so everyone has to work. There are 150 other children working at the quarry, some of whom will lose their sight because they do not have goggles to protect their eyes from stone splinters. Indira works five or six hours a day and then helps her mother with household chores such as cleaning and cooking. Her favourite food is noodles. She also attends school, which is thirty minutes' walk away. She does not mind working at the quarry but would prefer to be playing. She would like to be a Nepalese dancer when she grows up.

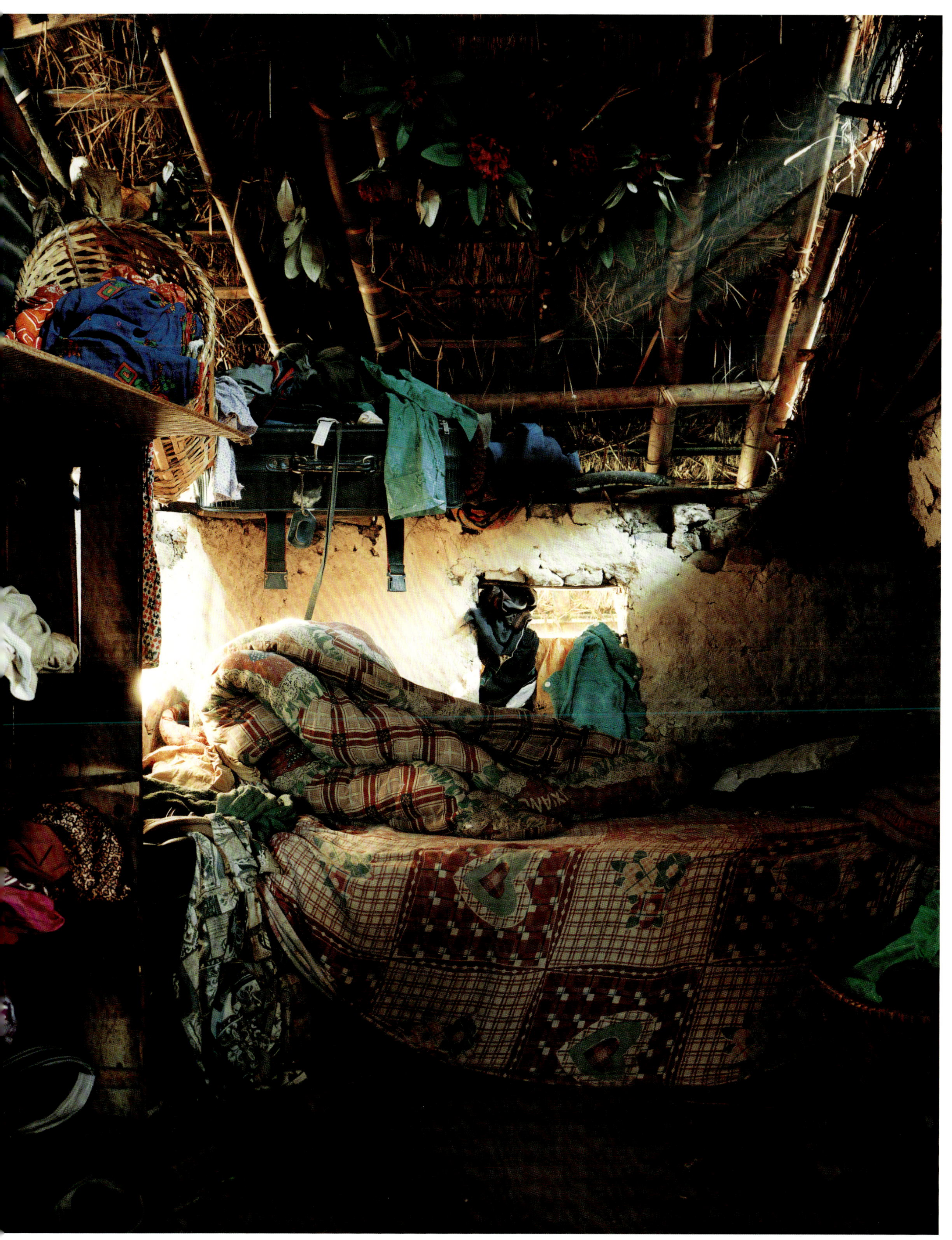

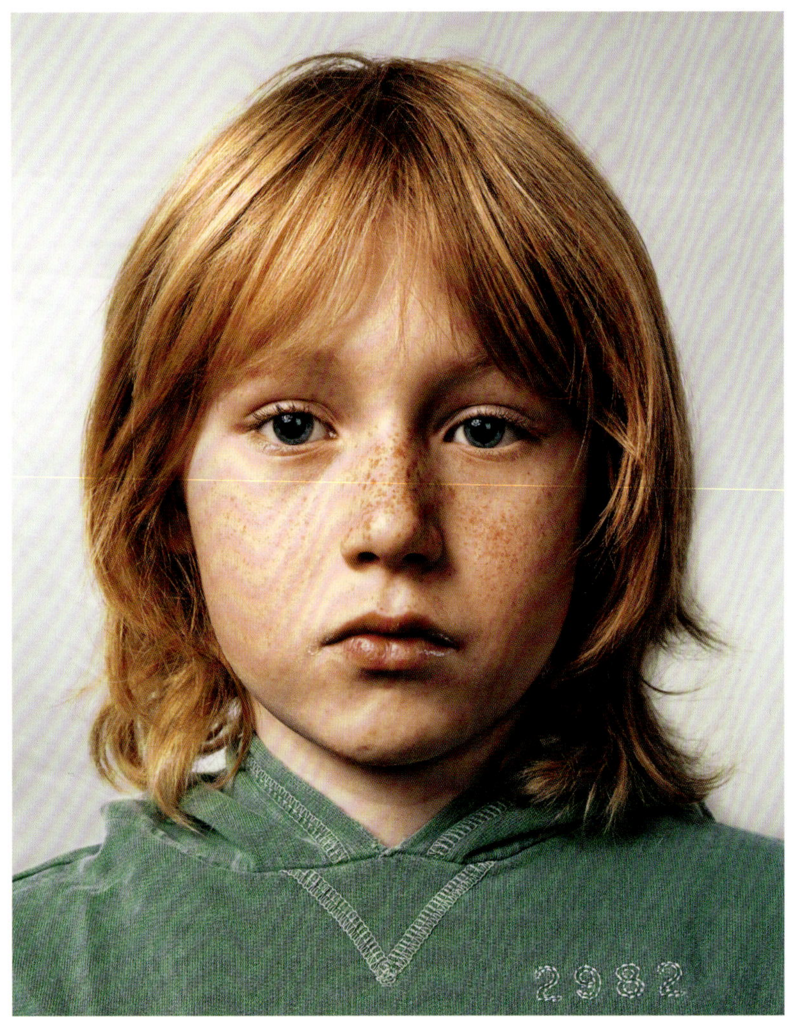

Tristan is seven years old and is an only child. His mother is a film maker, and his father is a pop cultural writer. They live in a small apartment in Manhattan, New York. They also own a beach house in New Jersey where they go for their summer holiday. Tristan attends an Eco-School, a state school run on environmental principles, just ten minutes' walk from his apartment. Here, there are no religious holidays – only the solstices and equinoxes are celebrated. Tristan had to pass several tests before he was accepted at the school, and his parents were also interviewed. This was the tenth school he had applied to. Competition for school places is fierce in New York. He enjoys school but does not like being told to clean up after lunch. Tristan's favourite food is bacon, and he has pizza every weekend. He has an unusual ambition for when he grows up – to be a creator of marmalade.

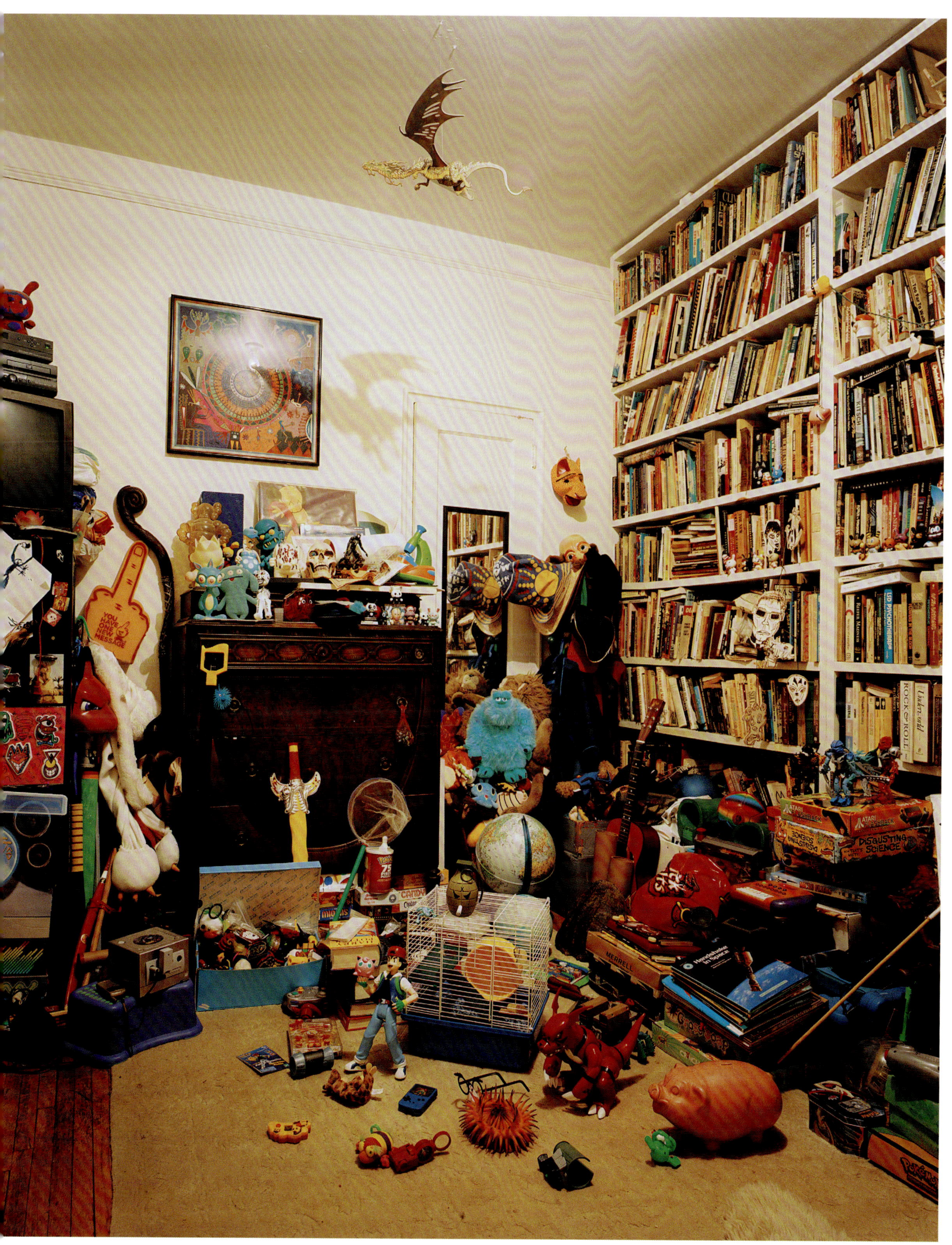
YOU HAVE ONE NEW MESSAGE
MERRELL
DISGUSTING SCIENCE

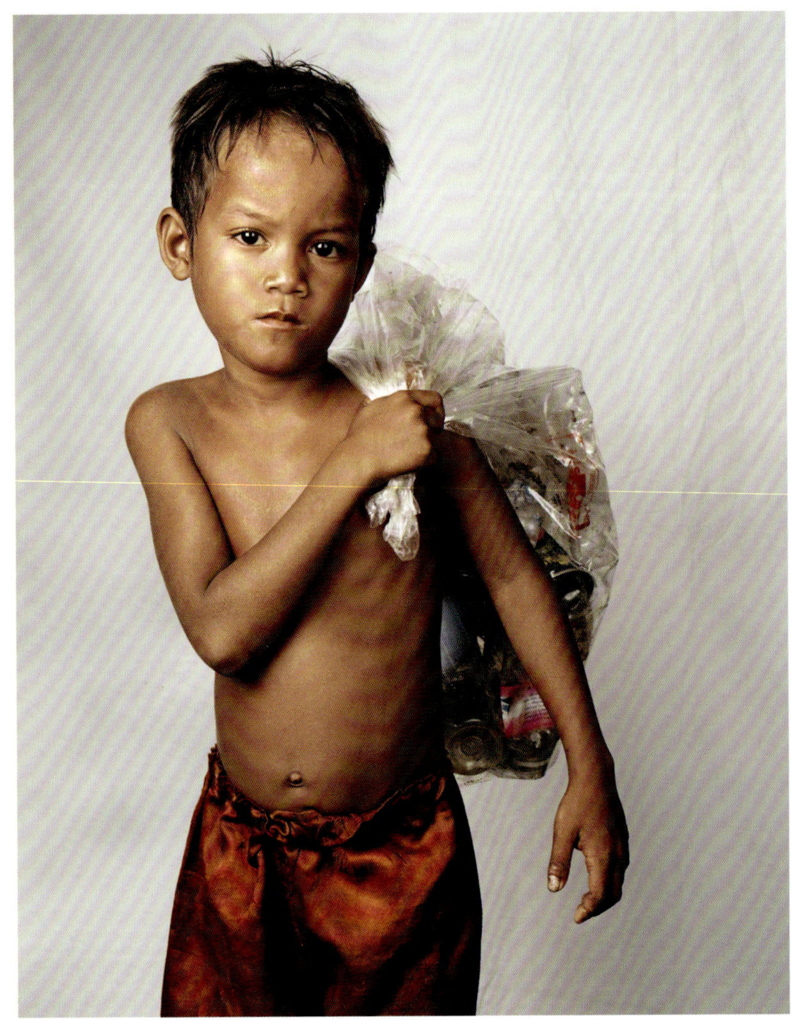

Roathy is eight years old. He lives on the outskirts of Phnom Penh, Cambodia. His home sits on a huge rubbish dump which is swarming with flies. They re-use whatever they can find. Roathy's mattress, for instance, is made from old tyres. The air is thick with the stench of decomposing waste, and the ground underfoot is soft and springy – one wrong step and it gives way to a poisonous black liquid. Five thousand people live and work and pay rent here. At six o'clock every morning, Roathy and hundreds of other children are given a shower and some breakfast at a local charity centre before they start work, scavenging through the rubbish for cans and plastic bottles which are sold to a recycling company. Breakfast is often the only meal of the day. On one occasion, Roathy's family suffered food poisoning after eating a chicken which his brother had found on the dump.

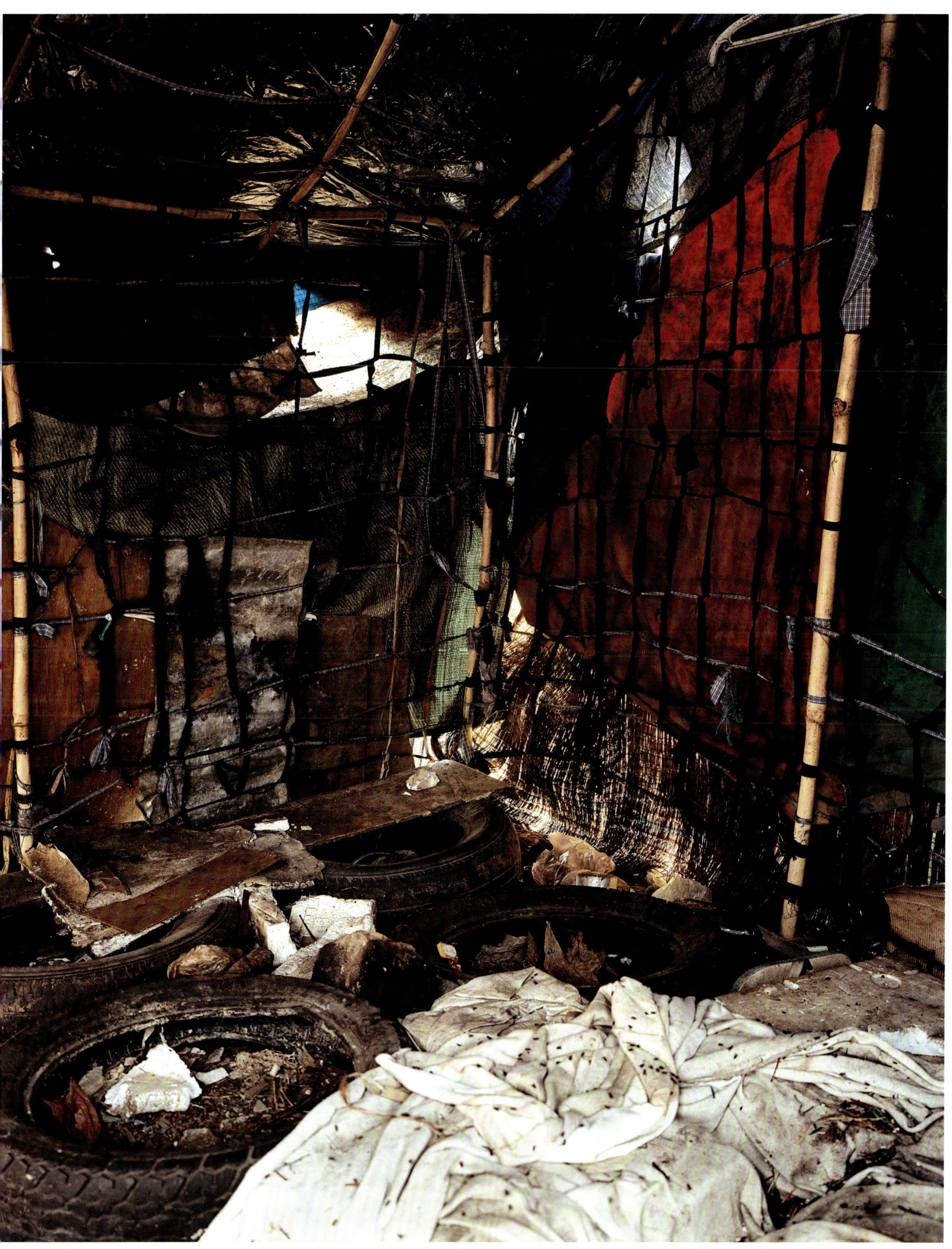

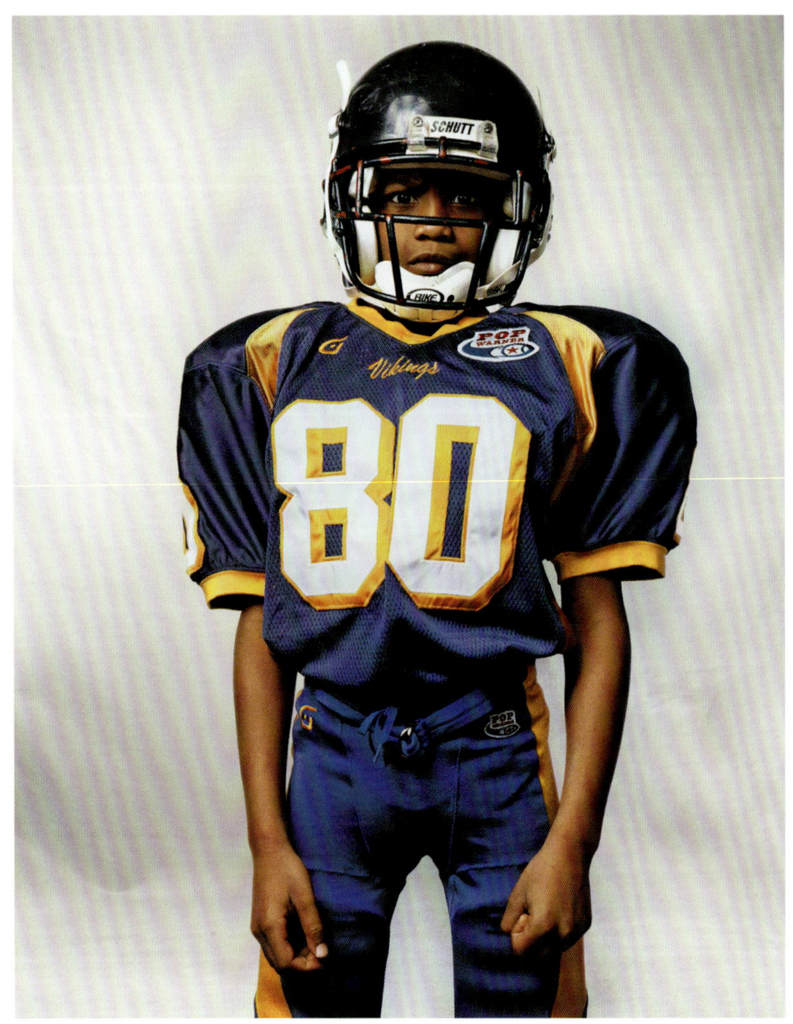

Eight-year-old Justin is passionate about sport, and his bedroom is decorated with a sports theme. He plays American football, basketball and baseball, and is active throughout the year, changing sports according to the season. During the football season he has to practise three times a week. This is his favourite sport. He has played for his local junior football team since the age of five. Justin's parents give him a lot of encouragement despite the expensive kit they have to provide for him. He goes to school on the school bus with other children from his neighbourhood. The family live in New Jersey, USA, in a four-bedroomed house, and they spend two weeks each summer on holiday on the Caribbean island of St Thomas. Justin has high expectations for his future. He would like to become the mayor of New Jersey. But if not, he would settle for being a poker player.

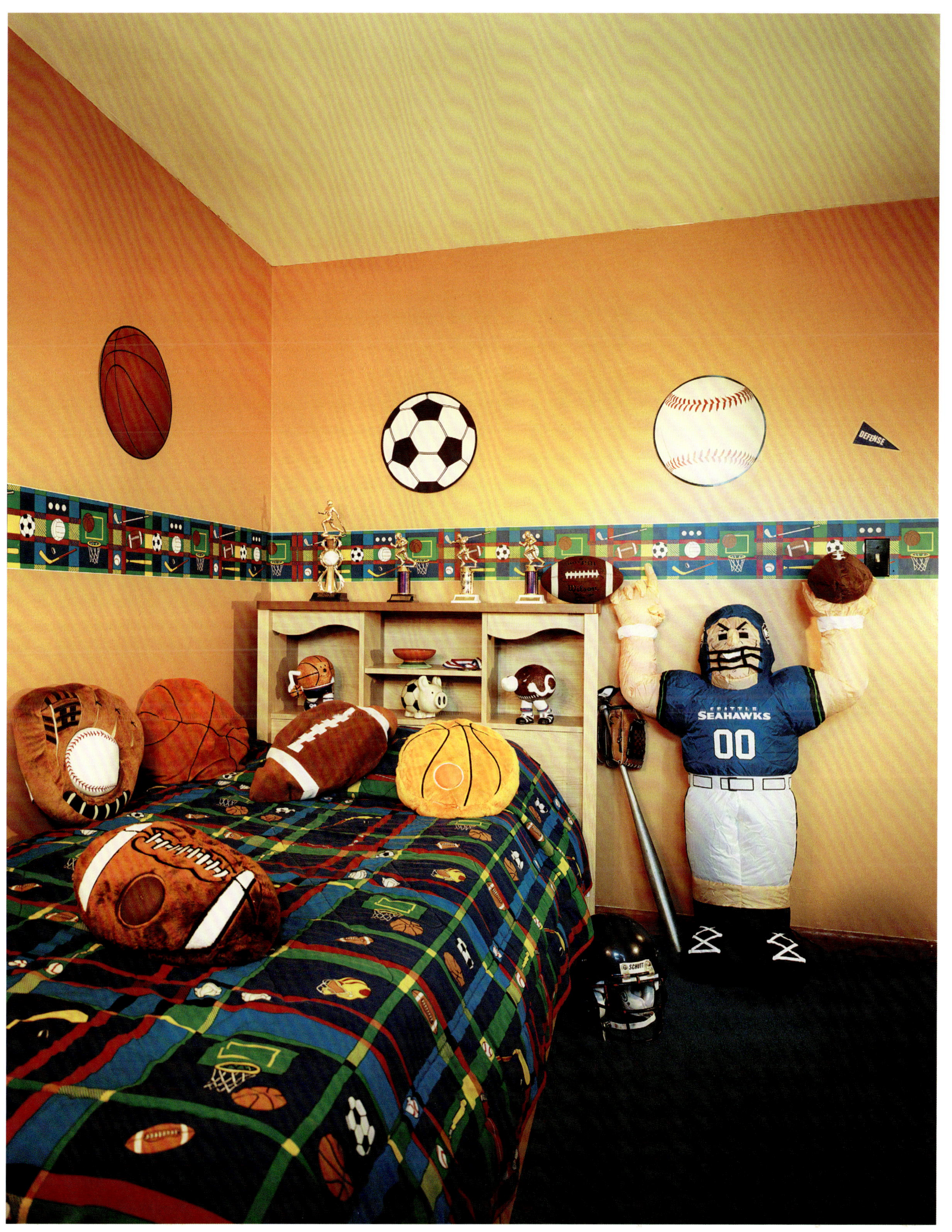
DEFENSE
SEAHAWKS
00

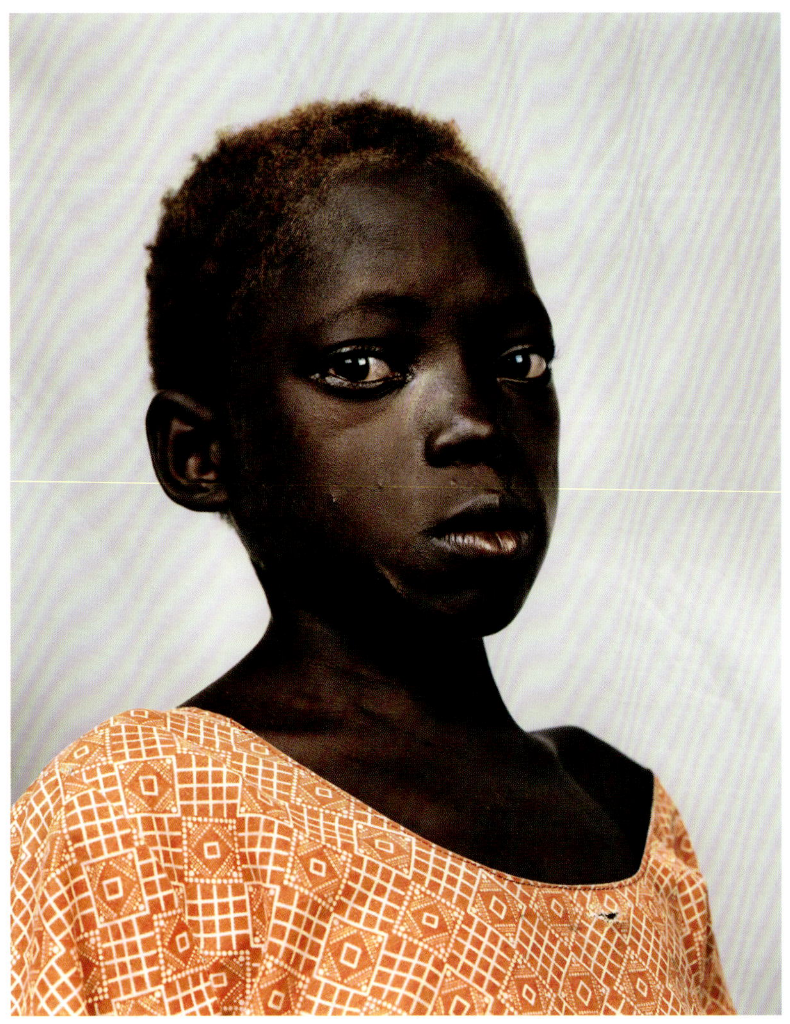

Syra is eight years old and lives with her parents and older sister in Iwol, a Bassari village in Senegal, western Africa. Syra does not really talk to people. She always looks sad. According to villagers, this is because two sorceresses chased her mother and stole Syra's and her sister's souls. Fearing for their lives, their mother travelled all around the area in a bid to cure them. She thinks she finally succeeded, but the villagers do not believe the sisters have really been cured. As a result of this witch-craft, no one will want to marry Syra now. As an unmarried woman, she will be cut off from the village, and forbidden to live under the same roof as women who can still bear children. This means she cannot stay with her mother. Syra's best hope is that her grandmother will take her in.

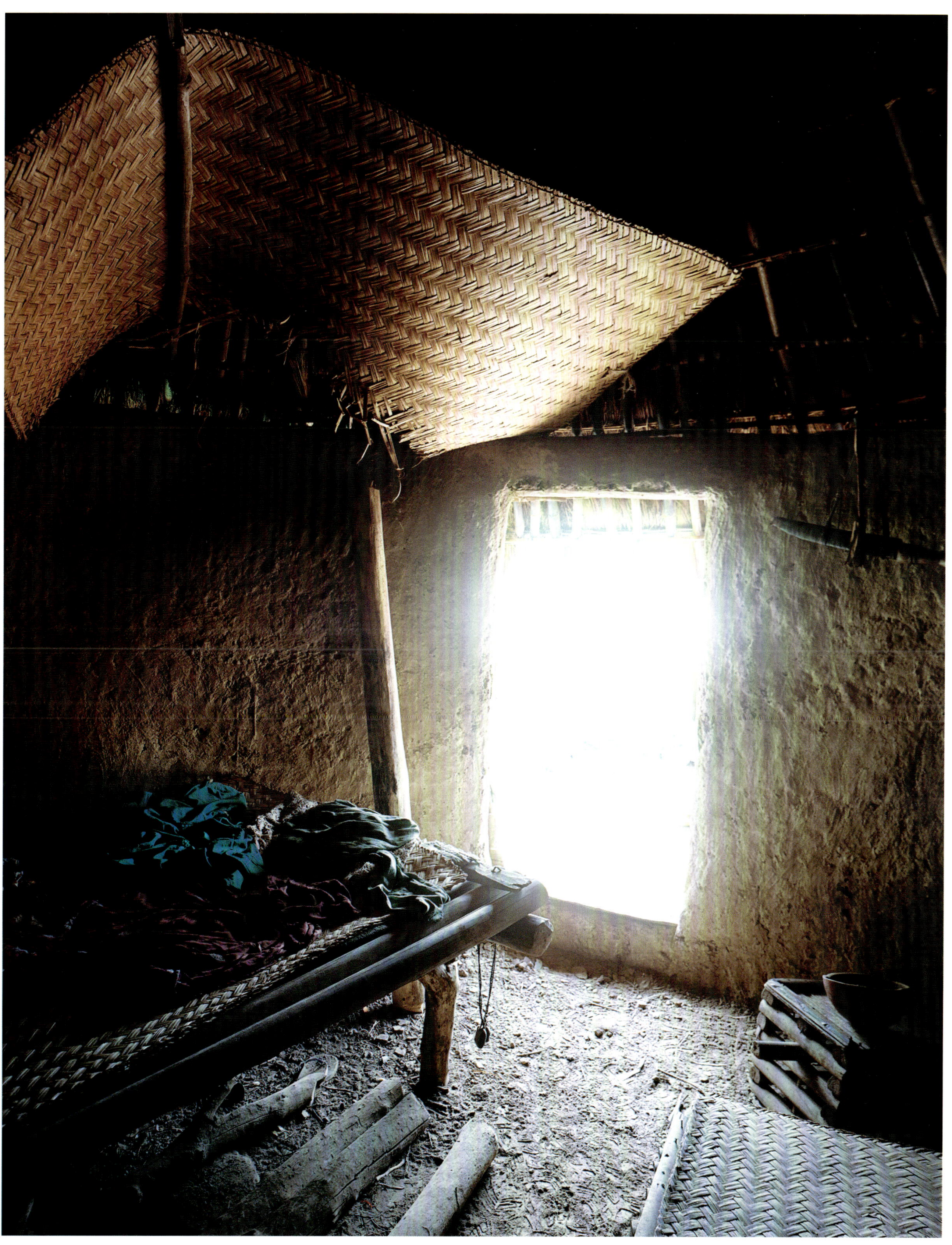

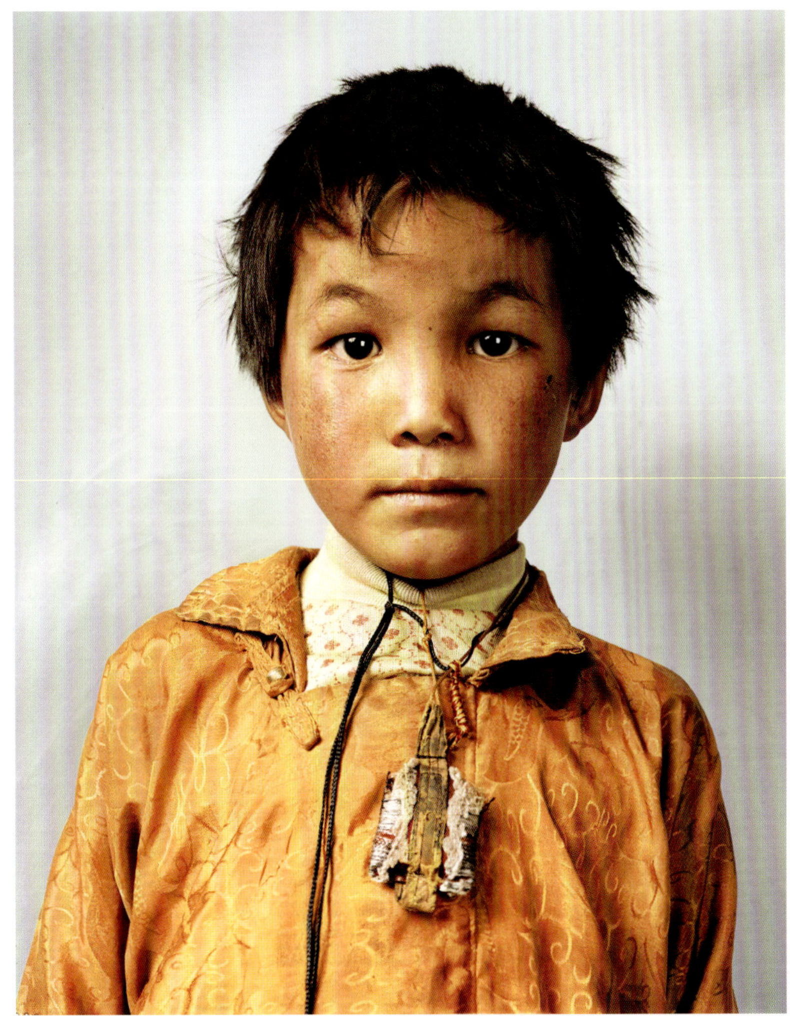

Lobsang is eight years old. He comes from Tibet but is currently staying in Nepal, while trying to make his way to India. There, he will have the opportunity to study in his own language and learn more about Tibetan culture. He cannot do this in Tibet, because the Tibetan language has been banned by the Chinese since they took over the country in 1949. Lobsang's father took him to the Tibetan border and arranged for him to travel to a reception centre in Nepal, where he will stay until he can complete his journey to India. The month-long trip into Nepal was hazardous, with the risk of frostbite or – worse – falling to his death down a mountain. Lobsang left behind his parents, two brothers, his sister and his grandparents. He has never been to school and is looking forward to it. Once he reaches India, he will be cared for by the monks at his new school until he is sixteen. He hopes to become a teacher and looks forward to returning to Tibet one day.

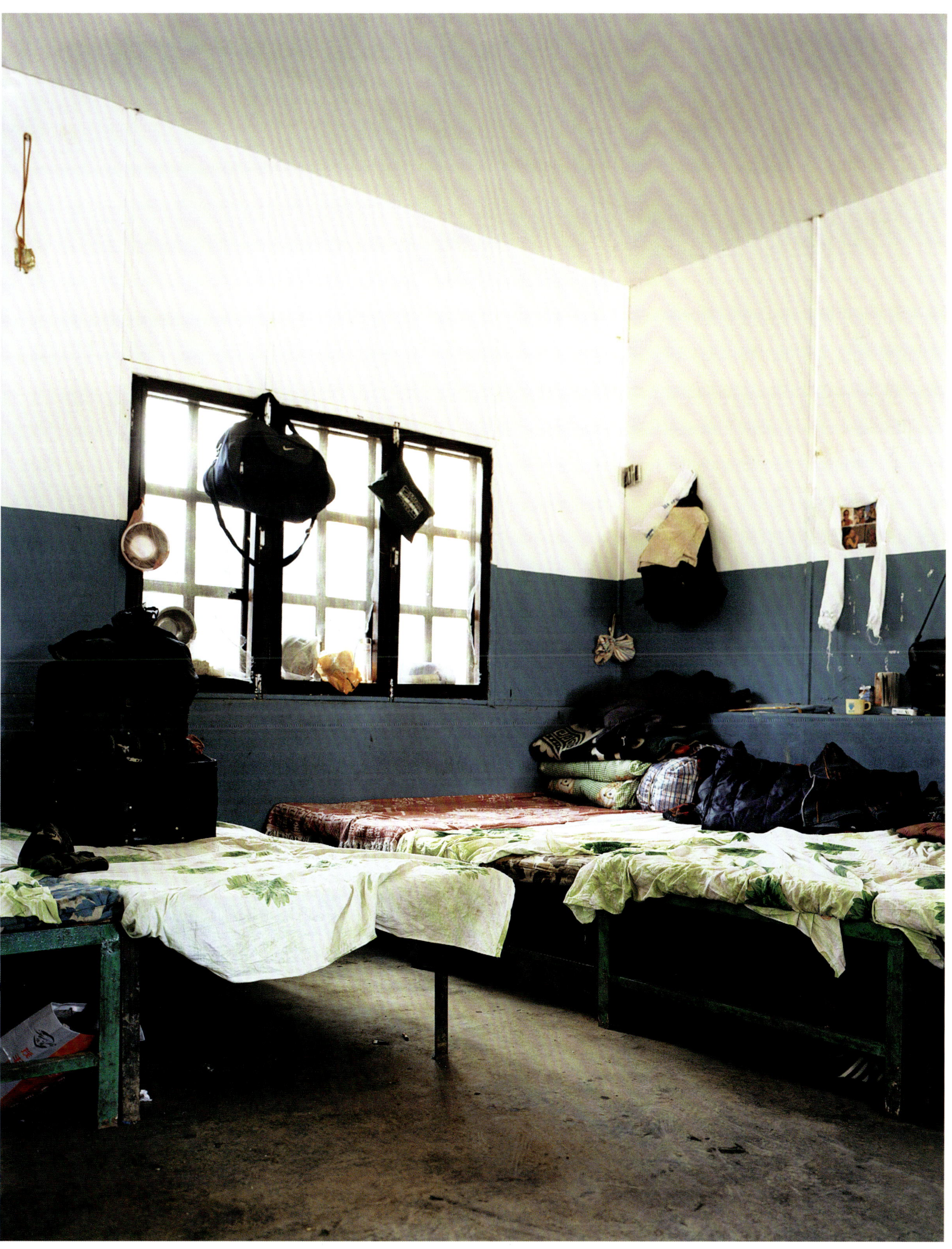

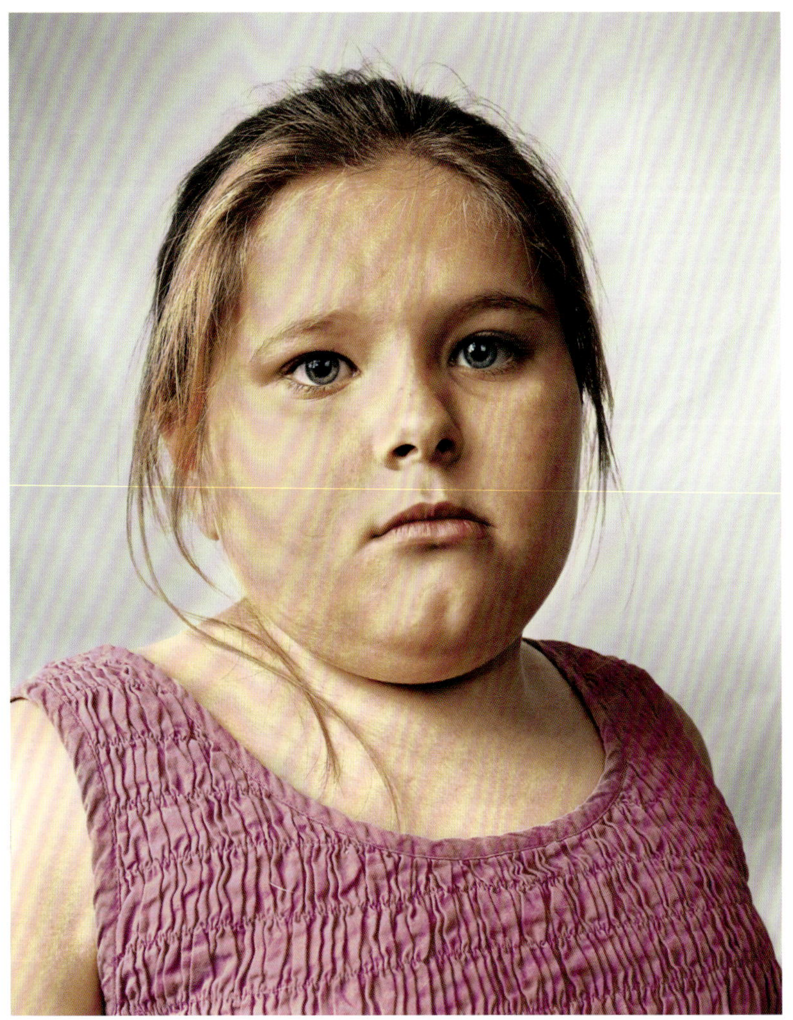

Alyssa lives with her parents in Kentucky, USA. She is an only child but her grandmother, uncle and orphaned cousin live close by. It is a beautiful, mountainous region known as Appalachia, but one of the poorest parts of America. Their small, shabby house, heated only by a wooden stove, is falling apart. The ceiling in Alyssa's bedroom is beginning to cave in. The family would like to buy a caravan instead, if they could afford it. Alyssa's mother works at McDonald's and her father works at Walmart, and everything they earn goes towards bringing up their daughter. She is lucky that her parents have jobs, even though they earn very little. Many local families are unemployed and have to rely on charity. There is a huge problem with drug misuse in the area, and two of Alyssa's relatives have already died from drug-related problems.

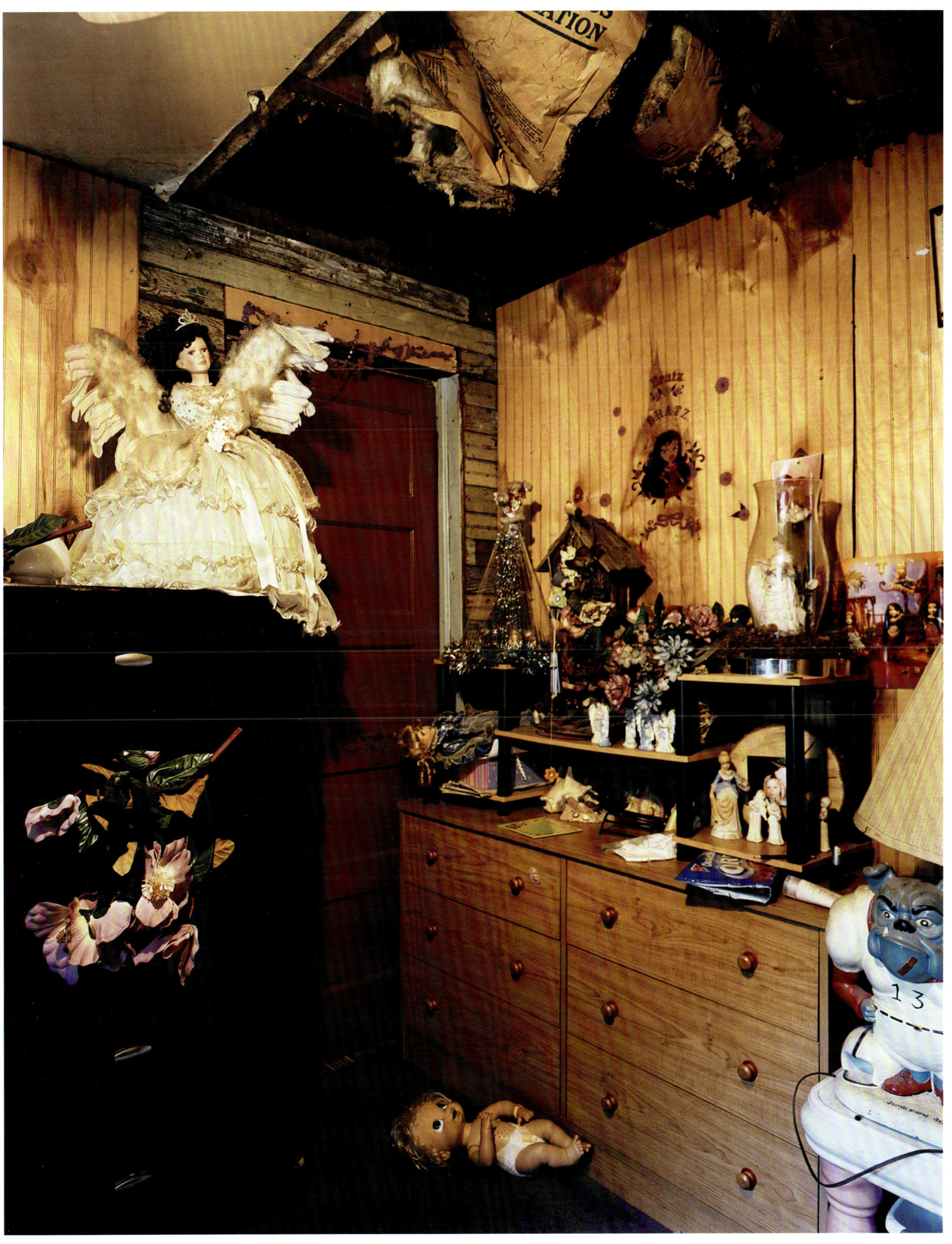
Bratz
BRATZ
13

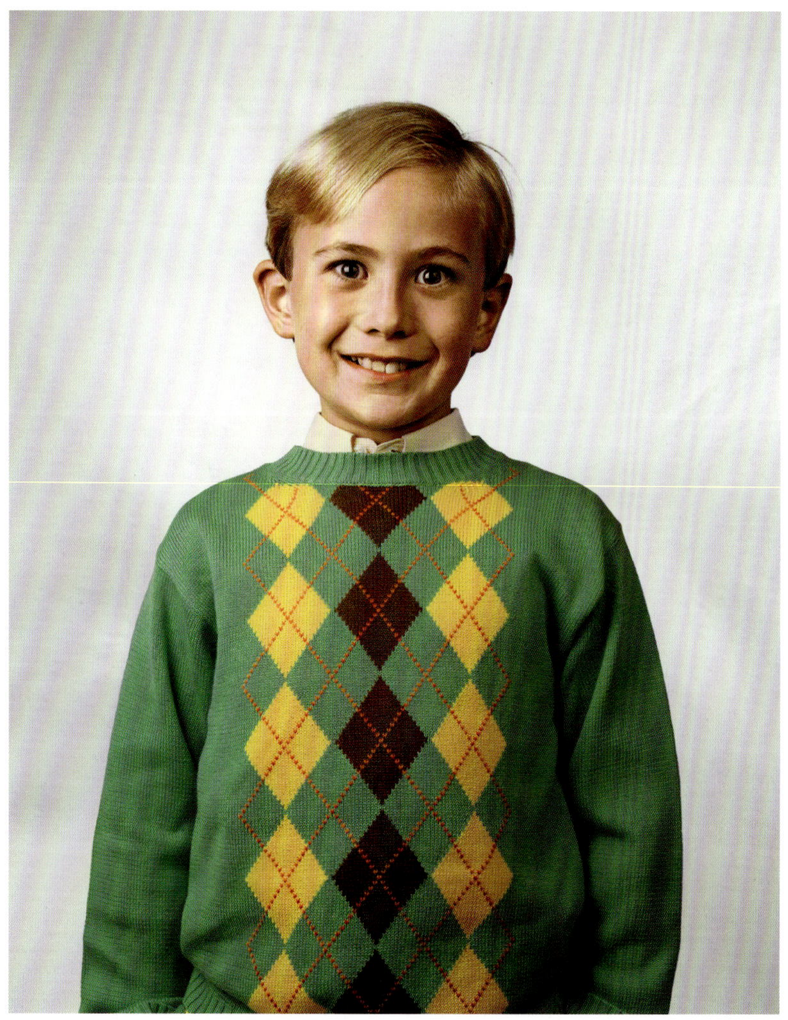

Harrison is eight years old and lives with his parents in New Jersey, USA. He is an only child. He attends a private school where hitting and teasing other children is banned. It takes two hours each way to get to school, but Harrison's mother enjoys spending this quality time in the car with him. Their house is a mansion with an elegant marble staircase. Harrison's bedroom has a big screen TV and en-suite bathroom. He has a separate playroom. The house is guarded by security men at the gates. Harrison is very special to his parents because they feared they would never be able to have children of their own. Harrison loves pizza and chocolate. He has several pets: two cats, a gerbil, fish and frogs. When he grows up he would like to become a vet.

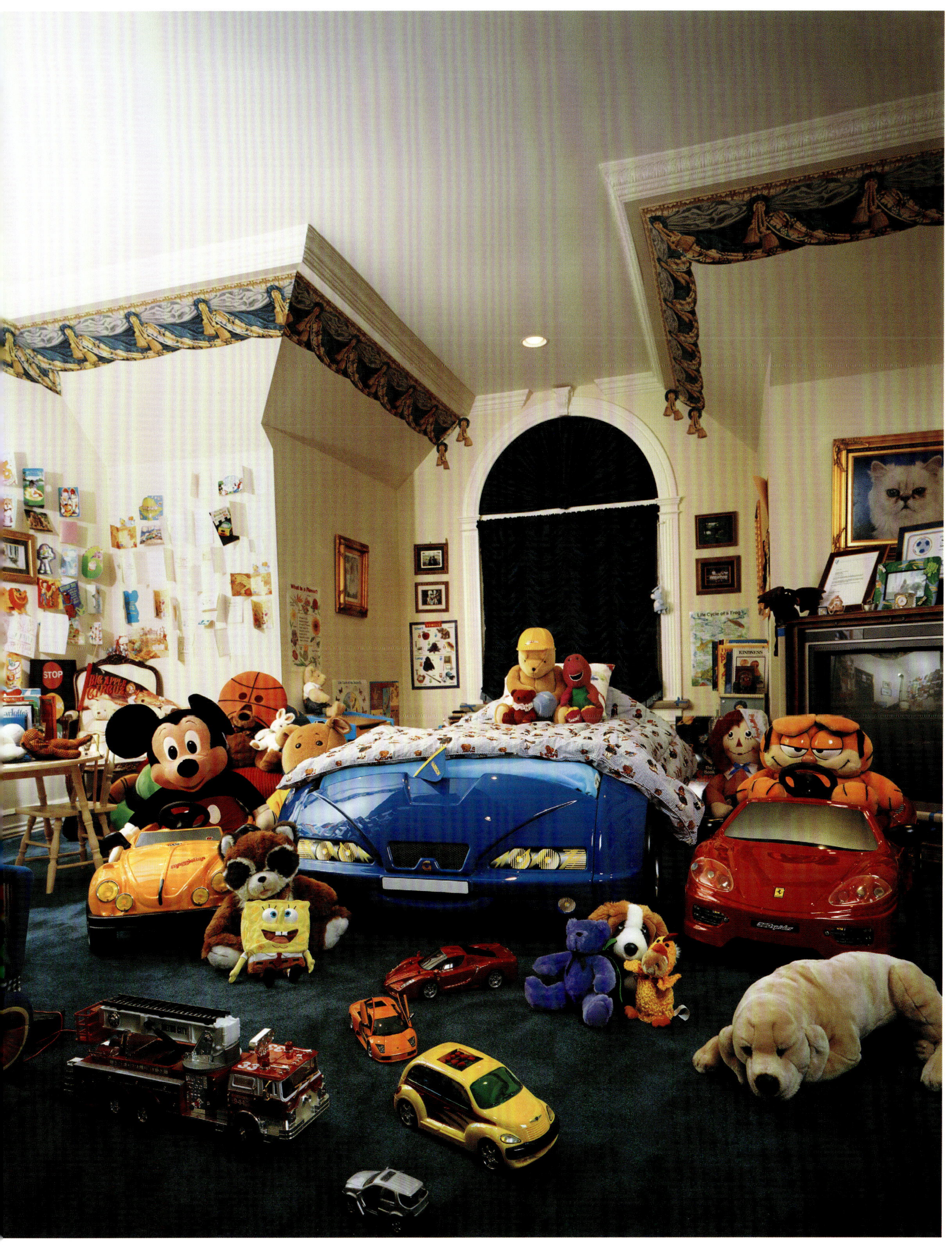
STOP
Life Cycle of a Frog
KINDNESS

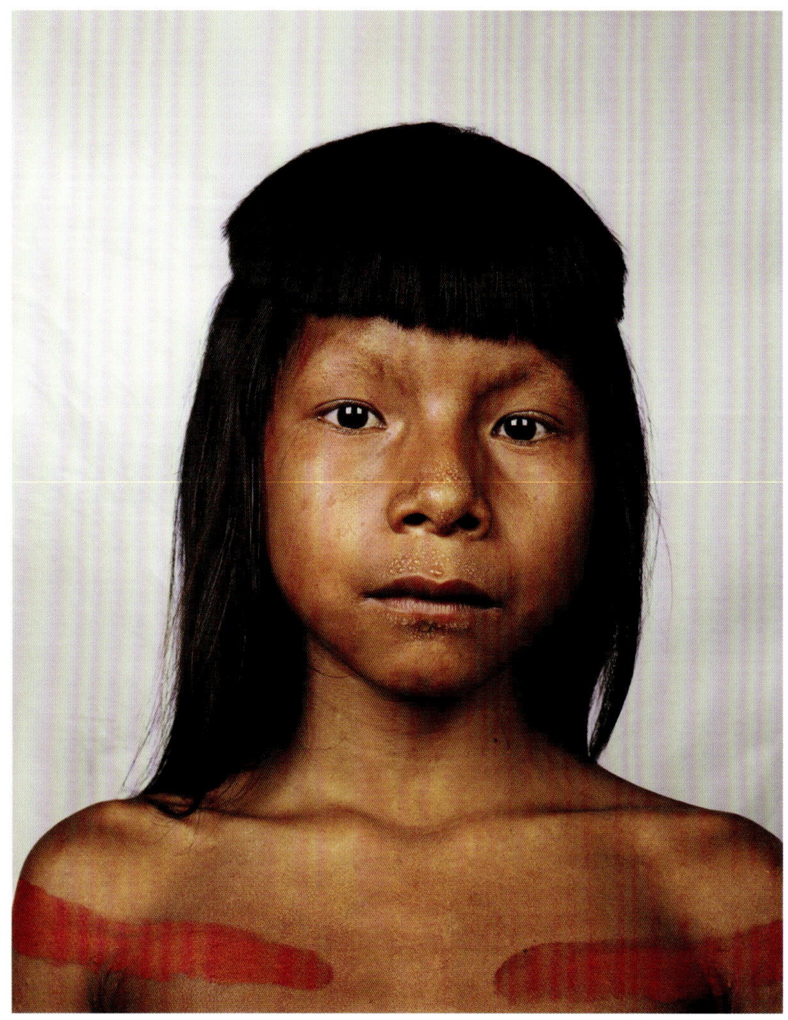

Ahkôhxet is eight years old and a member of the Kraho tribe, who live in the basin of the river Amazon, in Brazil. There are only 1,900 members of the tribe. The Kraho people believe that the sun and moon were creators of the universe, and they engage in rituals that are many centuries old. The red paint on Ahkôhxet's chest is from one of his tribe's rituals. The elders teach Ahkôhxet's generation to respect nature and their surroundings. Their huts are arranged in a circle, leaving space in the middle for gatherings and ceremonies to take place. The nearby river provides water for drinking and washing. The tribe grow half their food in the poor soil using basic tools. They also hunt. The rest of their food is bought using money earned from film crews and photographers who visit their camp. There is one car, shared between the whole tribe.

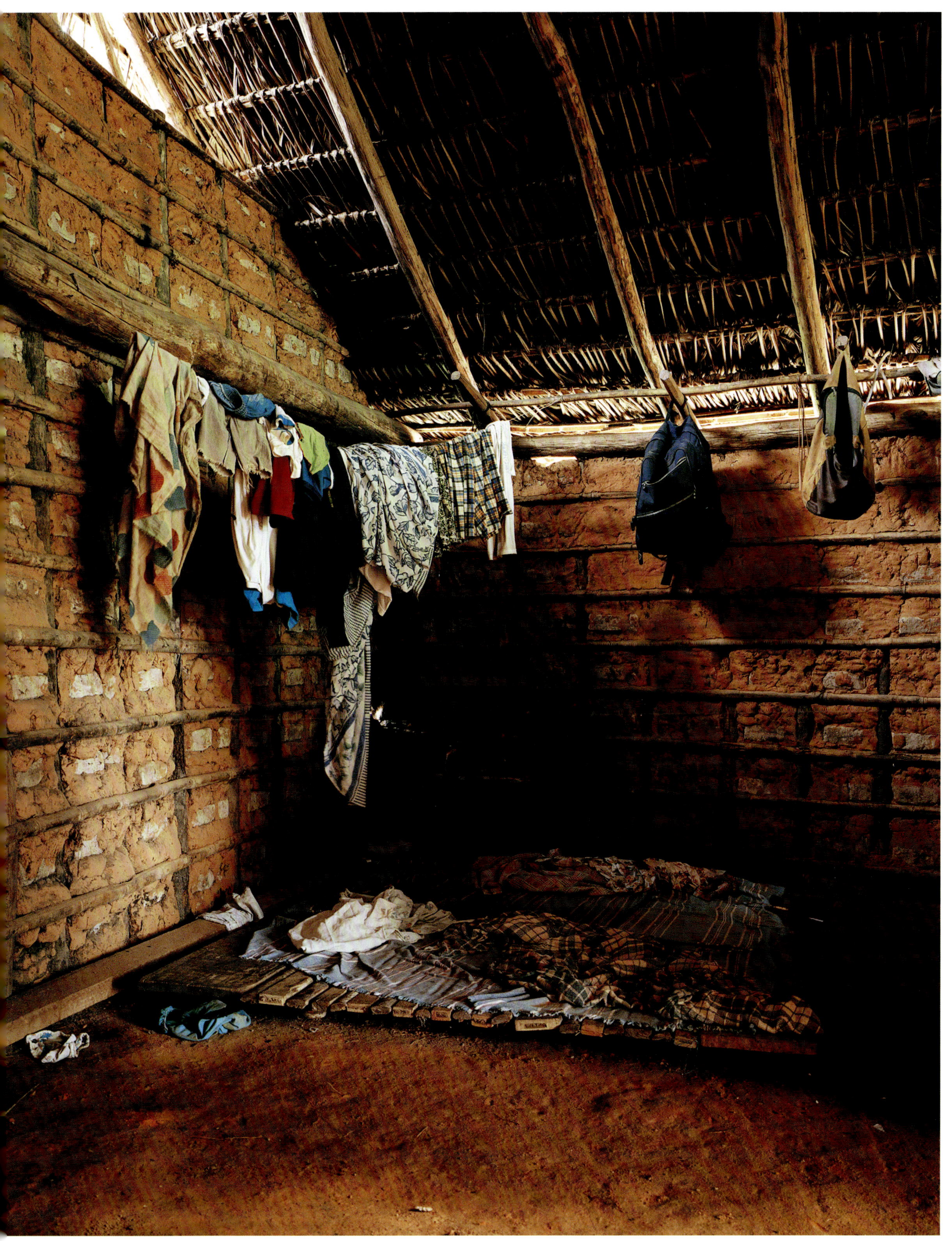

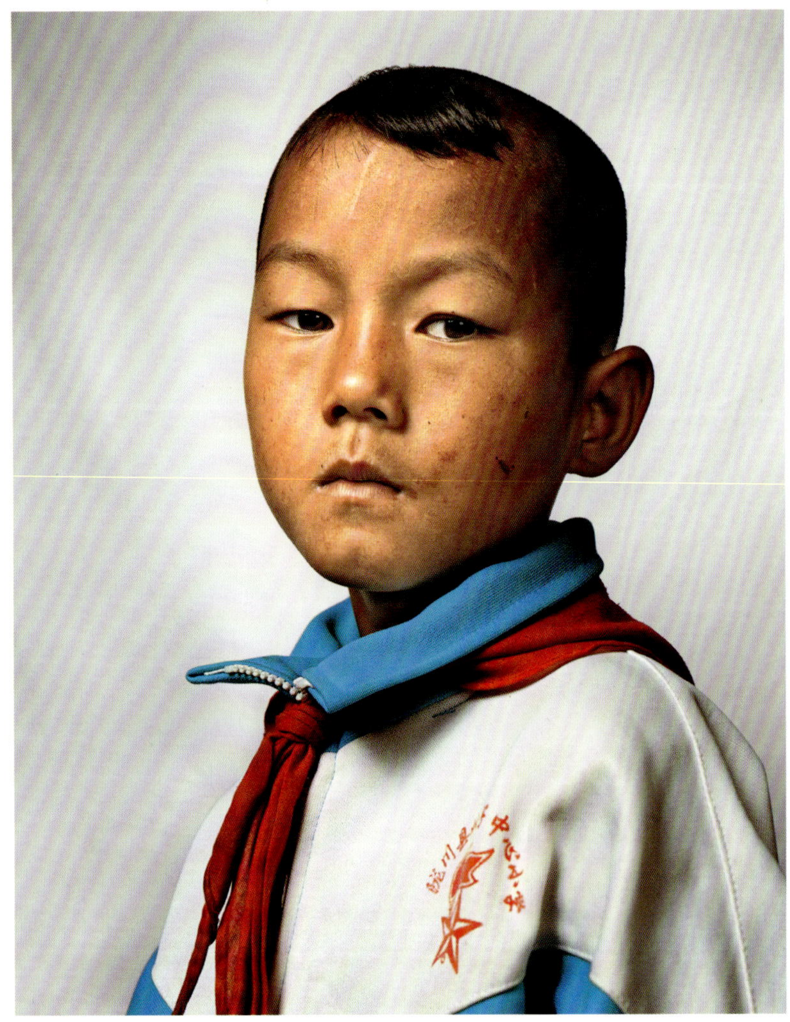

Dong is nine years old. He lives in the province of Yunnan in Southwest China, with his parents, sister and grandfather. He shares a room with his sister and parents. They are a poor family who own just enough land to grow their own rice and sugar cane. Dong's school is twenty minutes' walk away. He especially enjoys writing and singing. Most evenings, he spends one hour completing his homework and one hour watching television. His parents have to pay for his books and uniform but his tuition is free because he comes from a rural area. Dong's mother is pleased that her son can have an education, something she herself never had. Dong's favourite food is pork, sweets and ice cream, but the family also eat other meat, fish and vegetables. When he is older, Dong would like to be a policeman, because he'll be able to 'catch thieves and run around'.

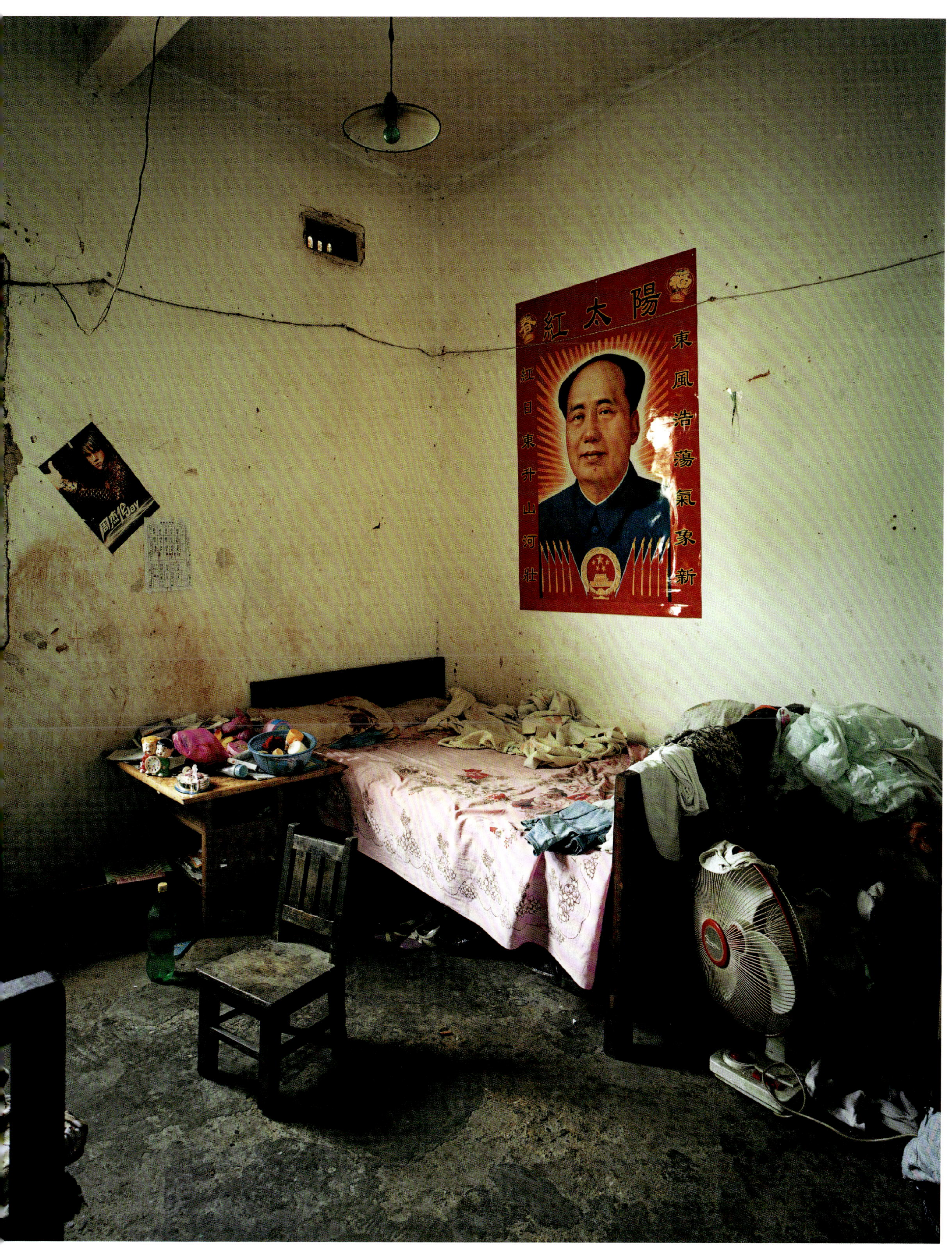
紅太陽
紅日東升山河壯
東風浩蕩氣象新
周杰伦Jay

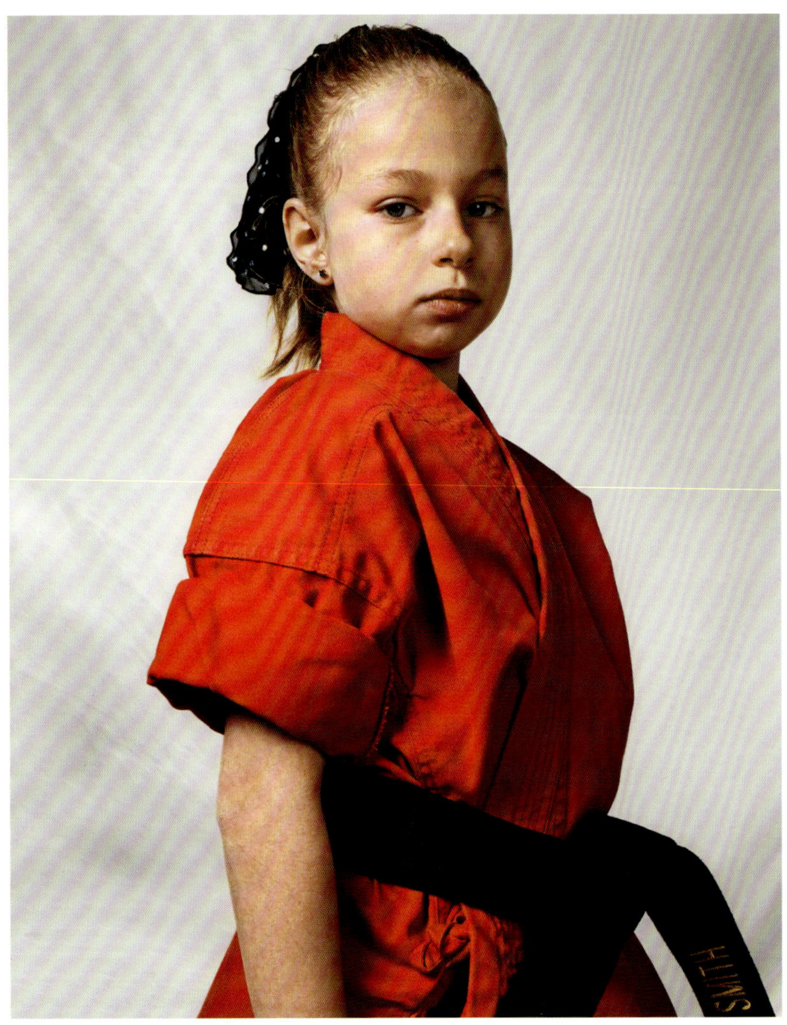

Samantha is nine years old. She lives with her parents, and her guinea pig and fish, in a detached house on Long Island, New York. Samantha has achieved a black belt – the highest level – in karate. She has been world champion three times. She first became interested at the age of three, when she saw a television advert featuring karate. She pestered her parents to let her learn and took her first lesson when she was four. She has now been in two adverts and a short film, and her bedroom is full of trophies she has won in competitions. Samantha's school is one mile away. Her mother takes her by car each morning so that she can have an extra few minutes' rest in bed. She spends four hours a day practising karate at the studio and also has an hour and a half of school homework each night. Samantha would like to become a karate movie star.

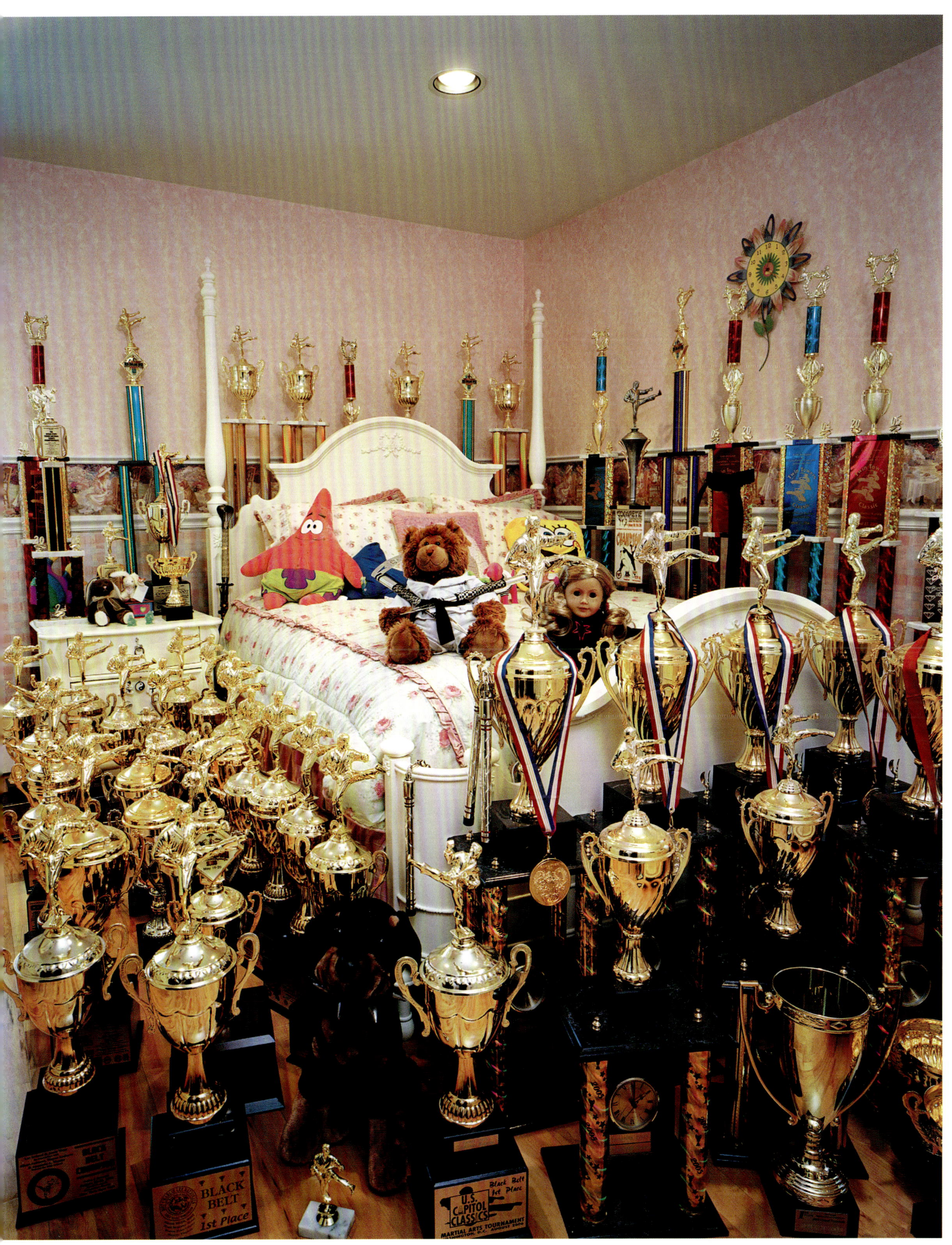
BLACK BELT 1st Place
Black Belt 1st Place
U.S. CAPITOL CLASSICS
MARTIAL ARTS TOURNAMENT
WASHINGTON, D.C. AUGUST 2006

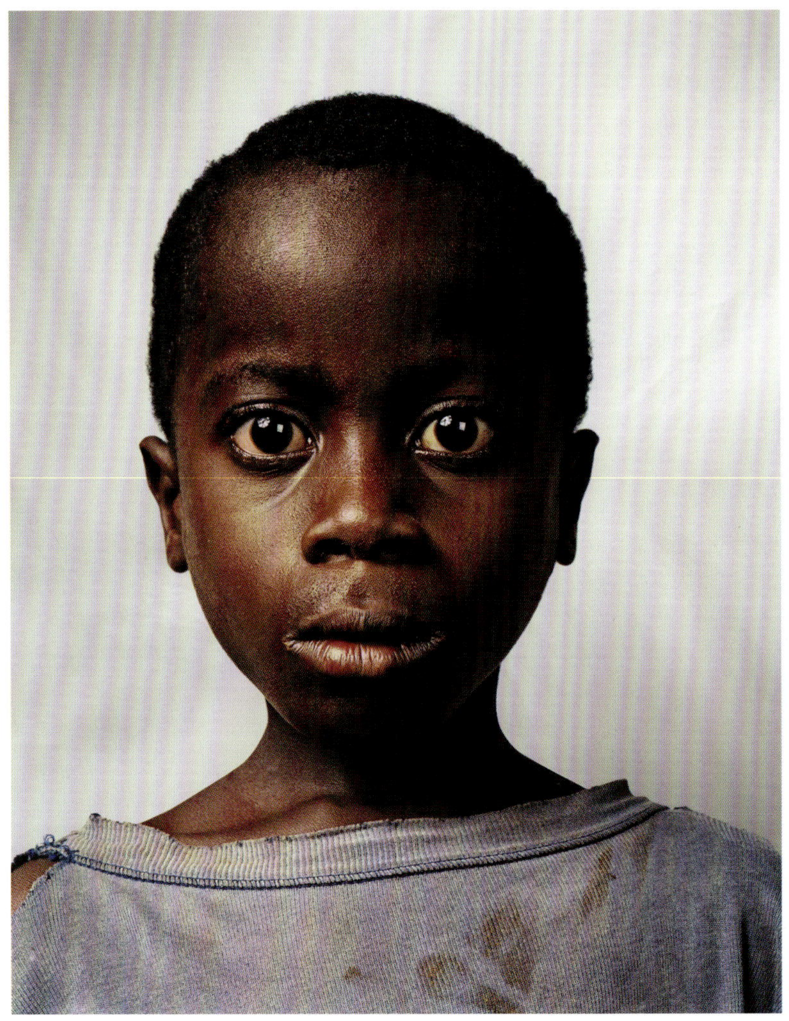

This nine-year-old boy is a refugee from war in Liberia, in western Africa, and goes to a school for ex-child soldiers in Ivory Coast. His name remains a secret in order to protect his identity. If it is revealed, his life could be at risk. Thousands of young children – many of them orphans – were recruited as soldiers to fight in the violent civil war in Liberia. They were tempted to become soldiers by promises of money, food and clothing. These child soldiers were then moved around the country during the conflict, causing them to lose track of their home villages. They became displaced. This boy is an orphan and has three brothers. He now lives in a concrete shack alongside other pupils from his school. His favourite food is rice with tomato, meat and fish ground up together. He likes football and would like to be a teacher when he is older.

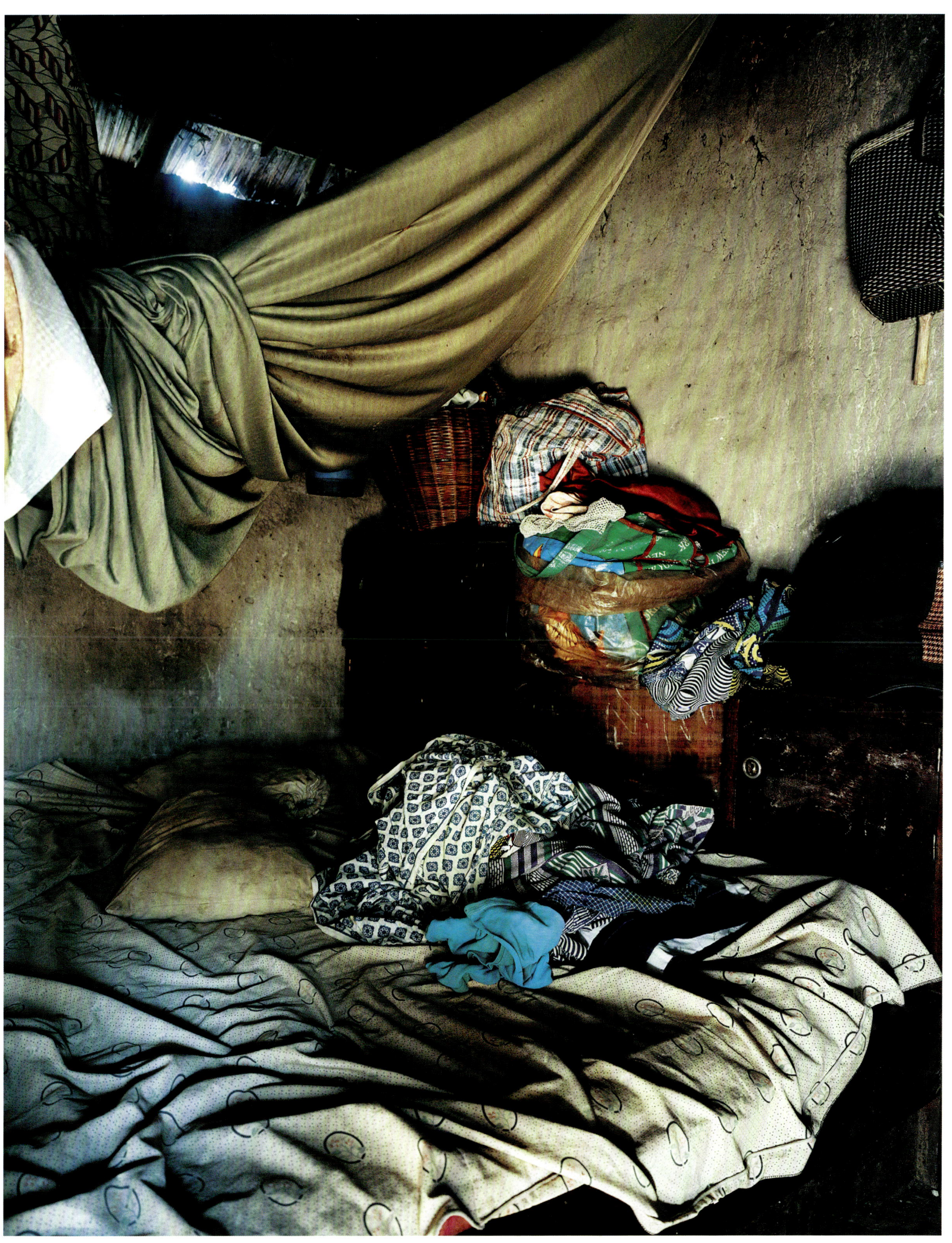

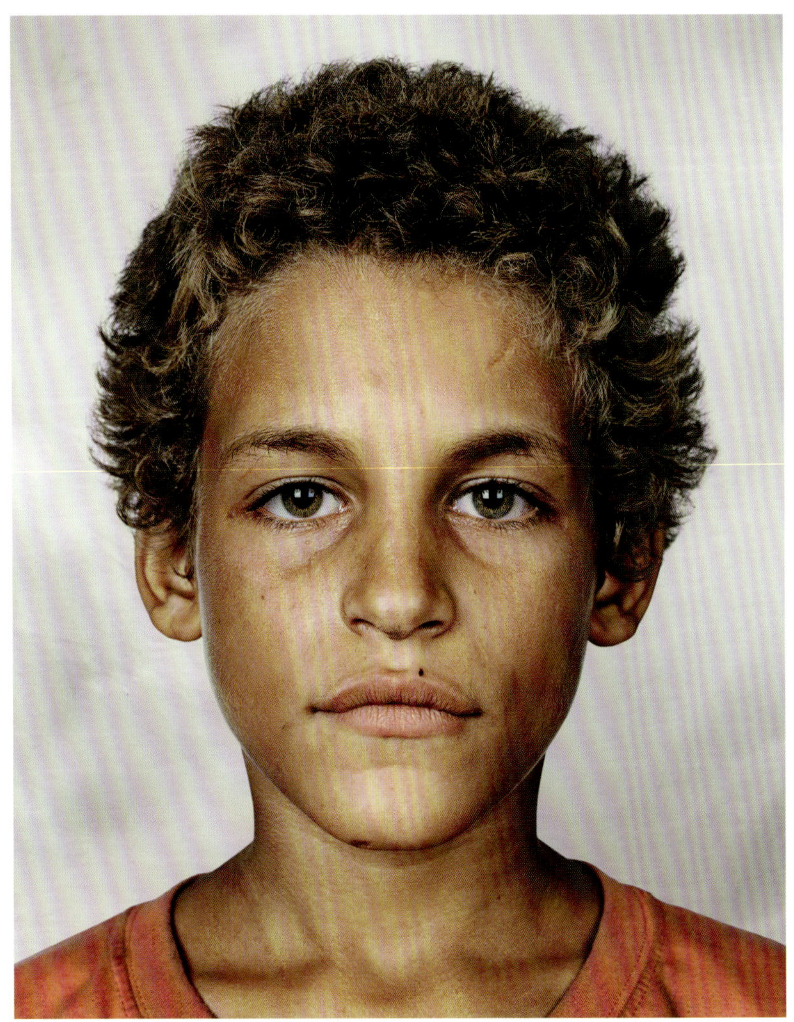

Alex is nine years old. He lives in Rio de Janeiro, Brazil. He does not go to school but spends his time begging on the city streets. He has found that the only way he can survive is to beg or steal. He admits that he sometimes steals from old people or from drivers waiting at traffic lights. As the drivers lean their arm on the window, Alex snatches the watch from their wrists. He is addicted to sniffing glue. Most of the time he sleeps outside, on an empty bench or discarded sofa if he can find one – otherwise on the pavement. Alex is still in touch with his family, and occasionally goes to see them to share a meal.

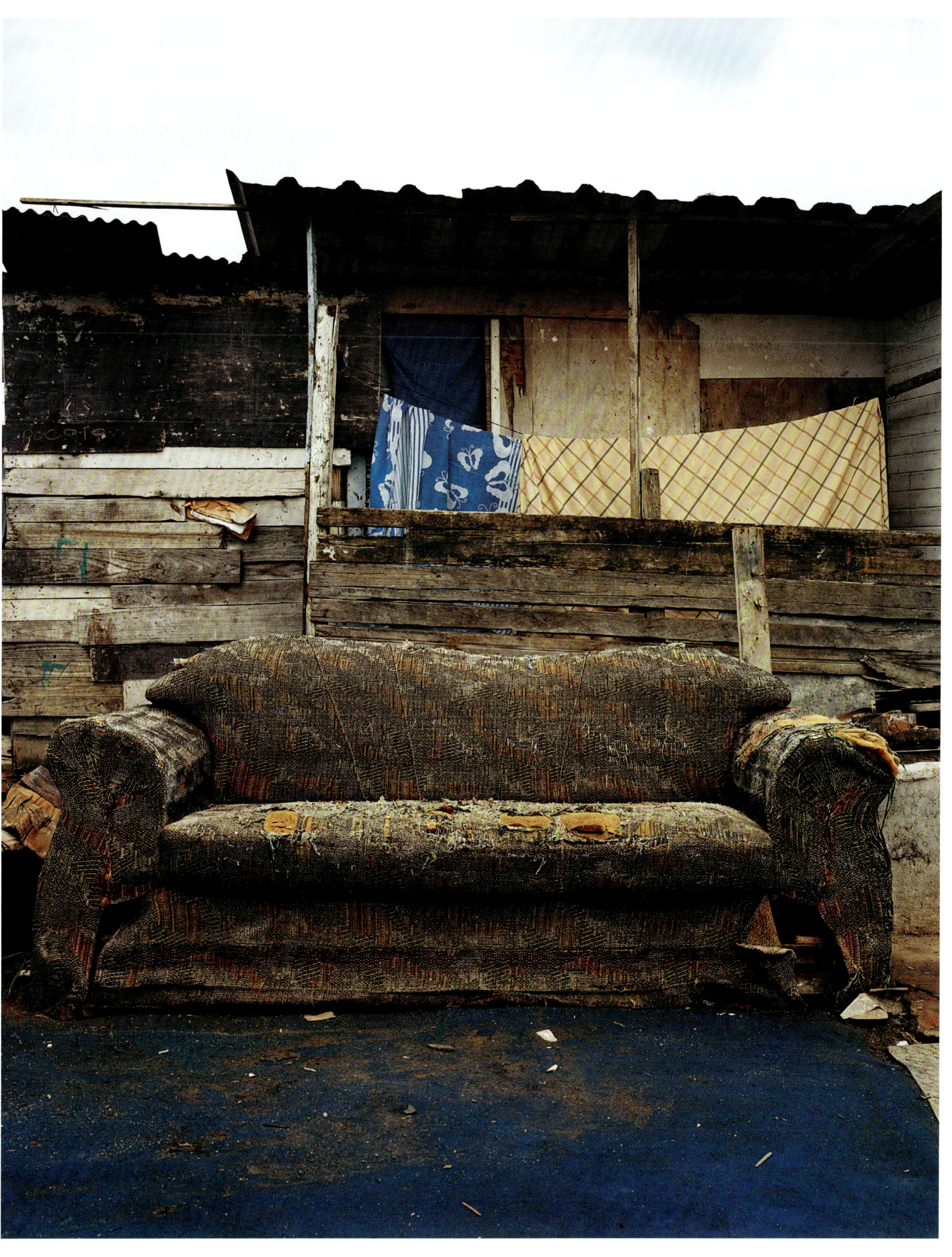

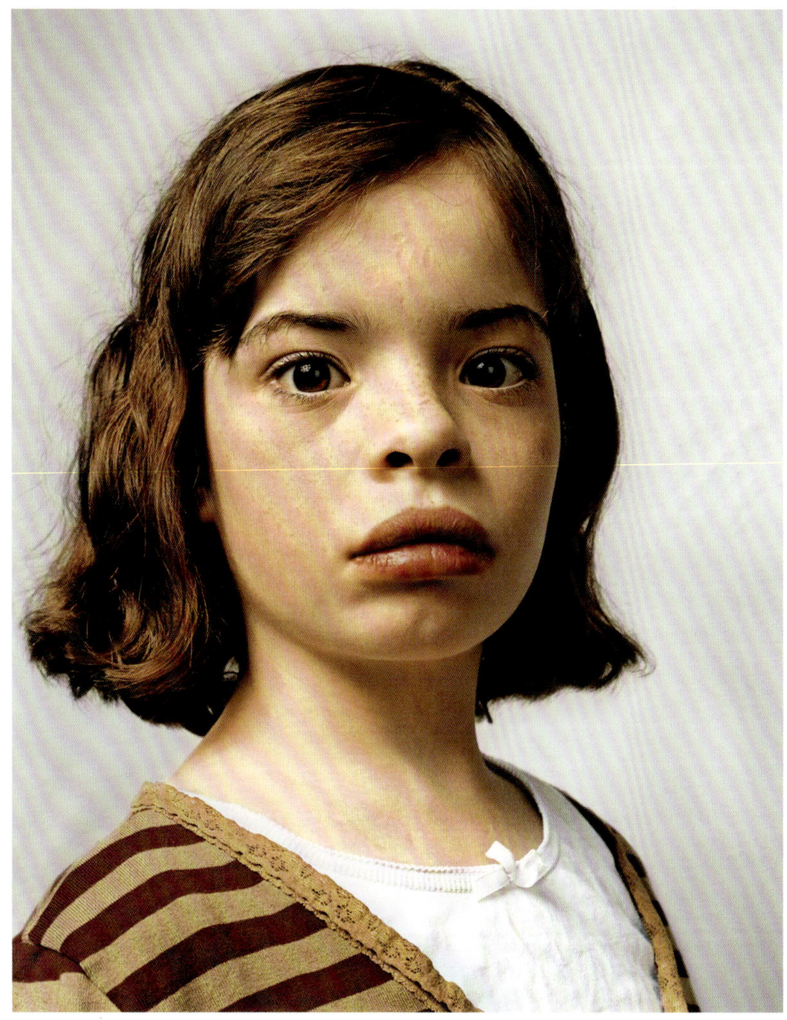

Nine-year-old Delanie lives with her parents and younger brother and sister, in a large house in New Jersey, USA. The children all have their own bedrooms. Delanie is very fussy about her appearance and she often takes hours in the evening choosing what to wear the next day. She and her brother travel to school together on the school bus, a journey of about ten minutes, but she does not like to sit with him. She enjoys seeing her friends in class but hates schoolwork. She only has fifteen minutes of homework each night but always leaves it until the last moment. Delanie's hobbies are shopping and dancing. She goes to church regularly and enjoys the happy atmosphere. When she grows up she would like to be a fashion designer and design her own clothes.

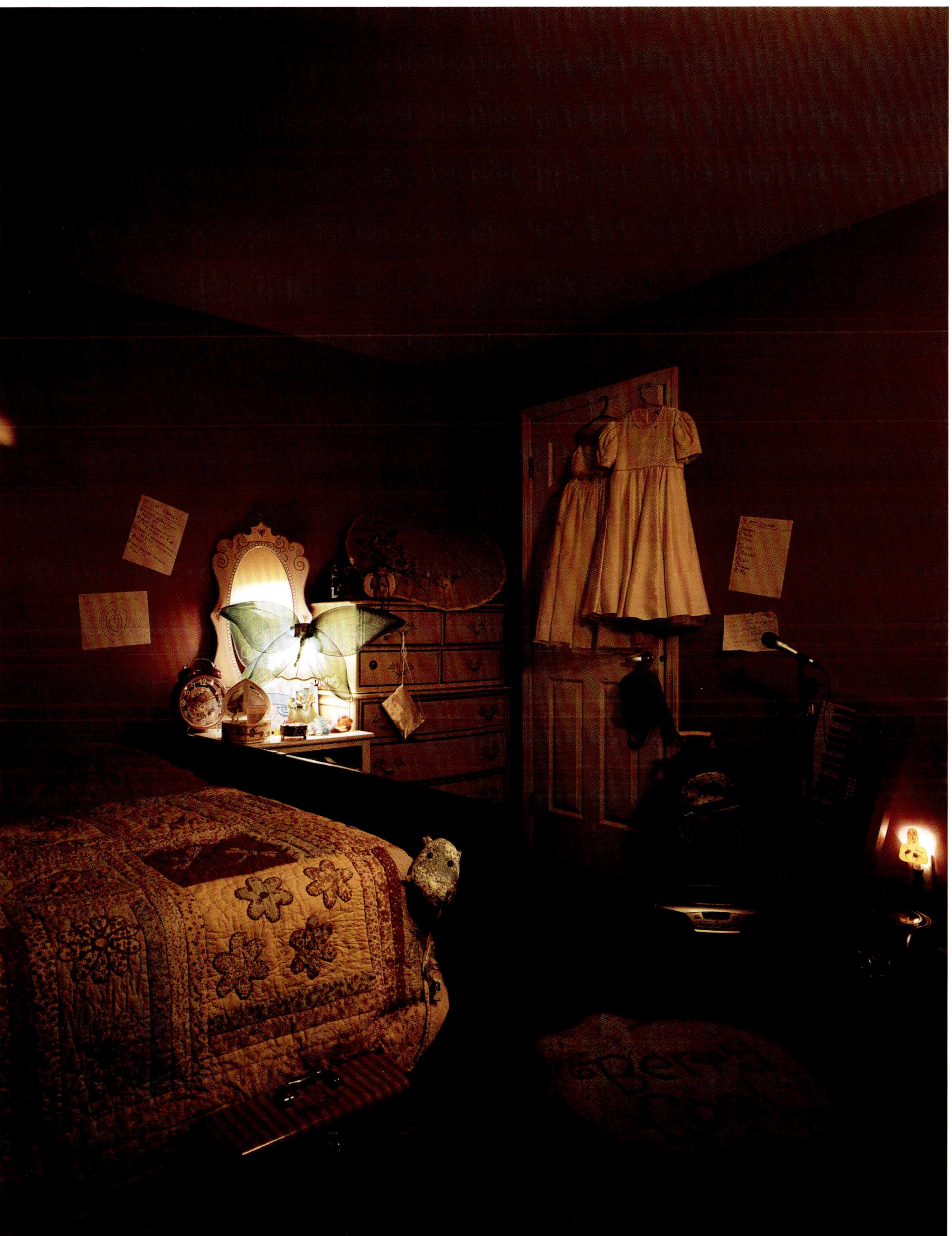

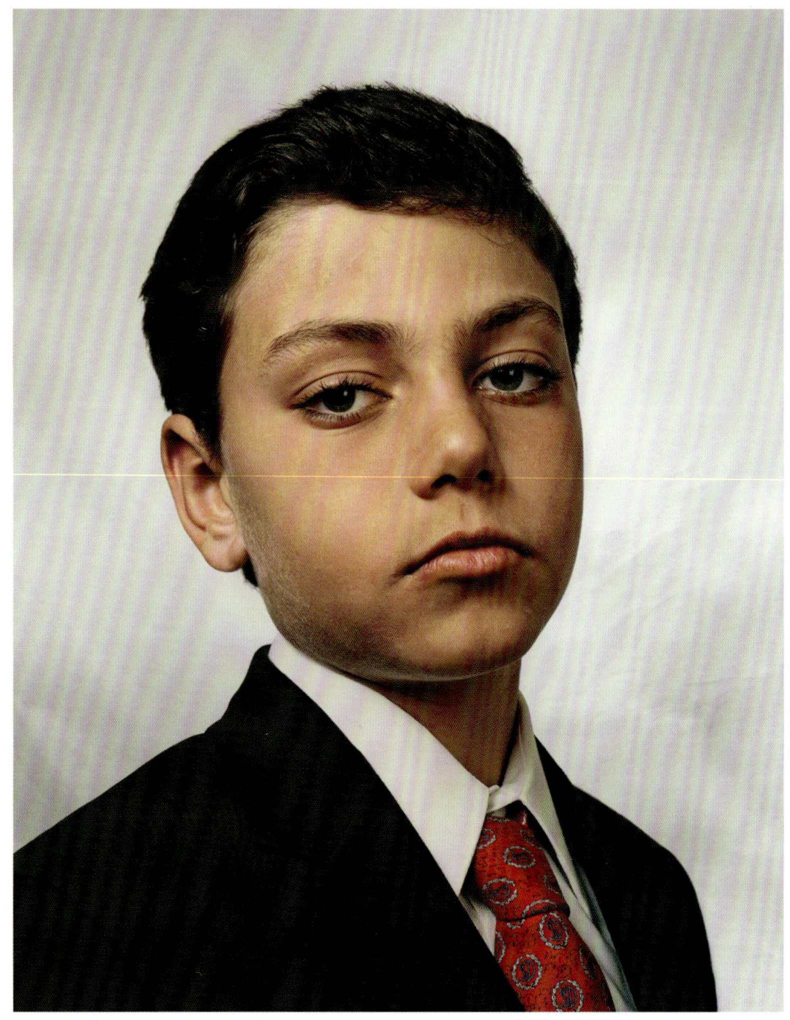

Jaime is nine years old. He lives in a top-floor apartment on Fifth Avenue in New York. His parents also own luxury homes in Spain and in the Hamptons on Long Island. He has a younger brother and sister who are twins. Places at Jaime's school are greatly sought after, even though the fees are very high. Jaime had to pass several tests before he was accepted. He is doing very well at his studies and particularly enjoys computer class, spelling and woodwork, but not geometry. He has an hour's homework each night and often finds it hard to fit this in with his other after-school activities. Wednesdays are particularly busy as he has judo and swimming lessons. In his spare time, apart from playing the cello and kickball, Jaime likes to study his finances on the Citibank website. When he grows up, he would like to be a lawyer like his father.

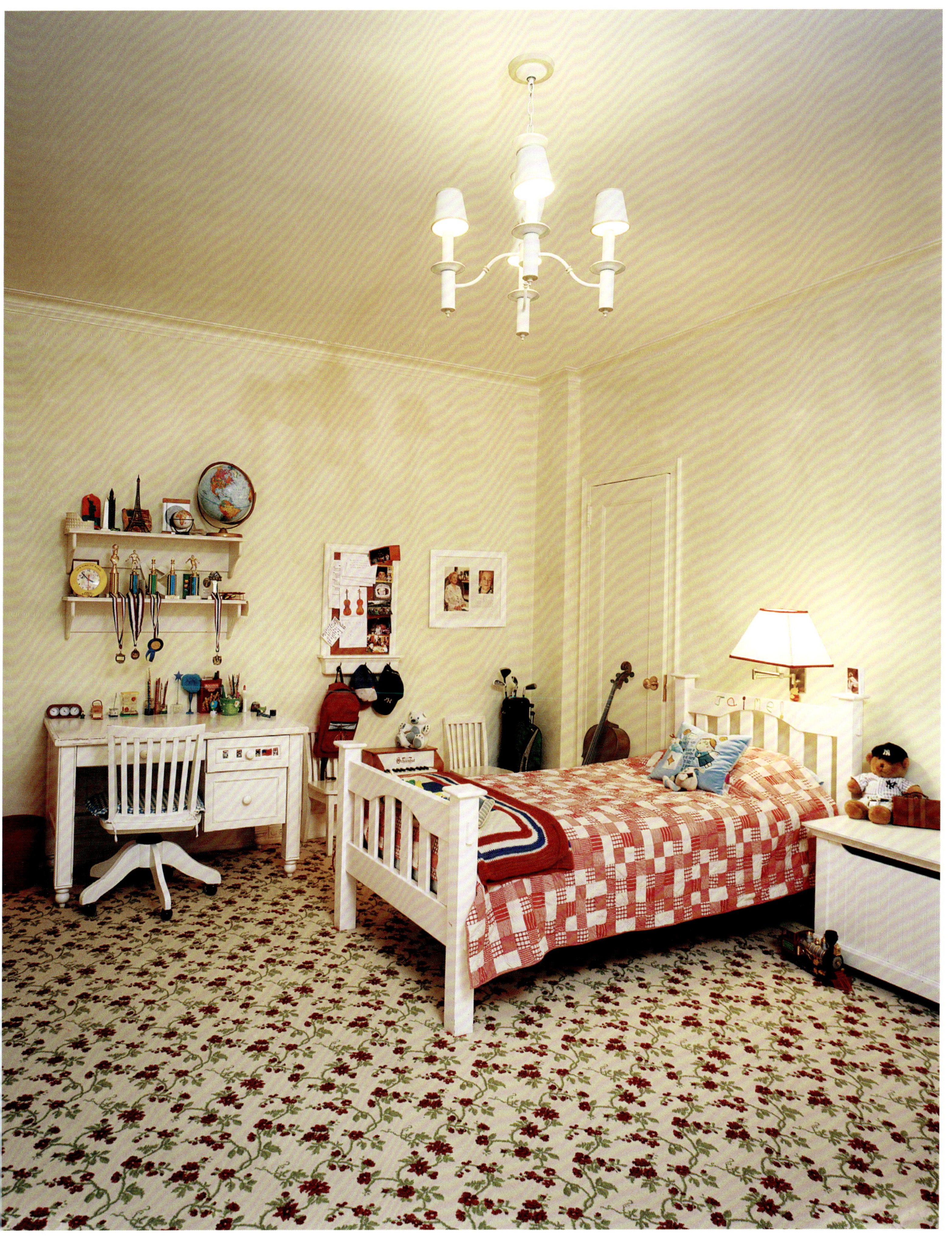
Jaime

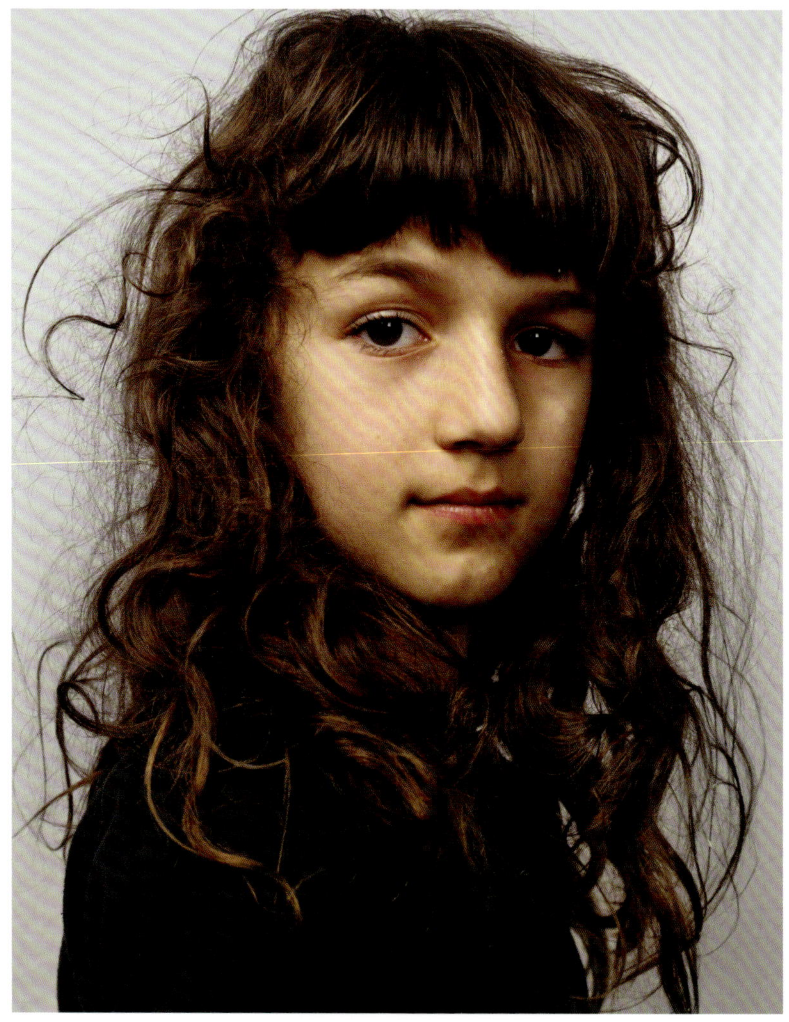

Ernesto, known as Nesty, is nine years old and lives with his parents and siblings in an old farmhouse in the countryside near Orvieto, Italy. They have six bedrooms and five bathrooms, yet the three children all sleep in one room. This helps to save money on heating bills and is also more convenient for bedtime stories. Bedtime is at eight o'clock. Nesty and his siblings occasionally help with washing dishes and folding the laundry, but mostly their mother does everything for them. Nesty can earn a star for his chart if he finishes his chores successfully. With enough stars, he gets a special treat. He attends the local school with twenty-three other children. His favourite subjects are woodwork, Italian and art. Nesty can speak four languages. He is sometimes teased about his long hair, which his mother brushes for him as he eats breakfast. When he grows up, he would like to be an ice cream seller, an artist or a rock star.

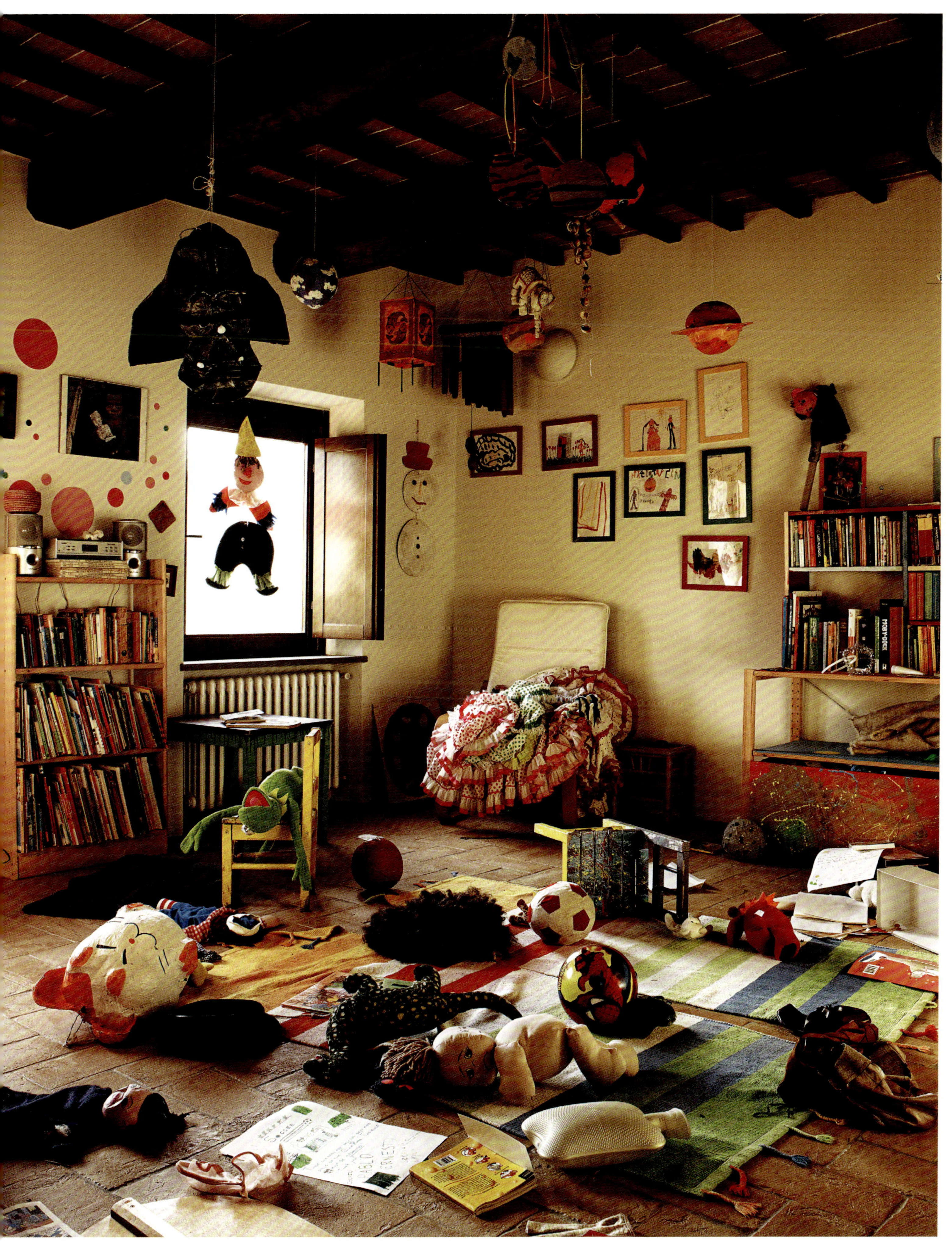
MOBY-DICK

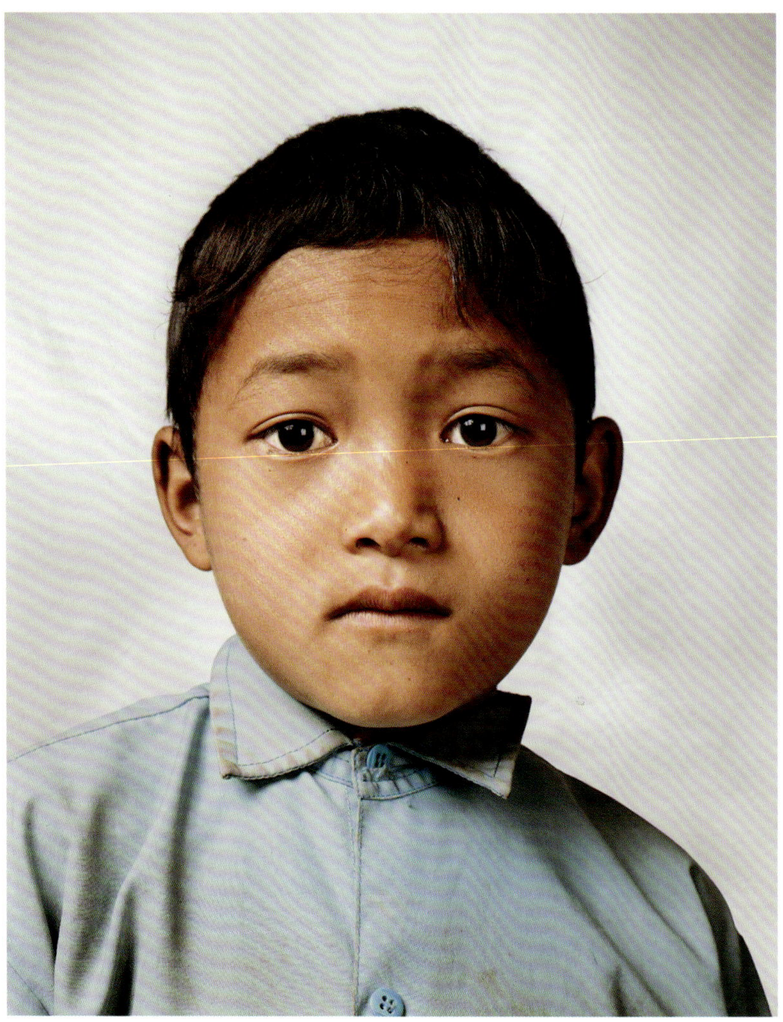

Bikram is a nine-year-old orphan. He lives with his grandparents, aunt, uncle and two cousins in the mountainous countryside of Nepal. His parents were both killed during the civil war. Bikram lives in a stone house which is a two-hour trek uphill from the nearest road. The ground floor of the building is a stable for the goats and buffalo. It is also the cooking area. The corn is stored upstairs to protect it from rats. Bikram and the rest of the family all sleep together in the corn store. There is no mains electricity, but they have a bedroom light powered by a car battery. The family own a small plot of land on which they grow the food which sustains them – wheat mash, lentils and vegetables. They are unable to afford meat or milk. Bikram works hard at school and enjoys general knowledge. He and his friend study together and play ball or fighting games. One day, he would like to be a doctor.

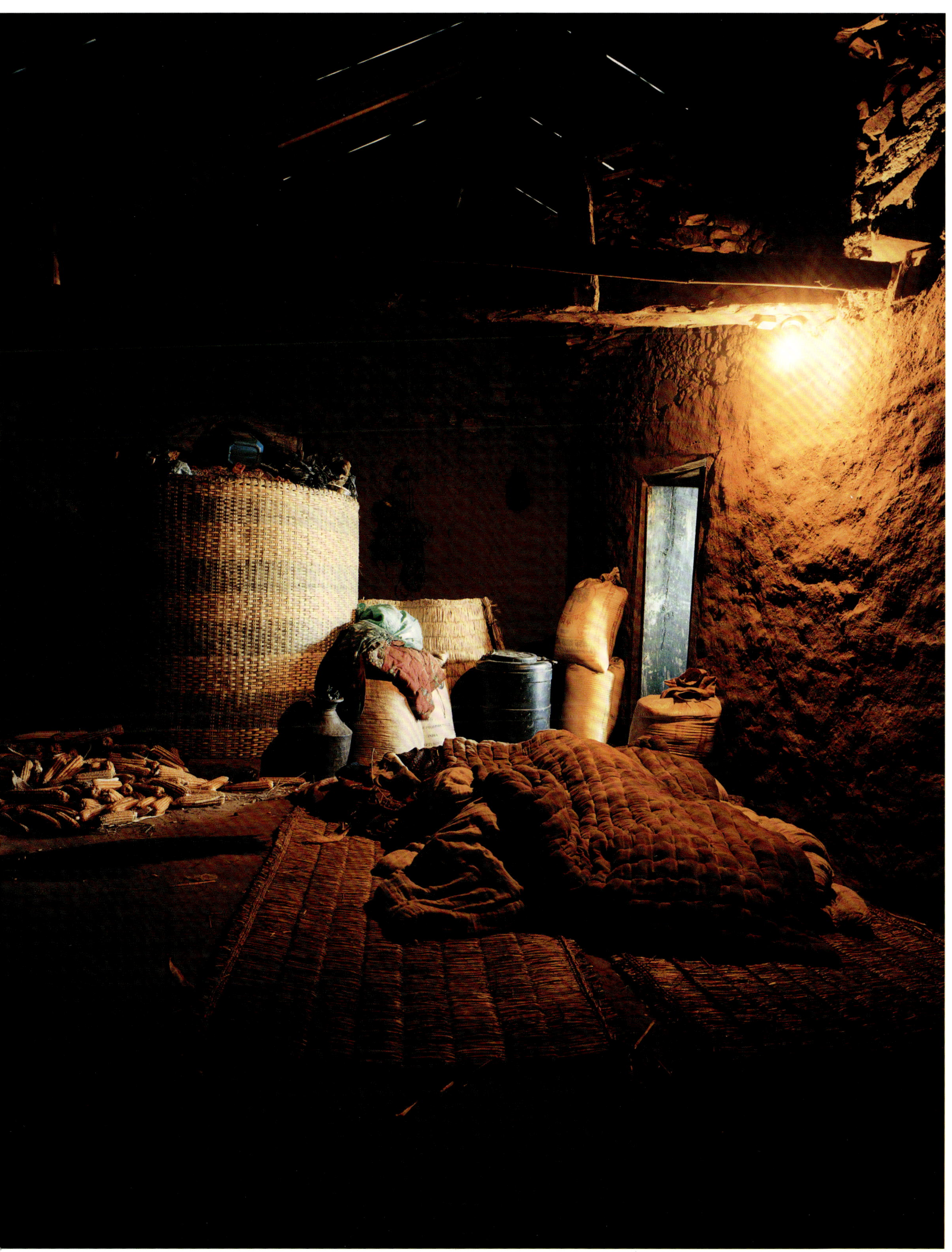

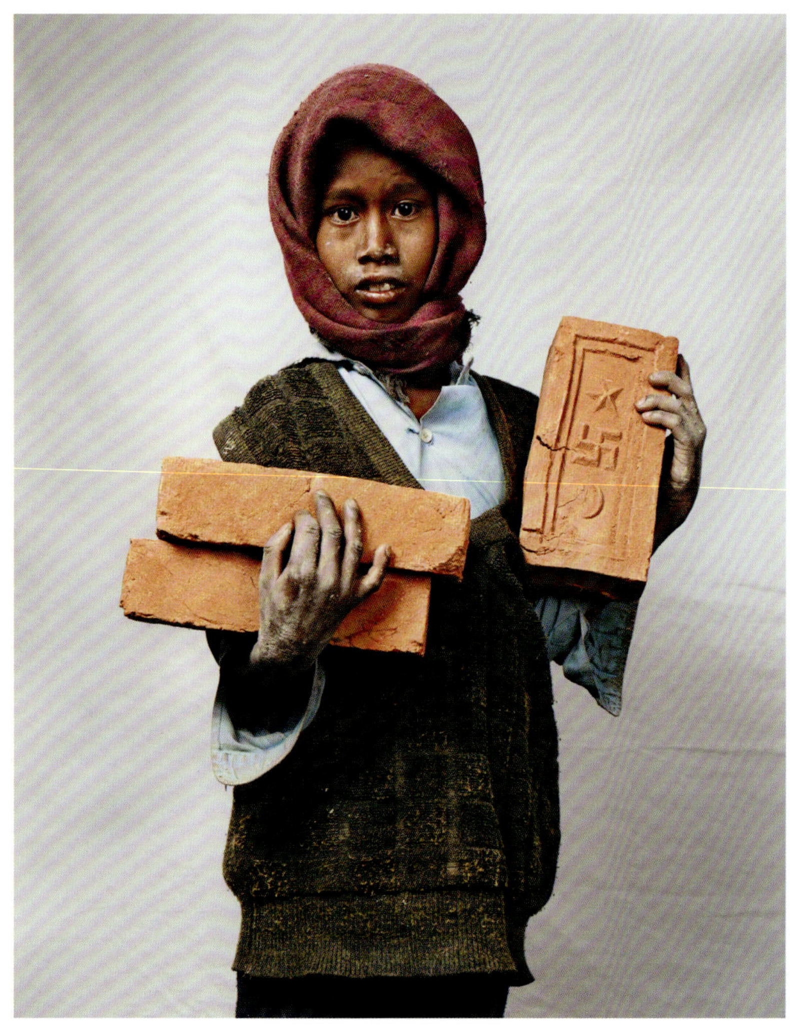

Ram lives with his parents and four brothers in the grounds of a brick factory in Kathmandu, Nepal, where they have all been working for six months. Ram is nine years old and makes over one thousand bricks each day. He also goes to school but has to fit it in between his shifts at the factory. He works from 5 am to 10 am in the morning, before walking for ten minutes to get to school, and then returning at 3 pm for two more hours' work at the brick factory. He does not like the job, because it is hard, dirty work. Ram and his family live in a tiny hut not much taller than Ram himself. It is impossible for an adult to stand upright inside. The hut has two very small rooms – a kitchen and a sleeping area. Ram's parents supplement their income by working as agricultural labourers, or acting as porters. The advantage of living here is that food is more easily available than in their home village. They eat rice and vegetables twice a day.

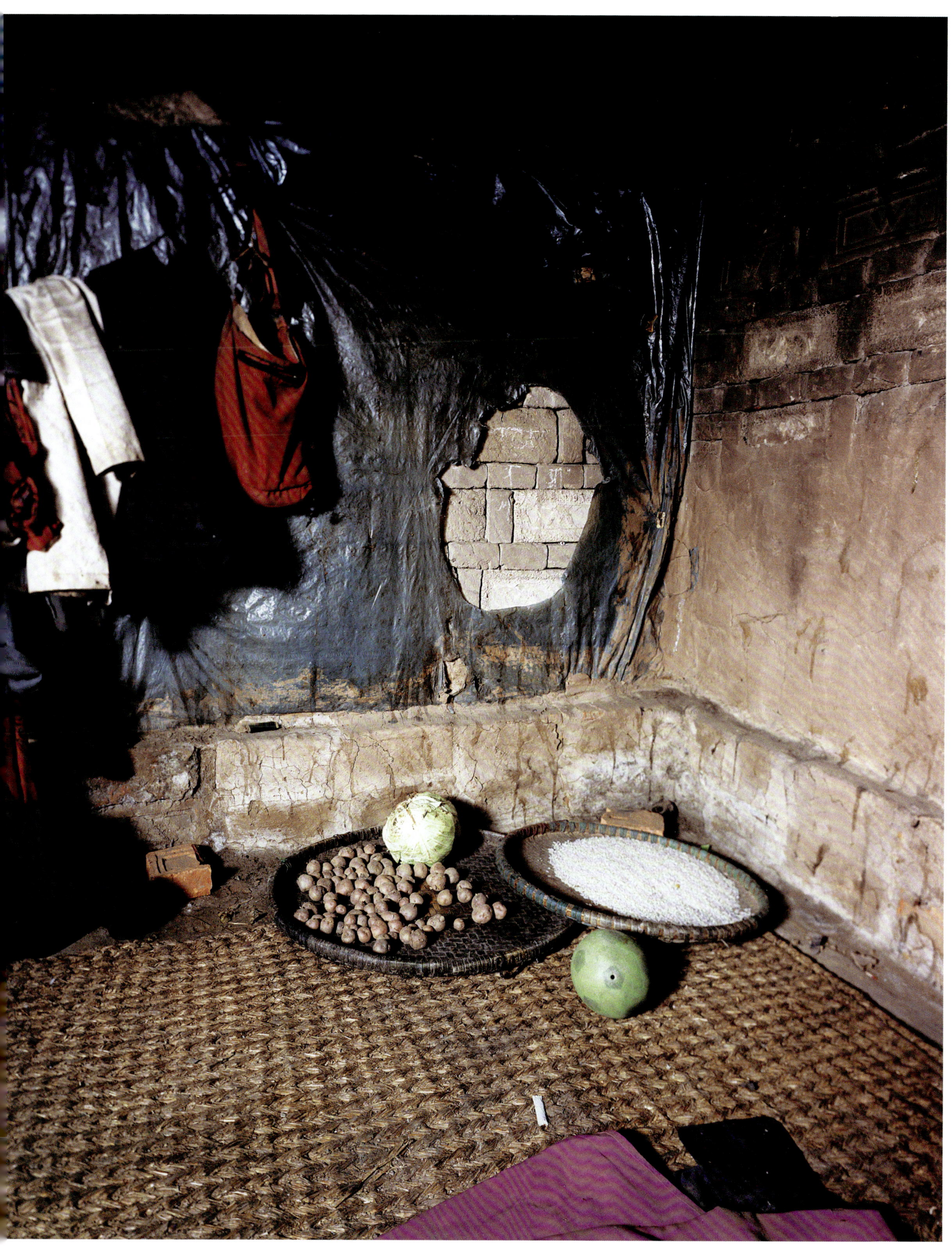

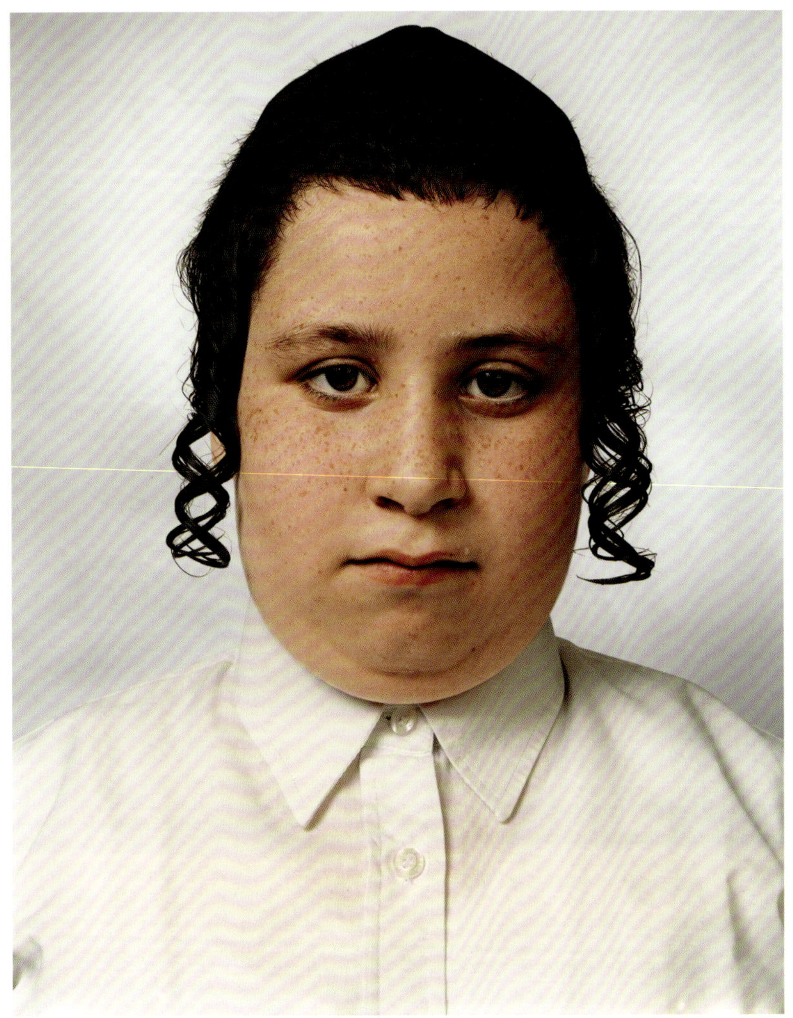

Tzvika is nine years old and lives in Beitar Illit, an Israeli settlement in the West Bank. It is a gated community of thirty-six thousand Haredi (Orthodox) Jews, who live their lives according to a strict religious code set out in the Jewish holy book, the Talmud. Televisions and newspapers are banned from the settlement. The average family has nine children, but Tzvika has just one sister and two brothers, with whom he shares his room. Like all good Haredi boys, Tzvika reveres God and wants to become a rabbi when he is older. He lives in a modern apartment block and is taken by car to school, a two-minute drive away. Religion is the most important subject, followed by Hebrew and maths. Sport is banned from the curriculum. Tzvika goes to the library every day and enjoys reading the holy scriptures. All the books in the library are religious books. Tzvika also likes to play religious games on his computer. His favourite food is schnitzel and chips.

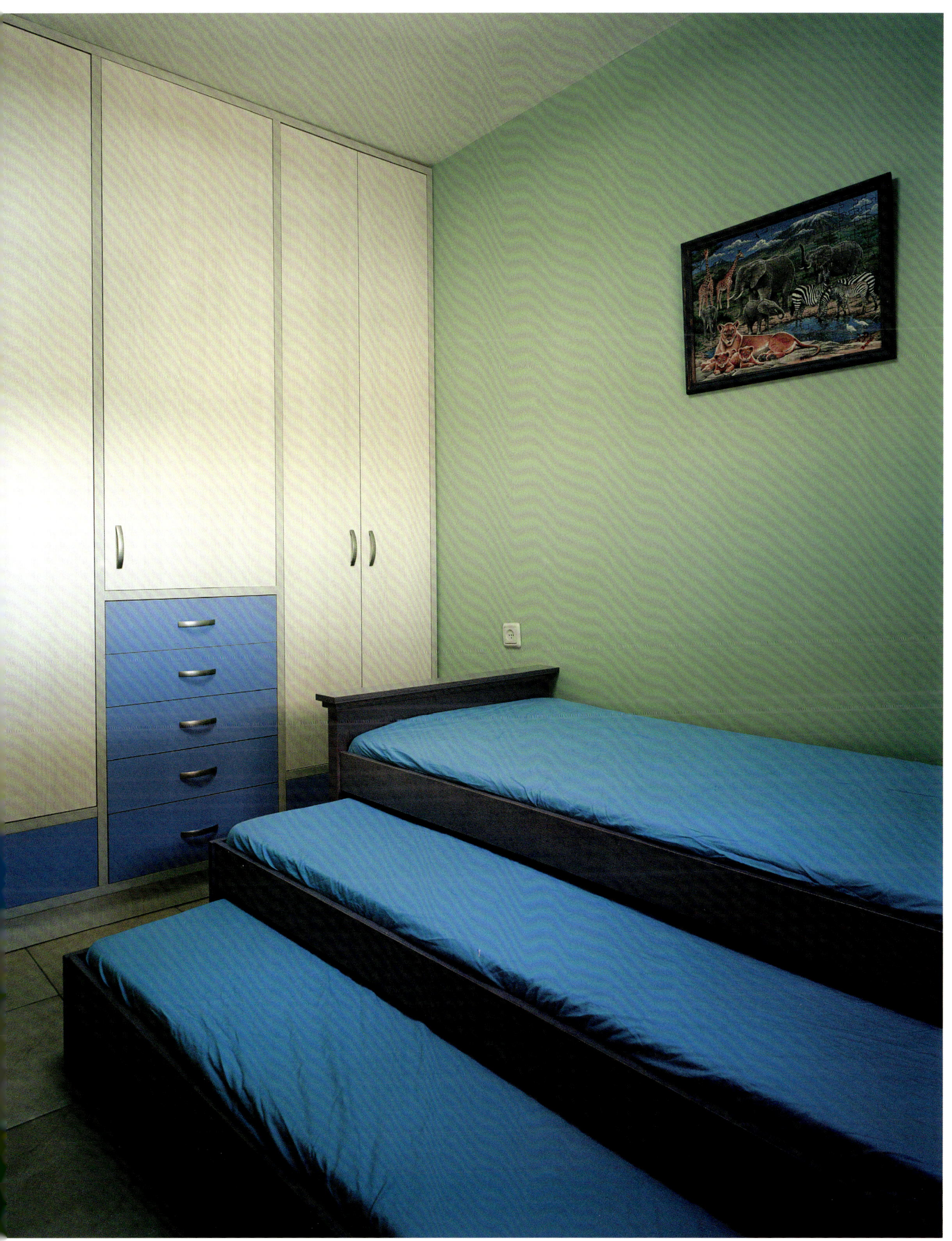

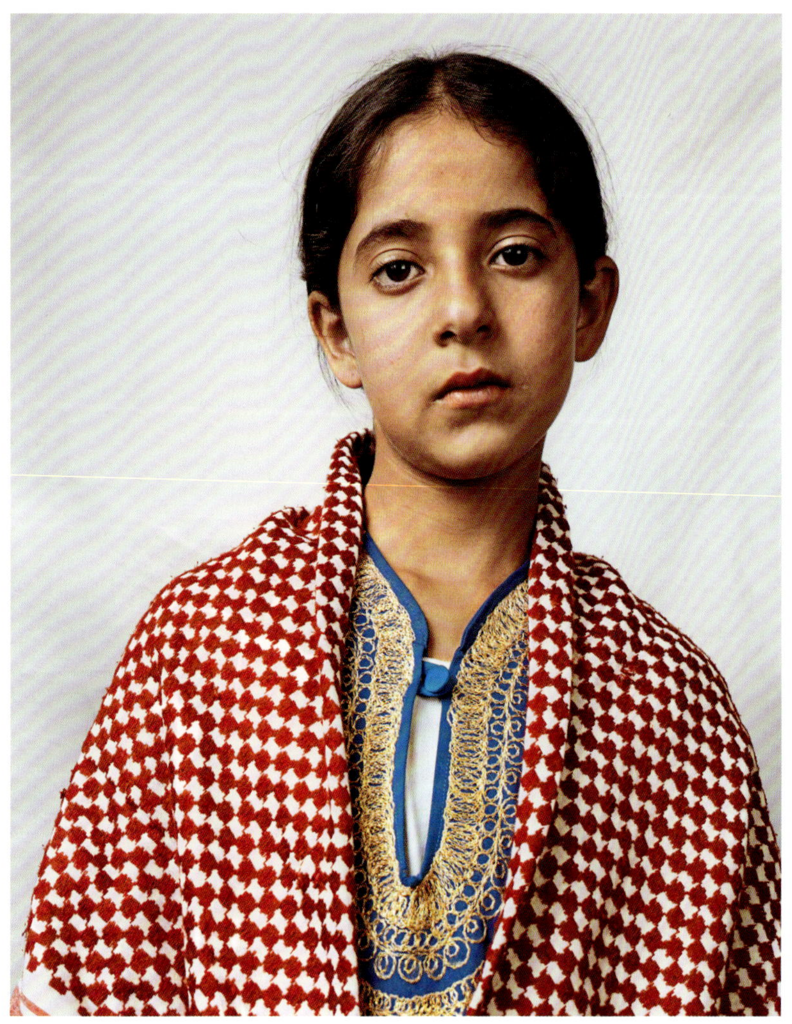

Douha lives with her parents and eleven siblings in a Palestinian refugee camp in Hebron, in the West Bank. She is ten years old and shares a room with all five of her sisters. The family diet mostly consists of green beans, meat, rice and lentil soup. Douha attends a school which is ten minutes' walk away. She works hard because she wants to be a paediatrician when she grows up. Douha's life has been severely affected by the conflict between Palestine and Israel. Her grandparents fled from their village in 1948, when Israel took over their land, and Douha's family has lived in refugee camps ever since. Douha was born in a refugee camp, and there has always been violence around her. Her brother Mohammed killed himself and twenty-three civilians in a suicide-bomb attack against the Israelis in 1996. Although no one in her family knew what Mohammed was planning, the whole family was punished for it: immediately after the bombing, the family home – including all their possessions – was destroyed by the Israeli military. Douha has a poster of Mohammed on her bedroom wall.

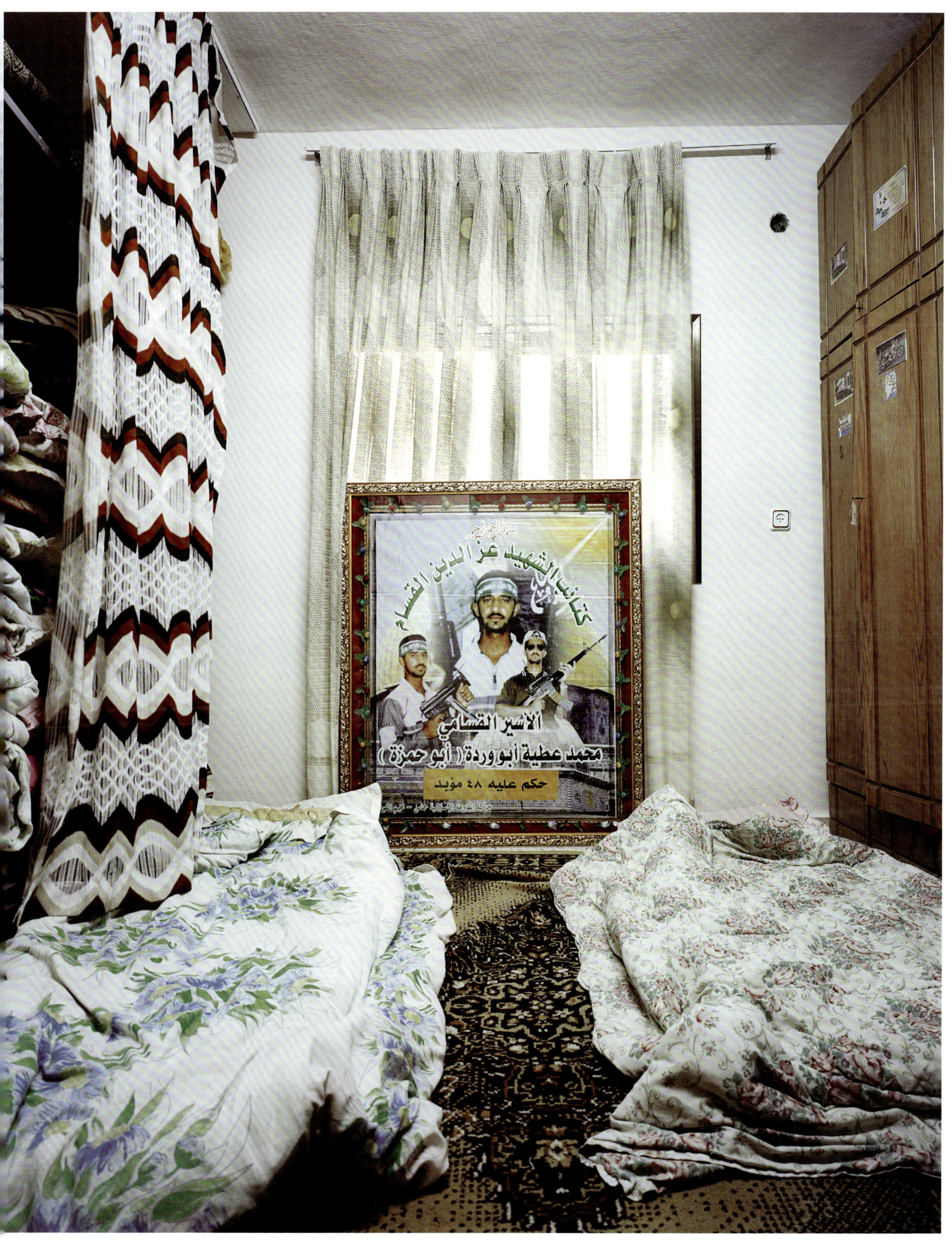
كتائب الشهيد عز الدين القسام
الأسير القسامي
محمد عطية أبووردة (أبو حمزة)
حكم عليه ٤٨ مؤبد

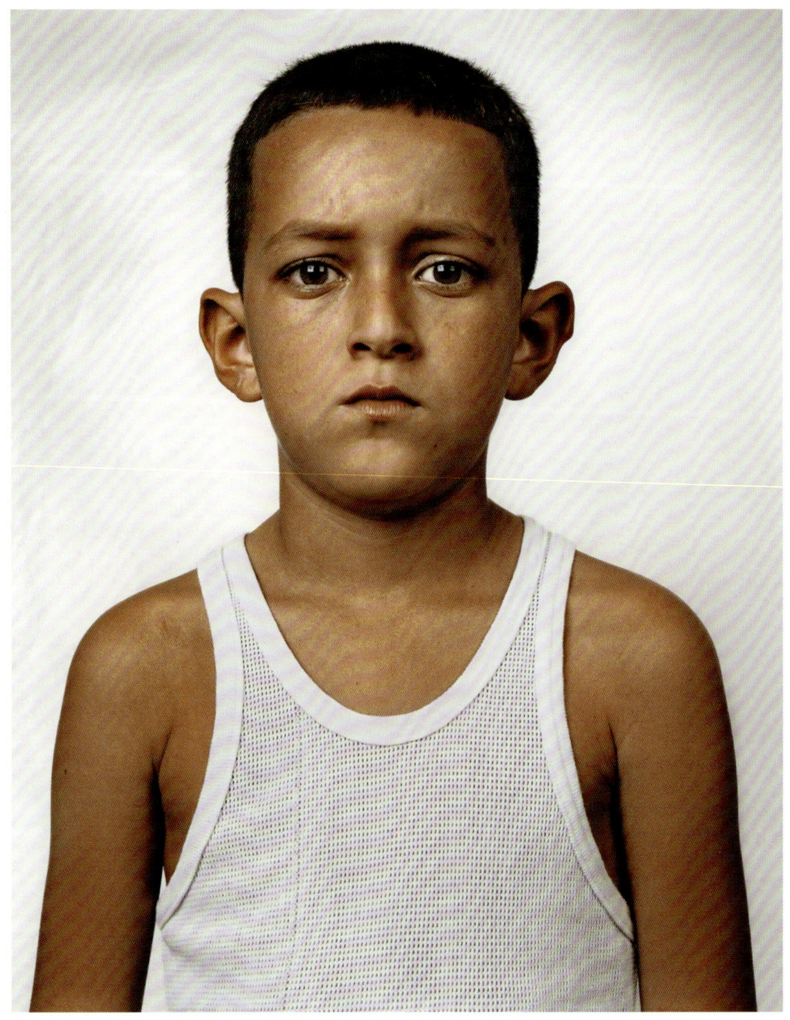

Juan David is ten years old and lives in a shanty town with his parents in Medellin, Colombia. He and his family are 'internally displaced persons', having fled from their former home town, where the community is severely affected by violence caused by the drug trade. Juan David's family now live with poor access to basic services like schools or hospitals. Their main food is soncoya, a spiky fruit which grows locally. Juan David's small shack was built by his father. It sits on wooden stilts on a steep hill crammed with other shacks just like it. The prospects for work here are very limited and his father struggles to get casual jobs as a car repairman. The family would love to move to America. Juan David is able to go to school. He enjoys playing football and would like to be a doctor when he grows up.

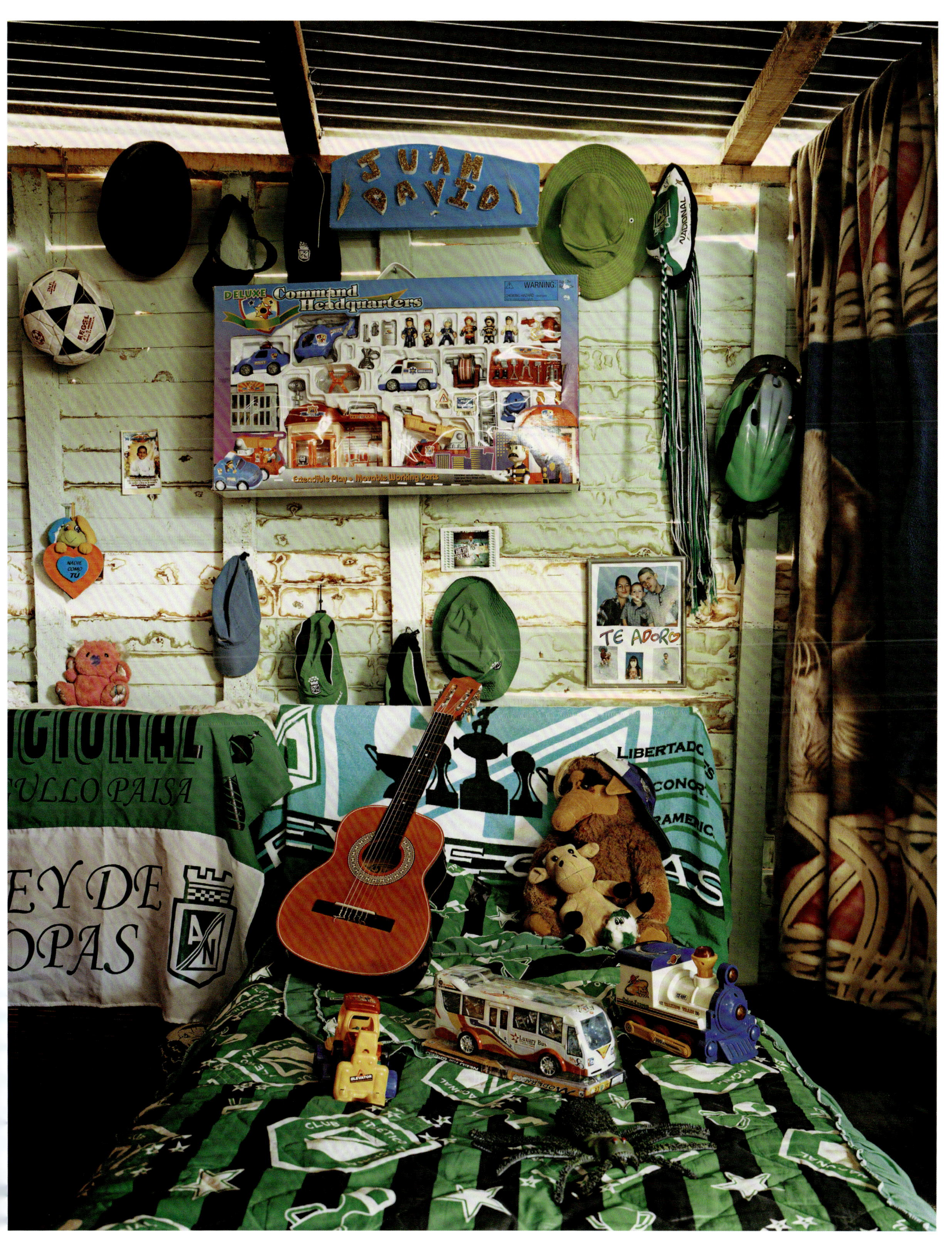

JUAN DAVID
DELUXE Command Headquarters
WARNING
Extendible Play • Movable Working Parts
NACIONAL
TE ADORO
LIBERTADO
ULLO PAISA
EY DE
OPAS
Luxury Bus
ELEVATOR

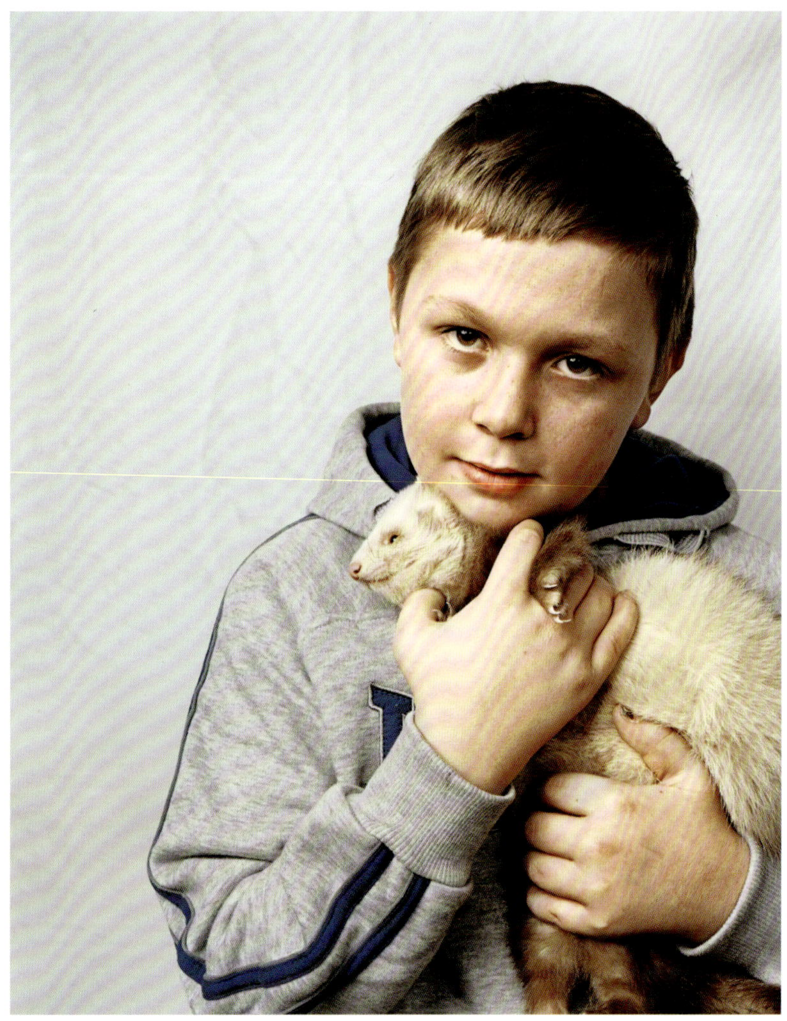

Ten-year-old Lewis lives with his parents and sister in a semi-detached house on the outskirts of Barnsley, in Yorkshire, England. He has been given an ASBO (Anti-Social Behaviour Order) because of his challenging behaviour. This means he is banned from going out at night, and must not possess drugs, alcohol, knives, or even a screwdriver. Lewis has a behaviour disorder known as ADHD (Attention Deficit and Hyperactivity Disorder) and has also been diagnosed with schizophrenia, both of which require daily medication. His aggressive behaviour has led to his being excluded from his special school seven times. His mother is quite exhausted after years of trying to control her son. As well as one-to-one counselling sessions, Lewis and his family receive family therapy from a psychologist. Lewis has felt happier since taking his medication but resents his curfew because he misses playing outside in the street with his friends.

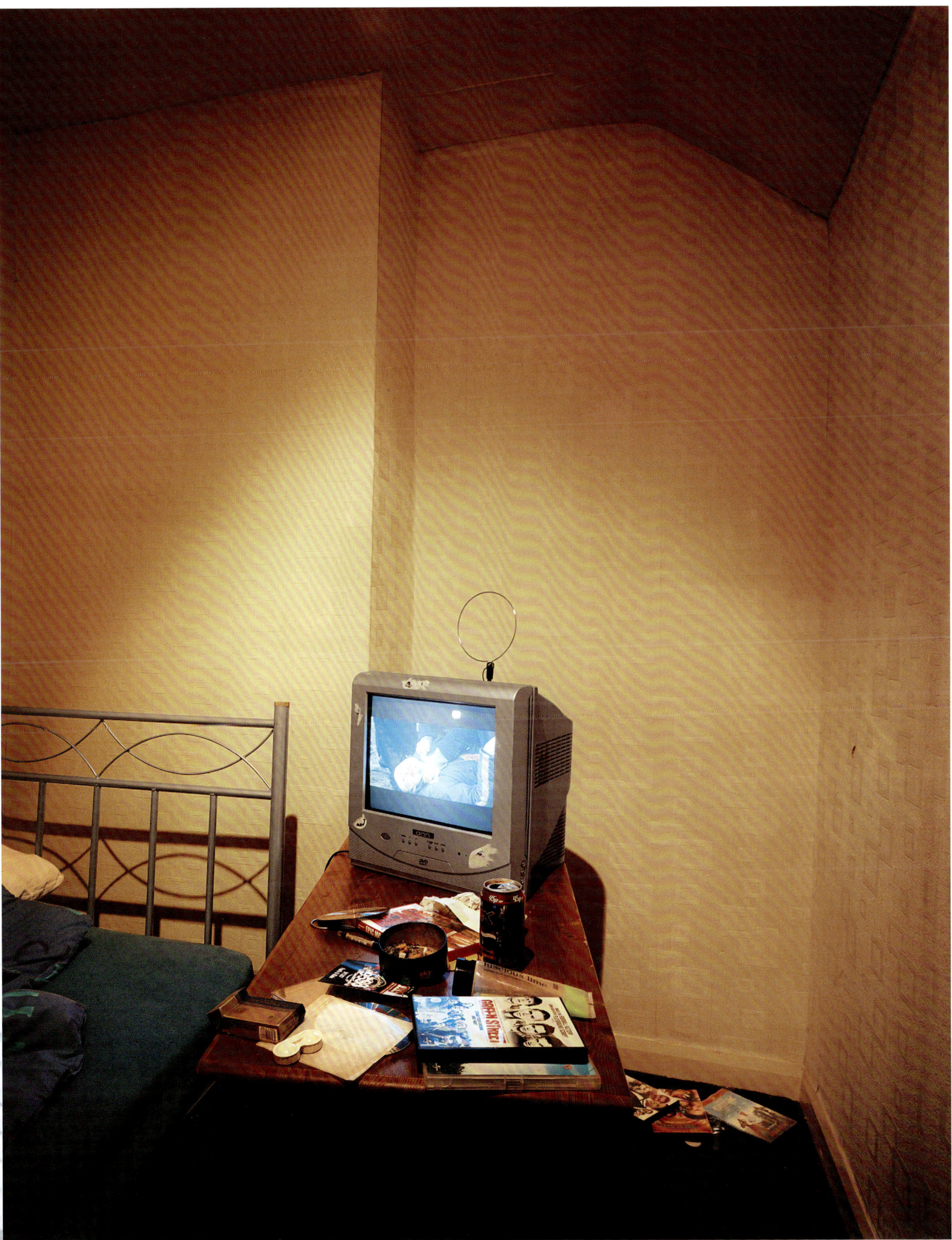
luscious lime
GREEN STREET

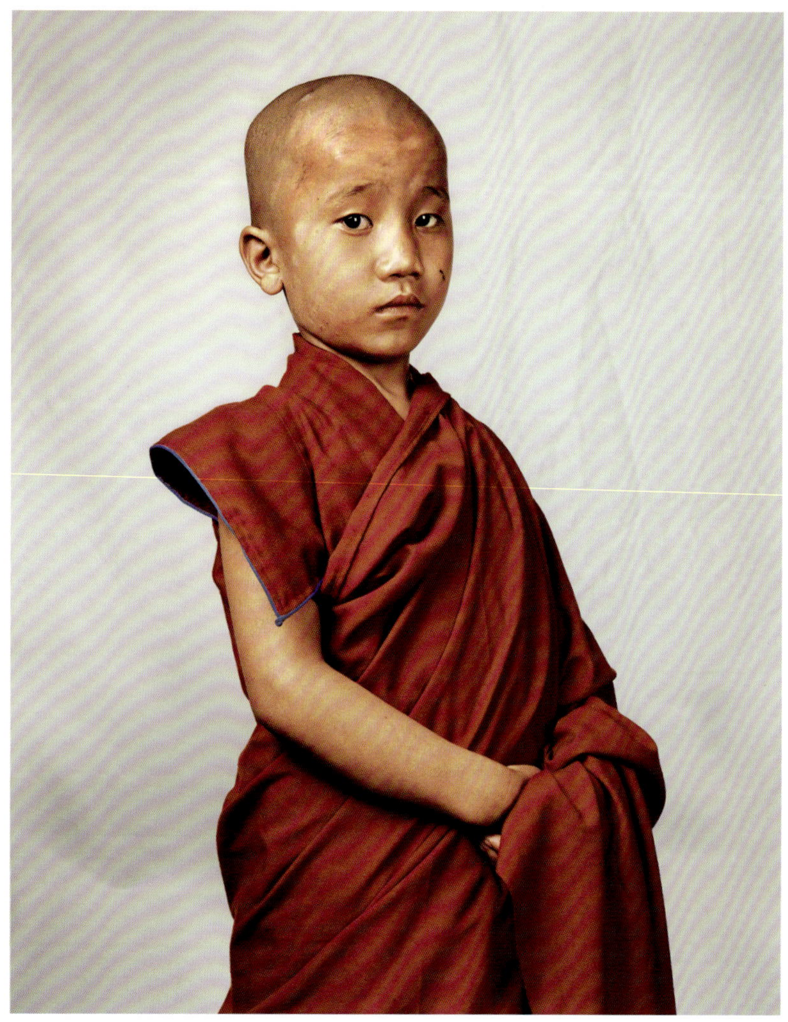

Sherap is ten years old. He lives in a beautiful Tibetan monastery in Kathmandu, Nepal, and shares a room with seventy-nine other boys training to be monks. The boys all sleep in bunk beds and have very few personal possessions. Sherap's parents sent him here because it is believed that good luck comes to families who offer a son to the monastery. It also means they have one less mouth to feed. Sherap has a long day. He gets up at 5.30 am to study, and finishes the day with an hour of chanting at 9 pm. He eats 'dhal bhat' (rice and lentil soup), 'thukpa' (noodle soup) and 'roti' (flat bread). He admires his teacher and would like to be a 'kempo' martial arts teacher one day but first he must finish school and then study privately for three years and two months.

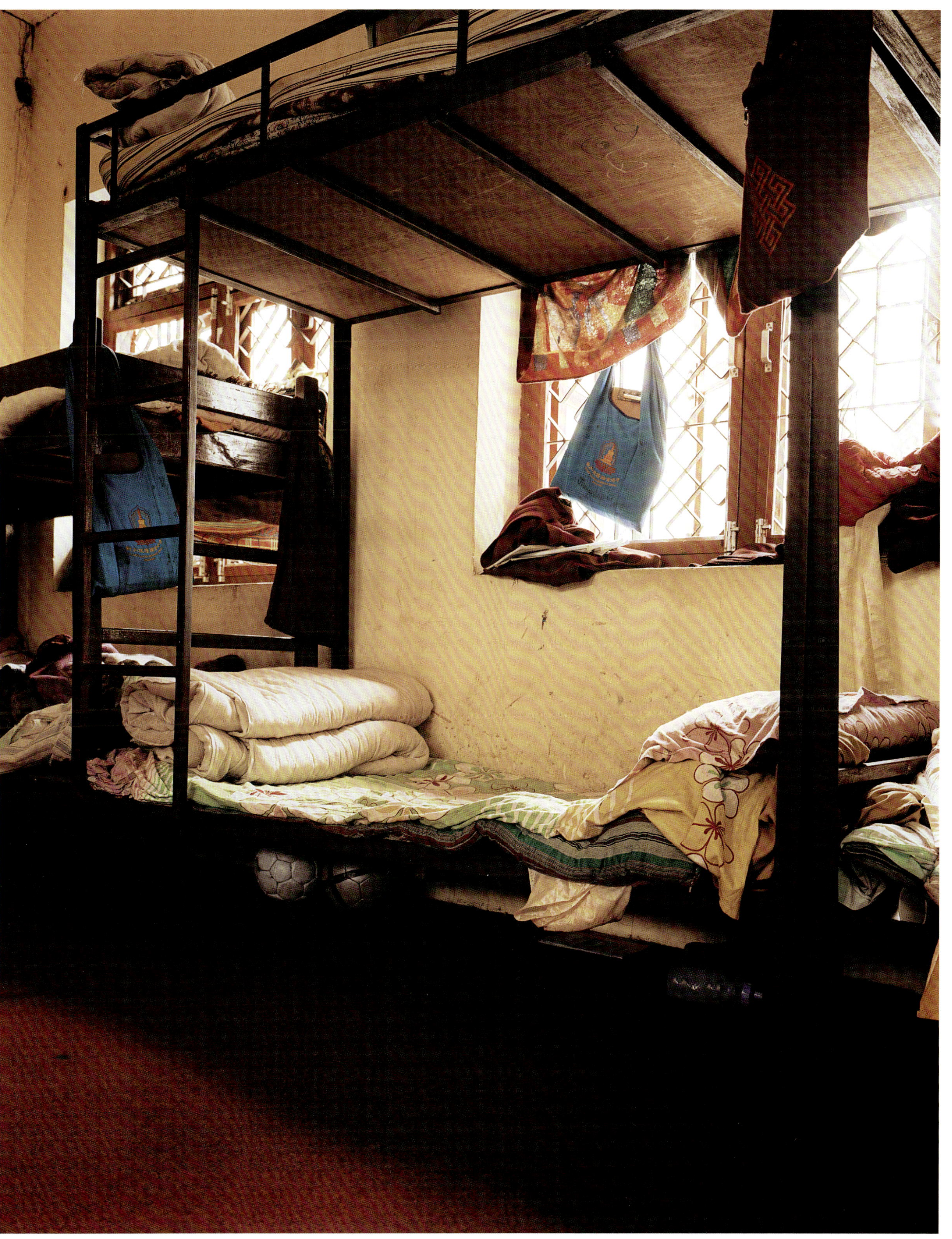

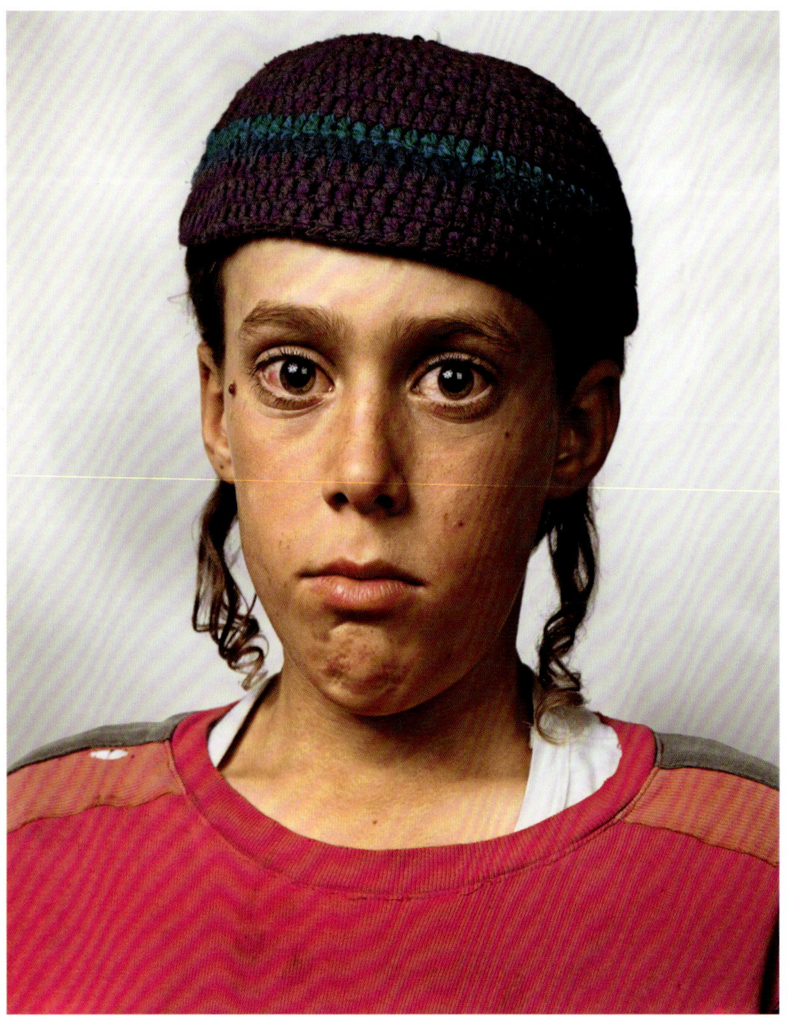

Yiftach lives in an impressive wooden house built by his father in the West Bank settlement of Bat Ayin (in occupied Palestine). This Israeli settler village is inhabited by religious Jewish Zionists, who believe that the land was given to them by God. Yiftach's parents helped to establish the community in which they live. They believe in combining a spiritual religious life with organic agriculture, but the land is steep and barely fertile – not easily suited to growing vegetables or cereal crops. The community have planted fruit and olive trees and they share goats and chickens. Yiftach is ten years old and attends school in the village, just five minutes' walk away. He enjoys studying solar energy and nature but dislikes maths. His father always carries a gun as he fears that Yiftach and his siblings are not safe from the Palestinians who live close by. Yiftach wants to become a pilot in the Israeli army when he grows up.

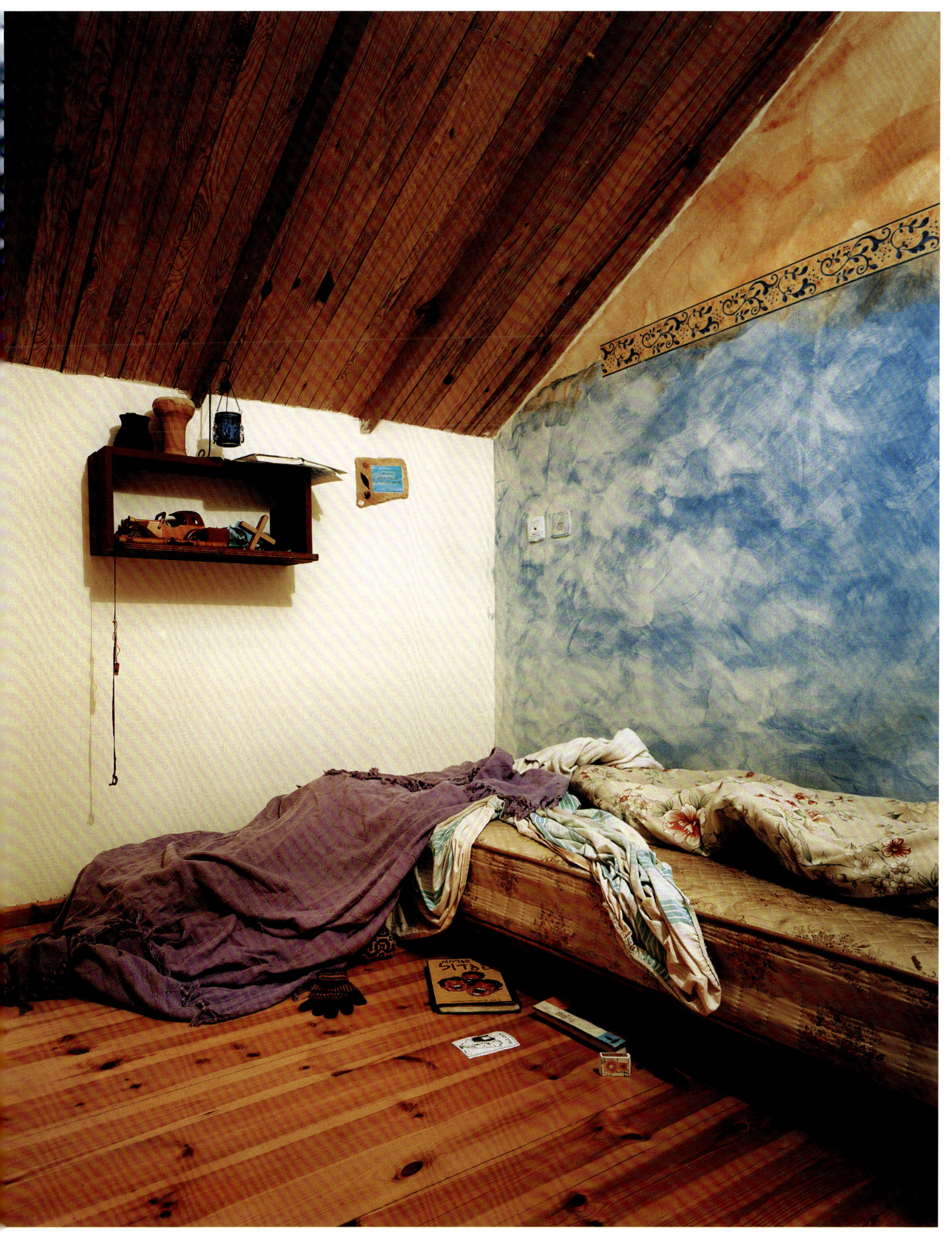

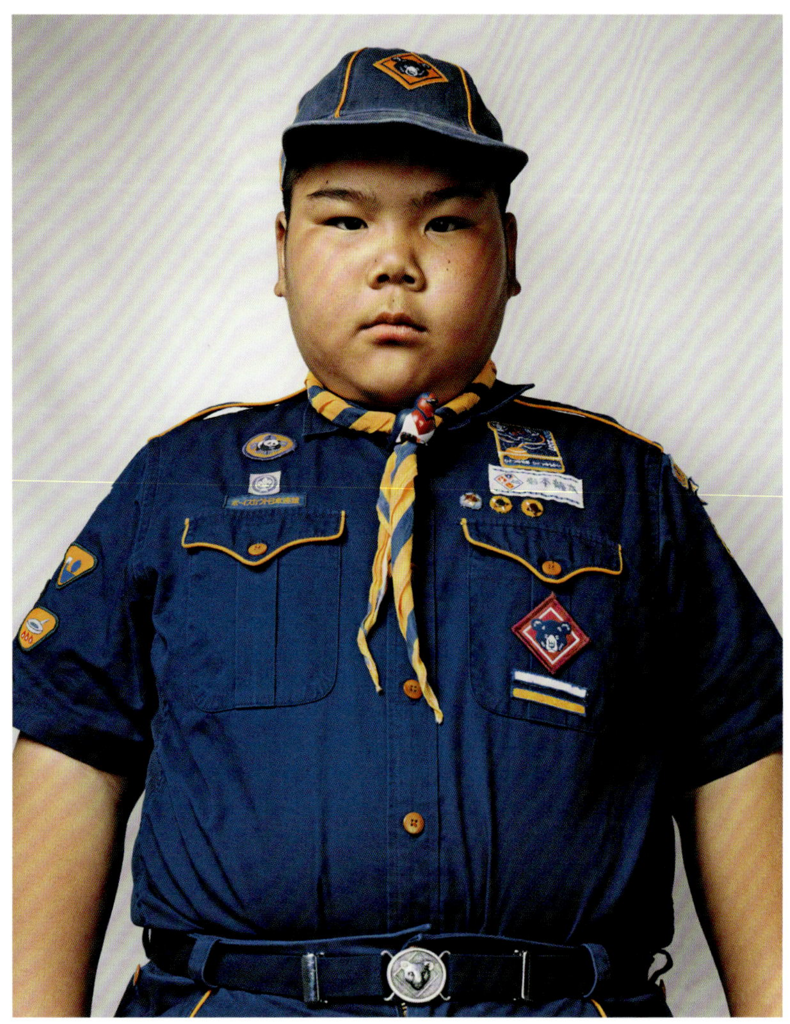

Ryuta is ten years old. He lives in Tokyo, Japan, with his parents and younger sister. He is a champion sumo wrestler and has been competing for seven years. He was very overweight at three years of age, so his parents decided to introduce him to sumo wrestling. He is currently one of the heaviest in his age group at sumo school. He is used to eating three large meals a day, including hot dogs and scrambled egg for breakfast, but he is becoming increasingly concerned about his weight, especially since one of his friends died of a heart attack linked to obesity. At school, his friends admire him because he never loses a wrestling match. Ryuta also belongs to the scout movement and enjoys outdoor activities like hiking, cycling and camping. In his spare time he likes to watch television or play computer games. Ryuta's ambition is to be a television host one day, and also to have a family.

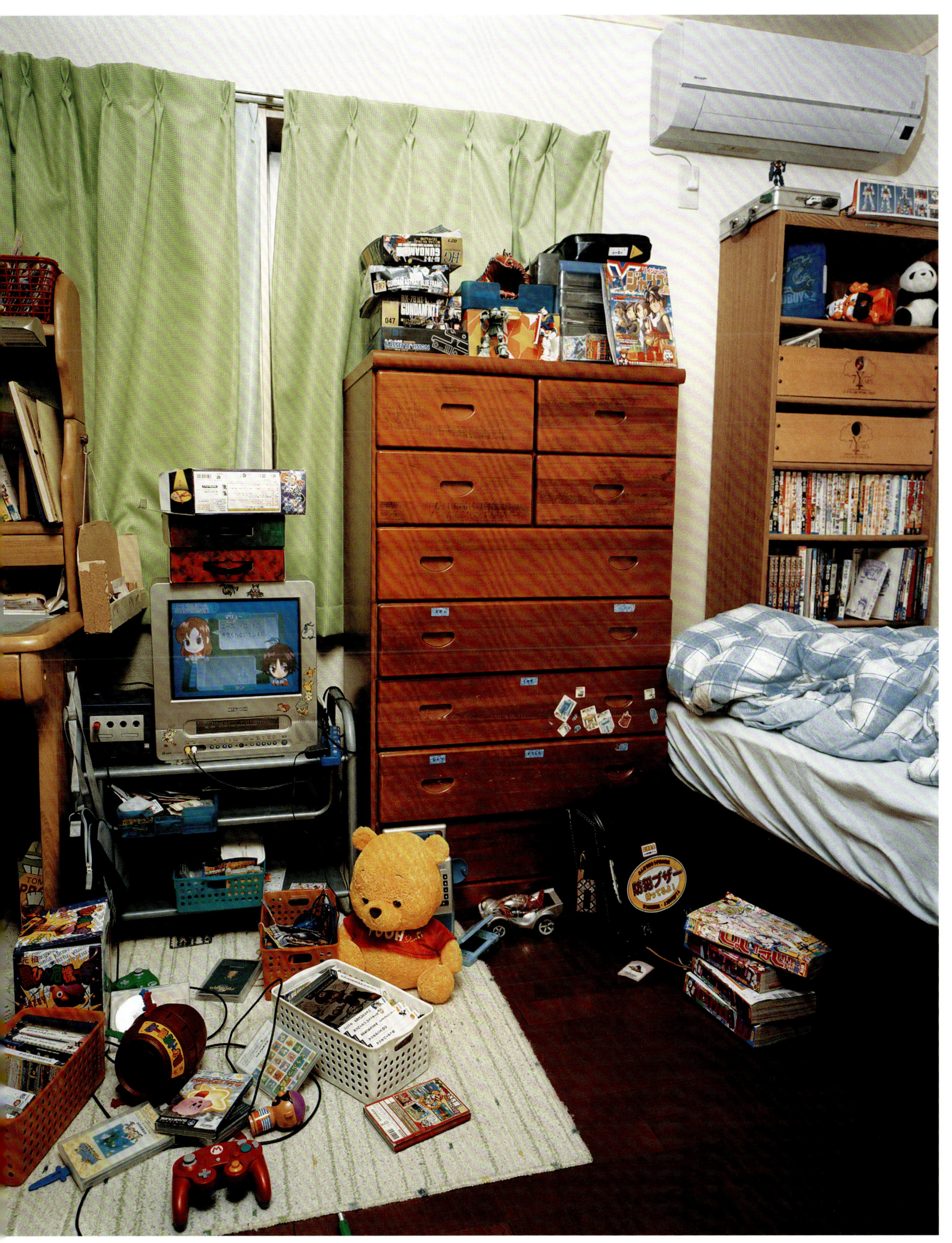

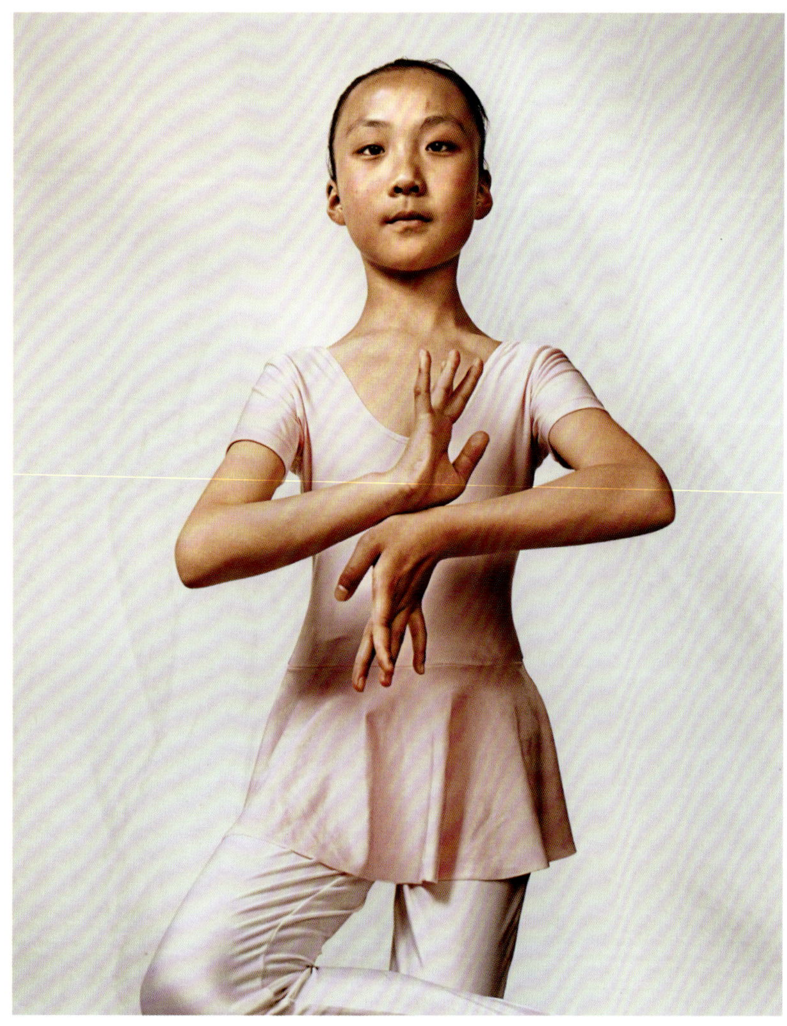

Li is ten years old and lives in an apartment block in Beijing, China, with her parents. She is an only child – as a result of the Chinese government's 'one child per family' policy, introduced to control population growth. Families with more than one child are usually penalized. Li goes to a school nearby, where she enjoys learning maths, singing and music. She is a perfectionist and will spend up to three hours each night completing her homework to the highest standard. She also attends ballet classes twice a week after school. Three times during her school life, she will have to attend a compulsory army summer camp organized by the People's Liberation Army. In preparation for this she has to attend army training. Li does not want to be in the army when she grows up. She wants to be a policewoman so that she can protect people.

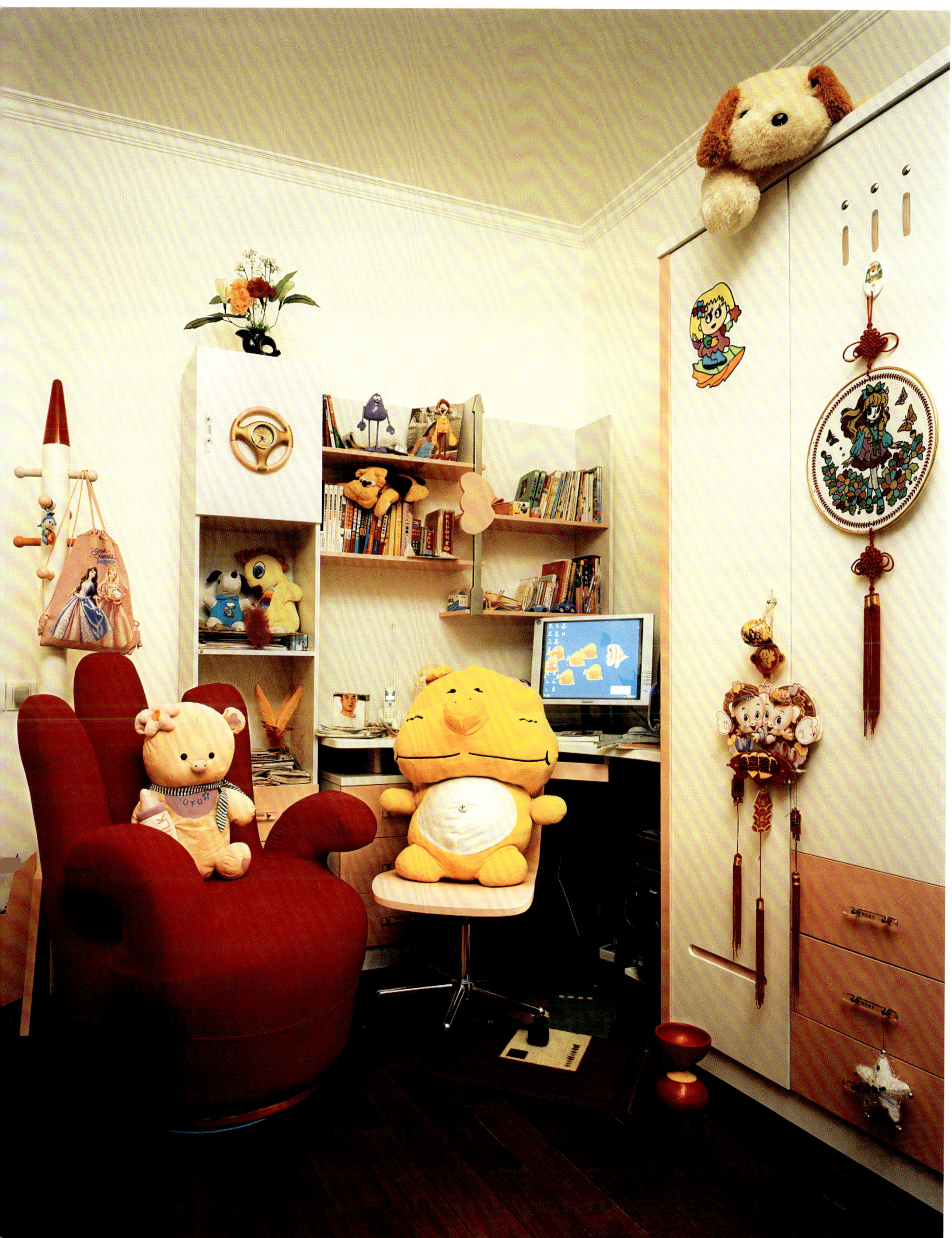

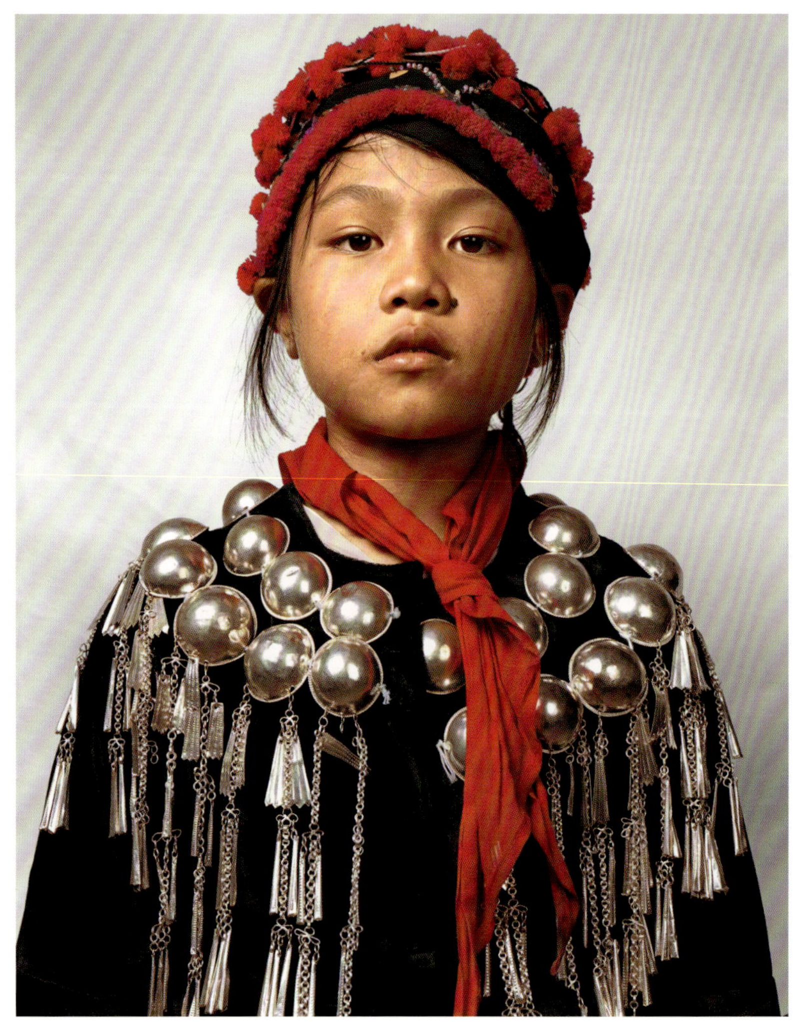

Eleven-year-old Lei lives with her grandparents, brother and two cousins, in the Yunnan province of Southwest China. Her parents, like many others, had to move to a large city to live and work – making Lei one of the millions of 'children left behind' – but they still visit their children once a week. Lei's grandparents are farmers and grow rice, sugar cane and vegetables. They now live in a city, which is far more convenient for schools, markets and hospitals. Lei walks to school, which is one kilometre away. She has thirty minutes of homework each night. Her grandmother wishes that Lei had a greater understanding of her ethnic background. She feels it is important for a person to recognize their own identity and pass on customs from generation to generation. Lei would like to be a doctor when she grows up and hopes that her parents will be able to borrow enough money to send her to university.

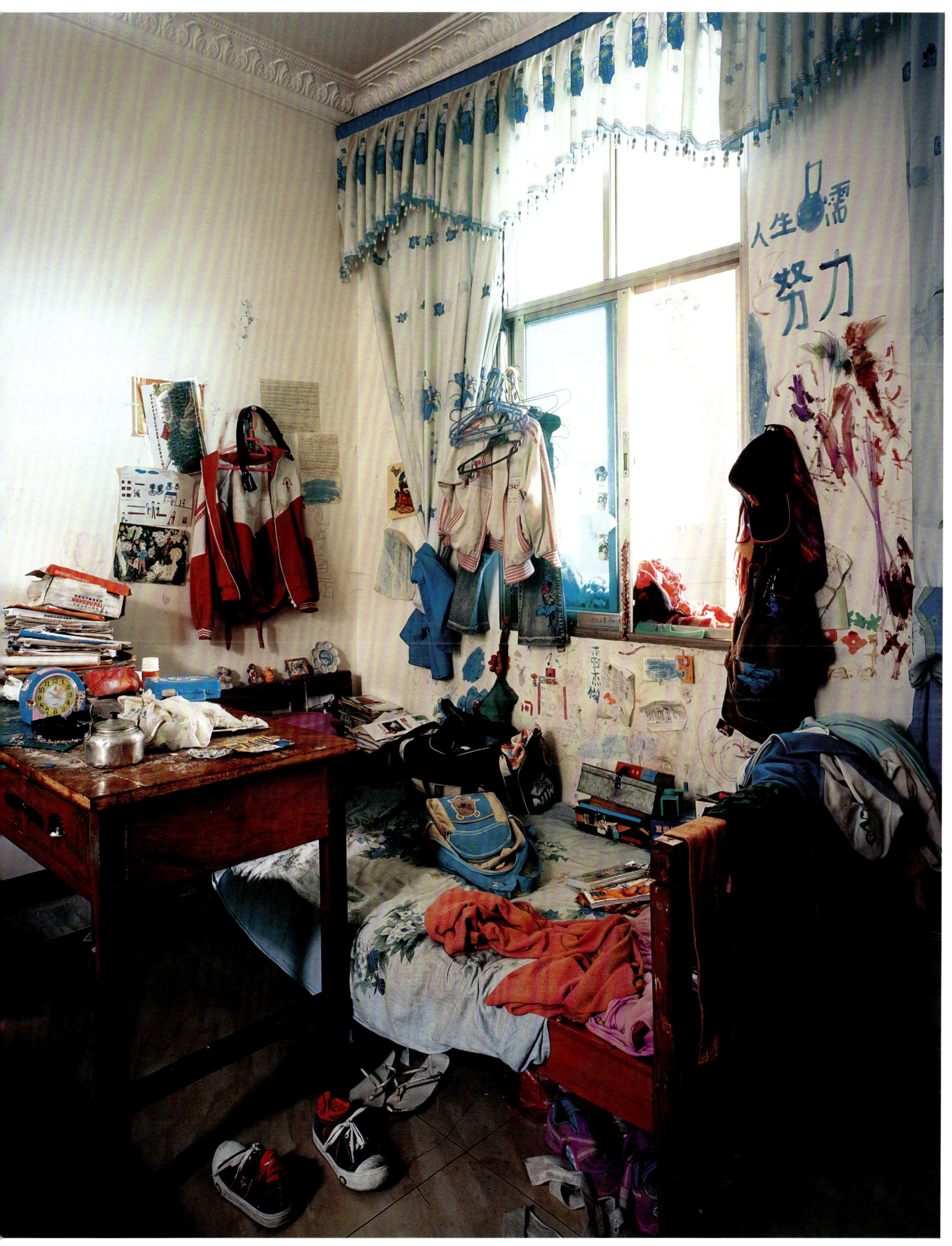
人生需
努力

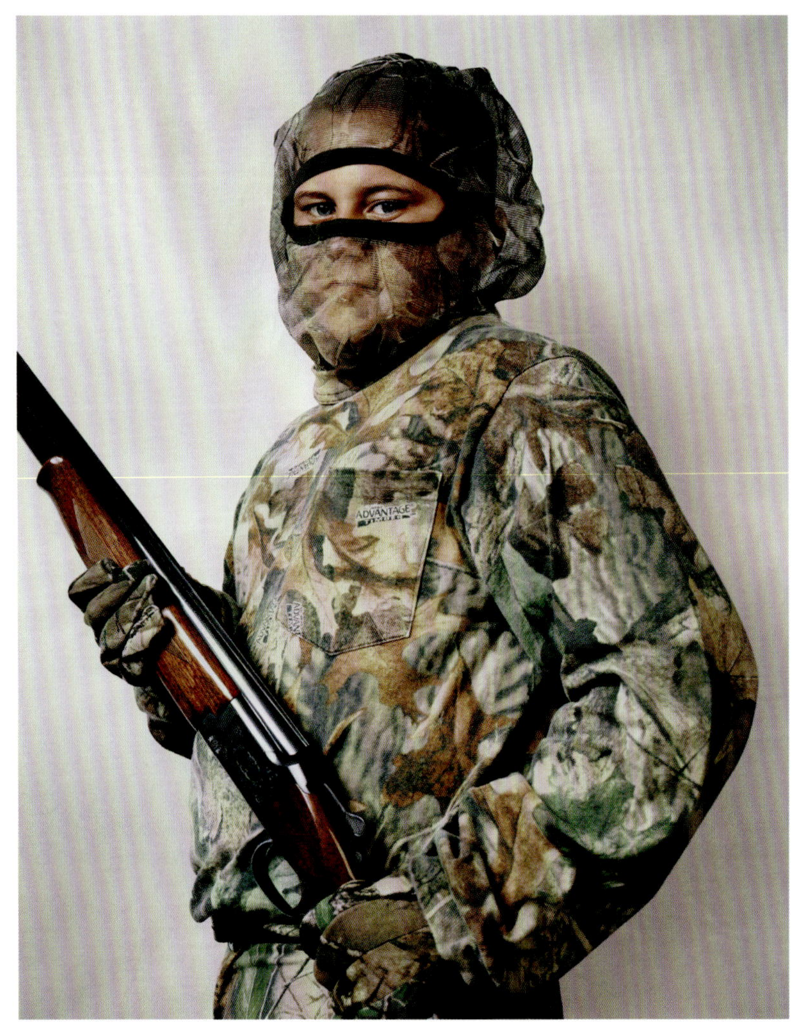

Joey lives in Kentucky, USA, with his parents and older sister. He is eleven years old. He regularly accompanies his father on hunts. He owns two shotguns and a crossbow and made his first kill – a deer – at the age of seven. He is hoping to use his crossbow during the next hunting season as he has become tired of using a gun. He loves the outdoor life and hopes to continue hunting into adulthood. His family always cook and eat the meat from the animal they have shot. Joey does not agree that an animal should be killed just for sport. When he is not out hunting, Joey attends school and enjoys watching television with his pet bearded dragon lizard, Lily.

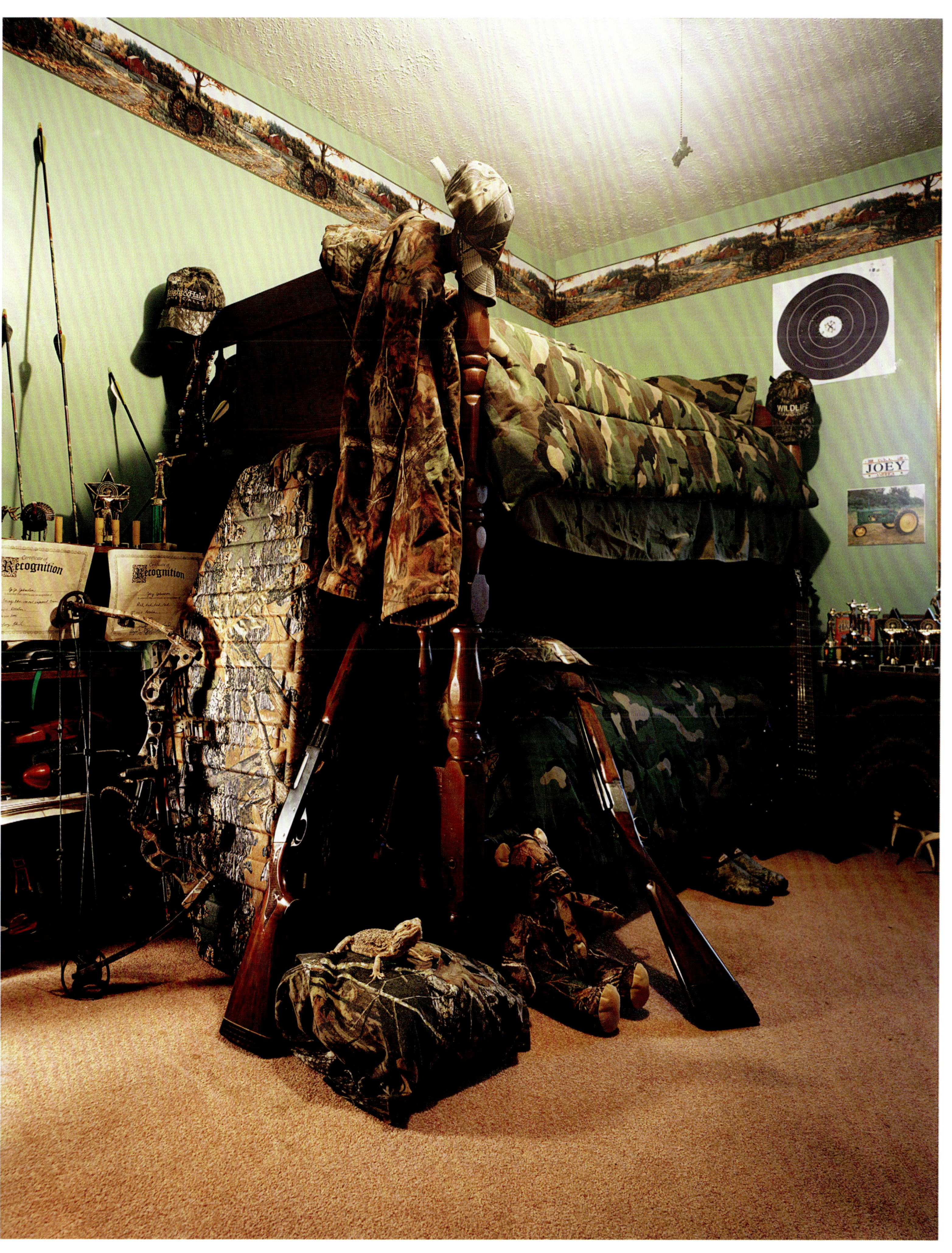
Recognition
Recognition
WILDLIFE
JOEY

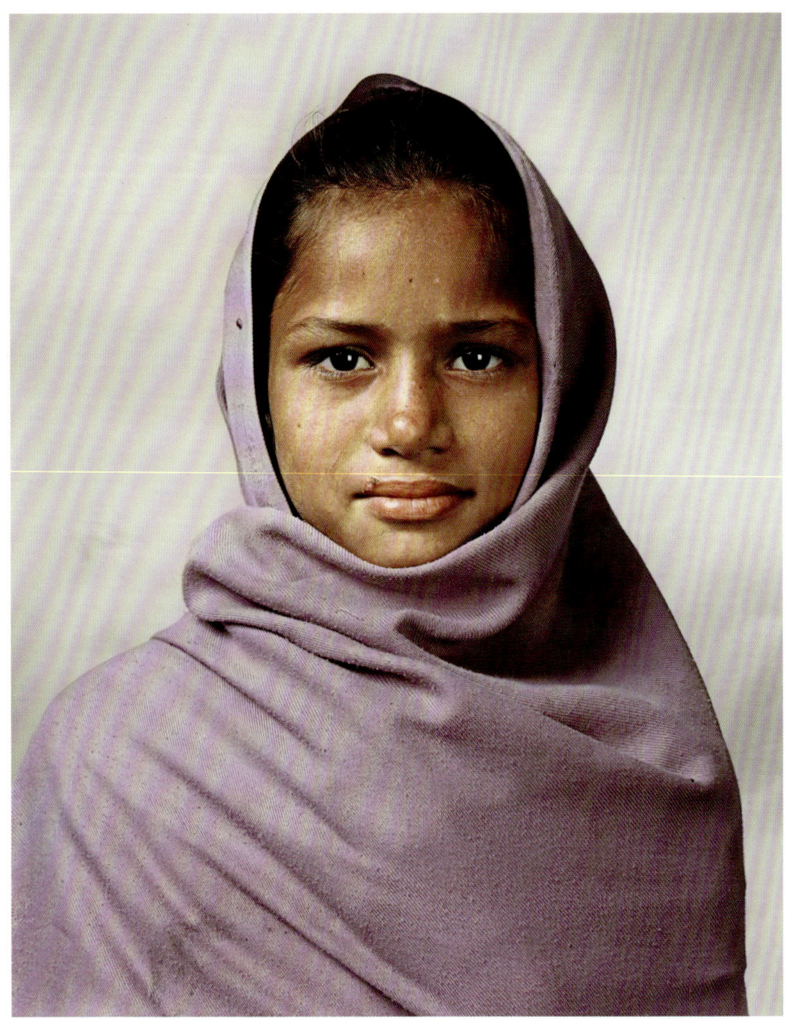

Netu lives in Kathmandu, Nepal, in an area known as 'Beggars' City'. She used to live in India with her parents, four sisters and brother. Her parents were unable to support the family and there was not enough food to survive, so they had to send Netu, the eldest, away to live with her aunt. They had hoped for better prospects for their daughter. They spent one week's salary on the bus fare for Netu to travel to Kathmandu. The journey took three days. Netu is eleven years old and now has to beg for money on the city's streets. It is only the tourists who are willing to donate anything and often she goes home with nothing. Her home is a plastic-sheeted shack. The room measures four metres by six metres and contains two beds. Four people sleep in one bed, three in the other, and four people sleep on the floor.

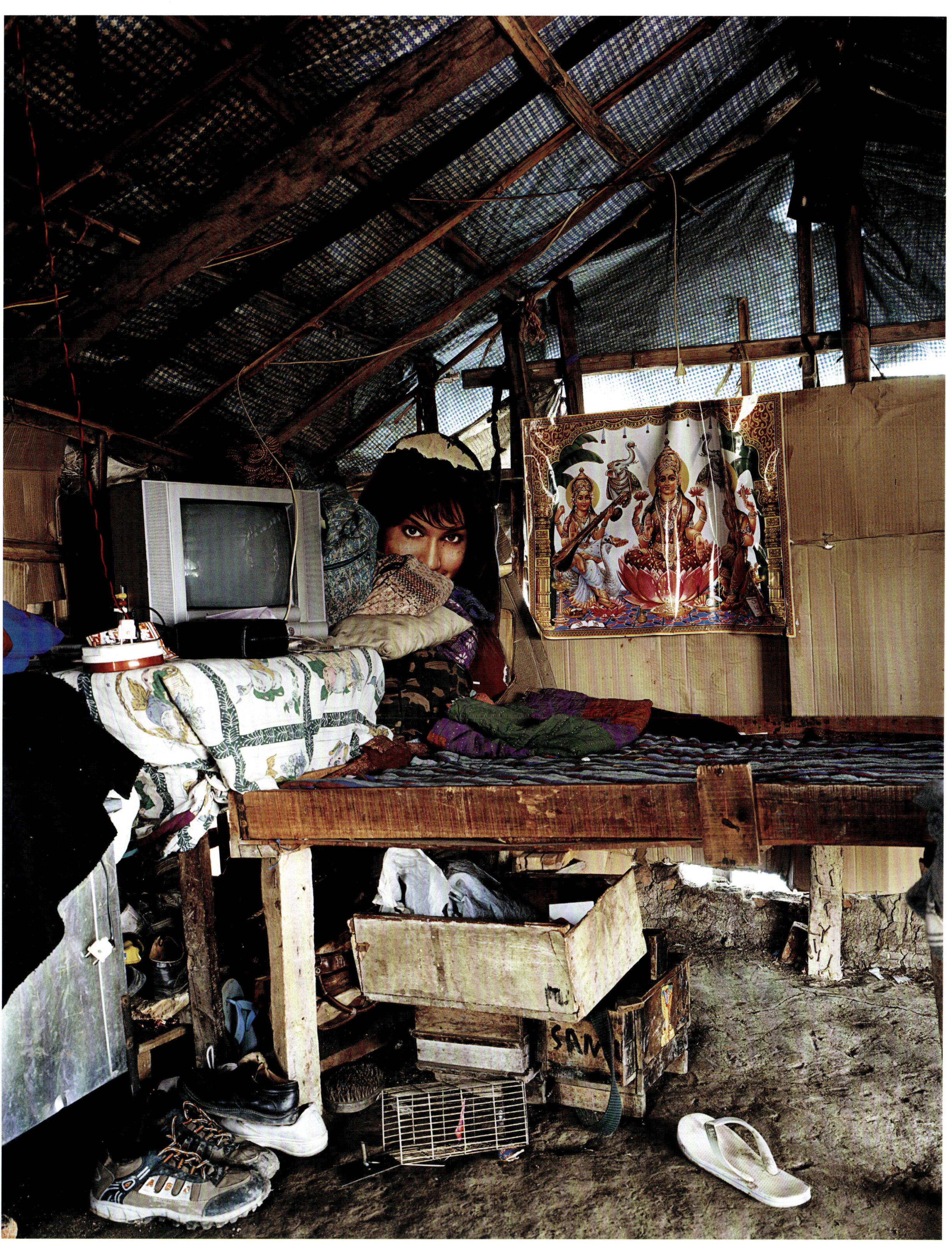

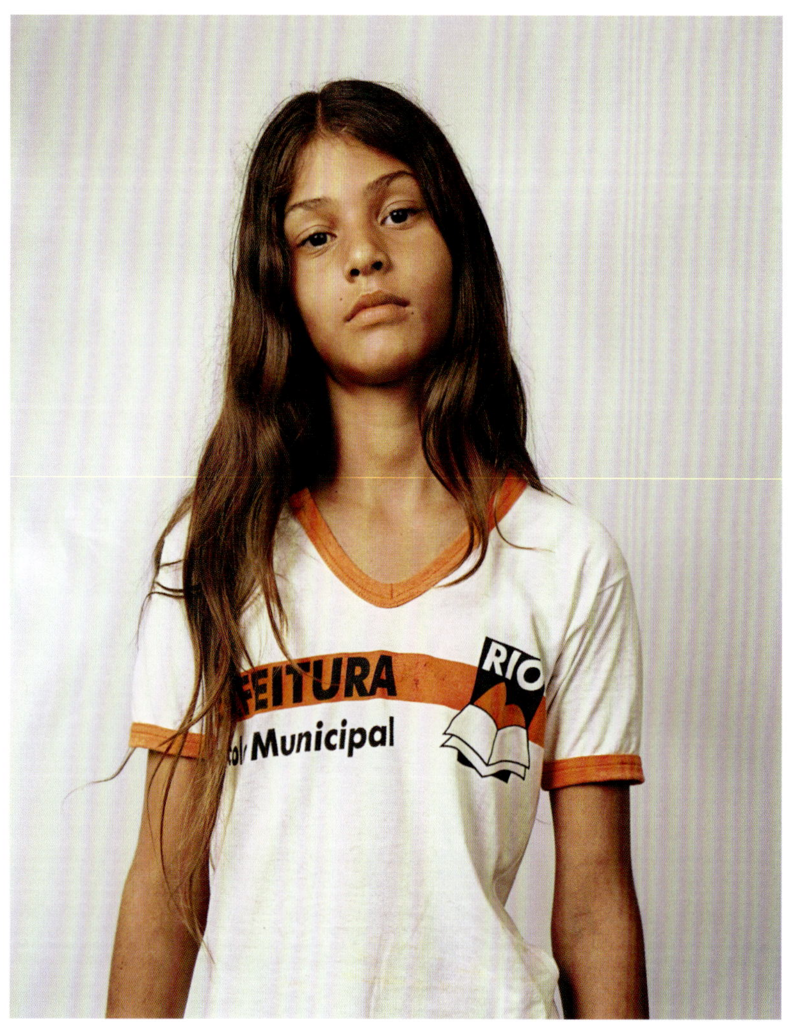

Thais is eleven years old and lives with her parents and sister on the third floor of a block of flats in Rio de Janeiro, Brazil. There are two bedrooms in the flat, so Thais has to share her room with her sister. They live in the Cidade de Deus ('City of God') neighbourhood in the western zone of Rio de Janeiro. It used to be a poverty-stricken, crime-ridden area, dominated by gang rivalry and drug abuse, but the 2002 film *City of God*, which was set in the neighbourhood, inspired major improvements. It is now a much safer place to live. Thais's parents are not well off but are able to support their family reasonably well. Thais is a great fan of Felipe Dylon, a Brazilian pop singer. She has his posters all over her bedroom wall. She also admires the Brazilian model and actress, Gisele Bündchen, who is thought to be the highest-paid model in the world. Thais would like to be a model when she grows up or, alternatively, a paediatrician.

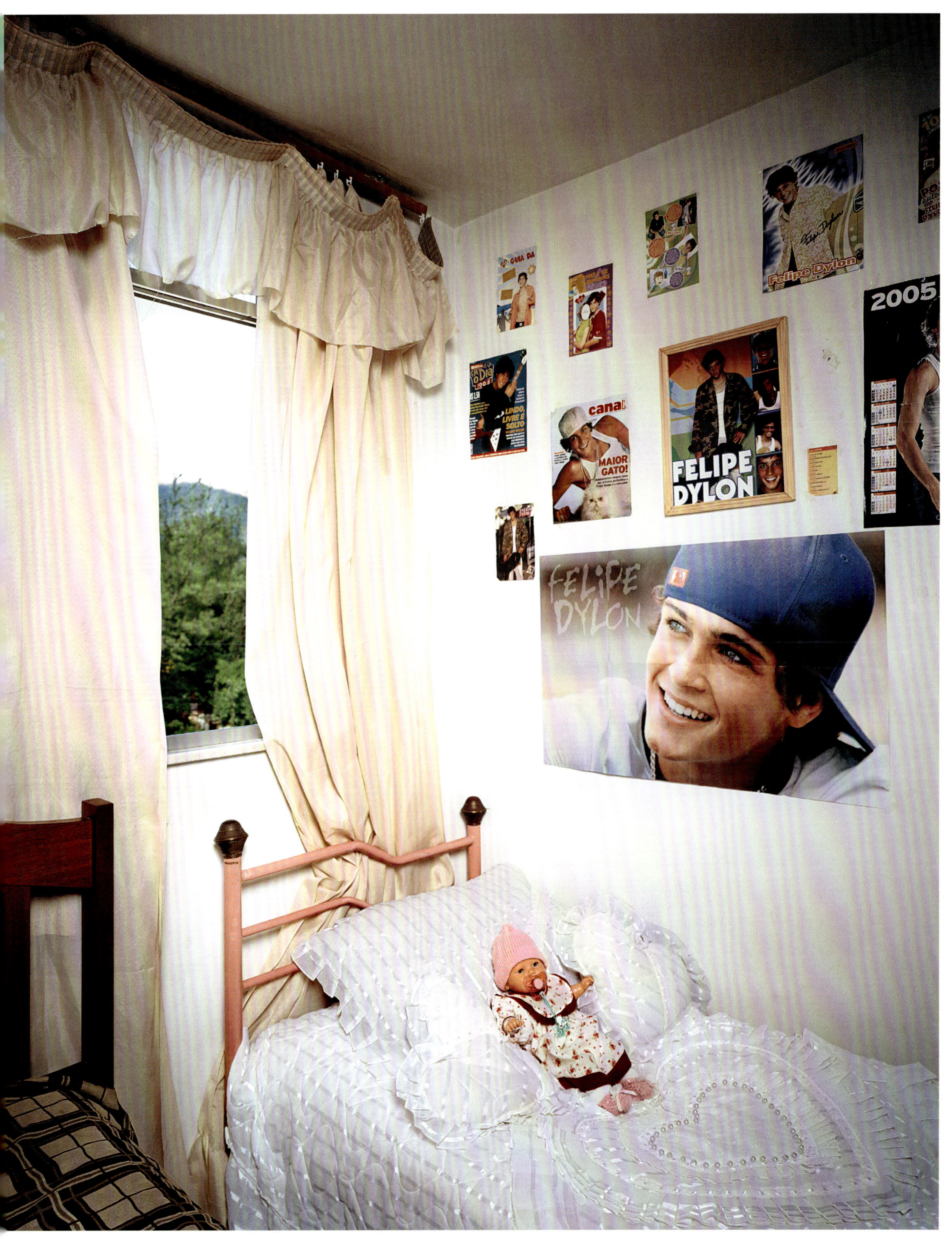

Felipe Dylon
2005
canal
MAIOR GATO!
LINDO, LIVRE E SOLTO
FELIPE DYLON
FELIPE DYLON

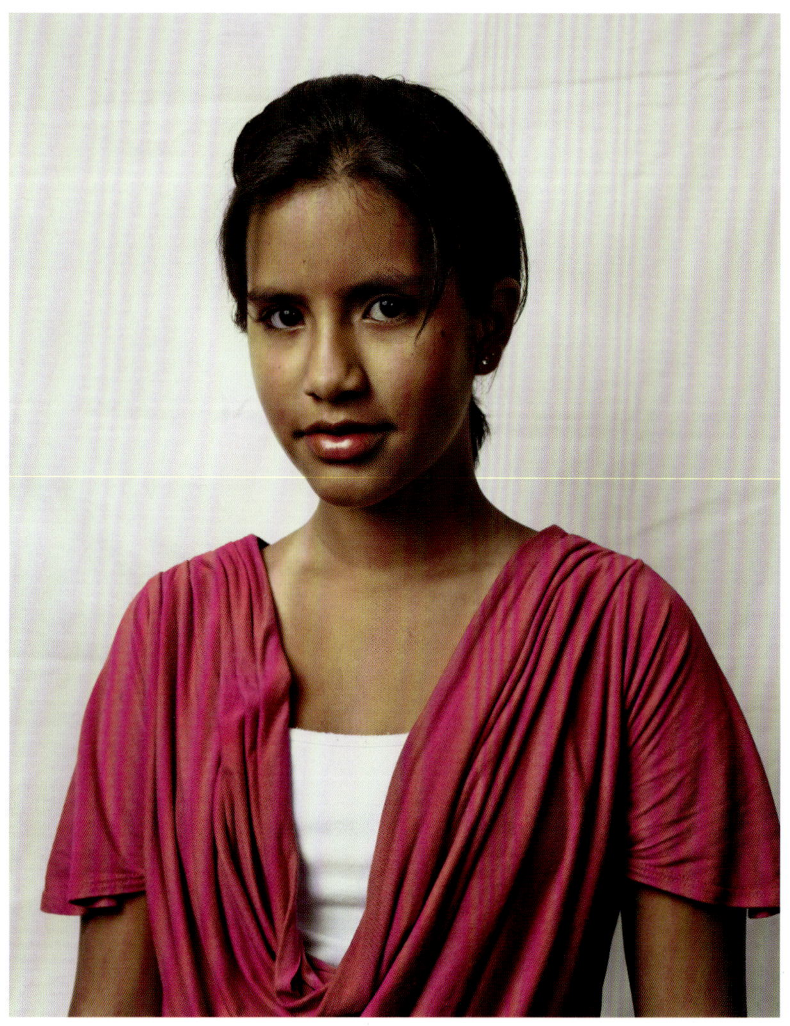

Maria lives in Mexico City with her parents and older sister. Their home has three storeys and is set around a courtyard, behind security gates. The family has taken security very seriously ever since one of her cousins was kidnapped by a gang. Maria is twelve years old and attends a private school twenty minutes' drive away. The school is run by Americans, so the children celebrate American holidays such as Thanksgiving. She learns a mixture of Spanish and English. She has one hour of homework every school-night except for Friday. Maria enjoys socializing with her friends at school but does not like working hard. Her hobbies include all types of dance – tap, ballet, Irish – but she would like to be a professional jazz dancer one day. Maria has two stereos, an iPod, a cellphone and her own private doorbell outside her room. Apart from Lucha Libre (Mexican wrestling), she does not watch television very much but prefers to play on her Xbox.

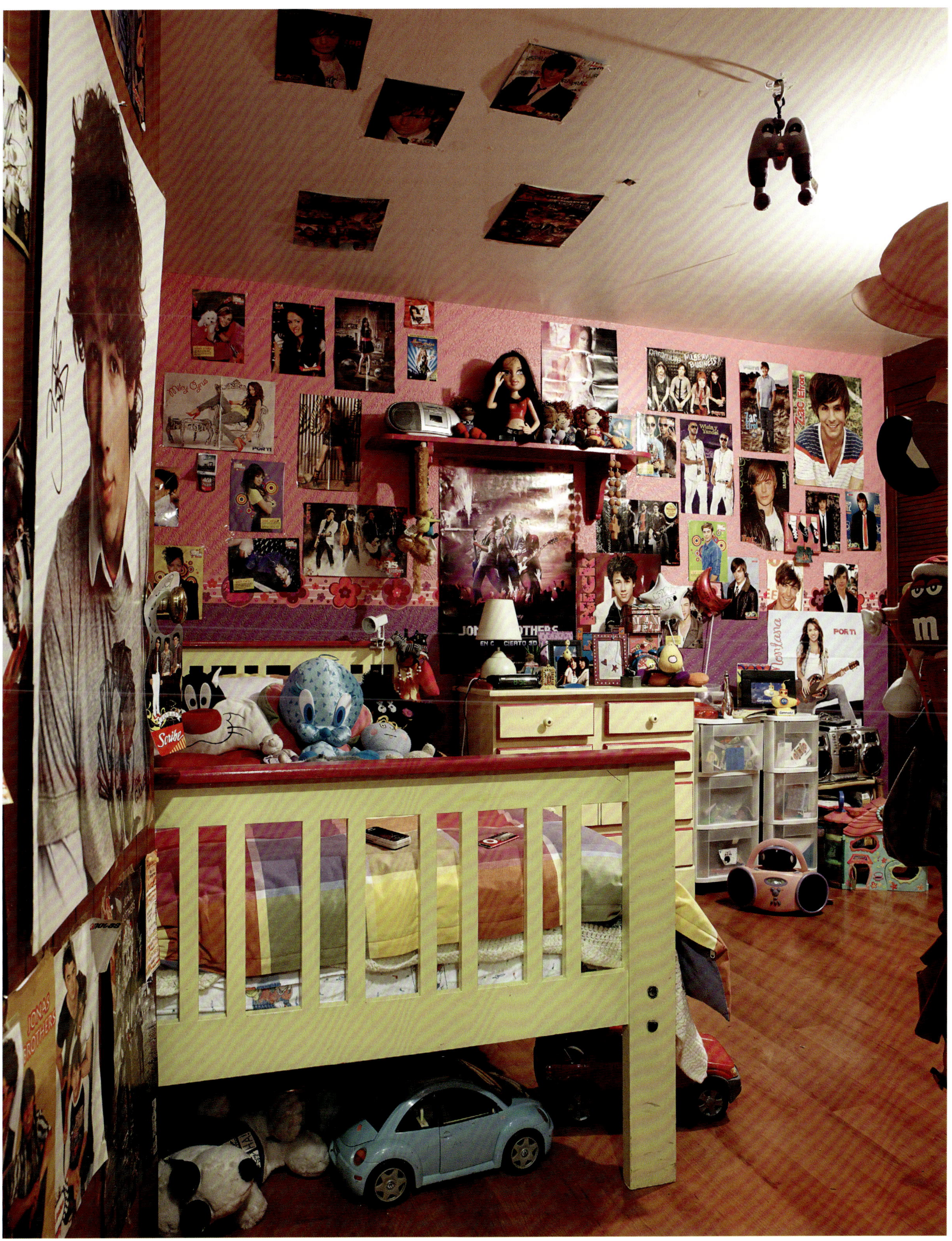

Zac Efron
POR TI
JONAS BROTHERS
Scribe

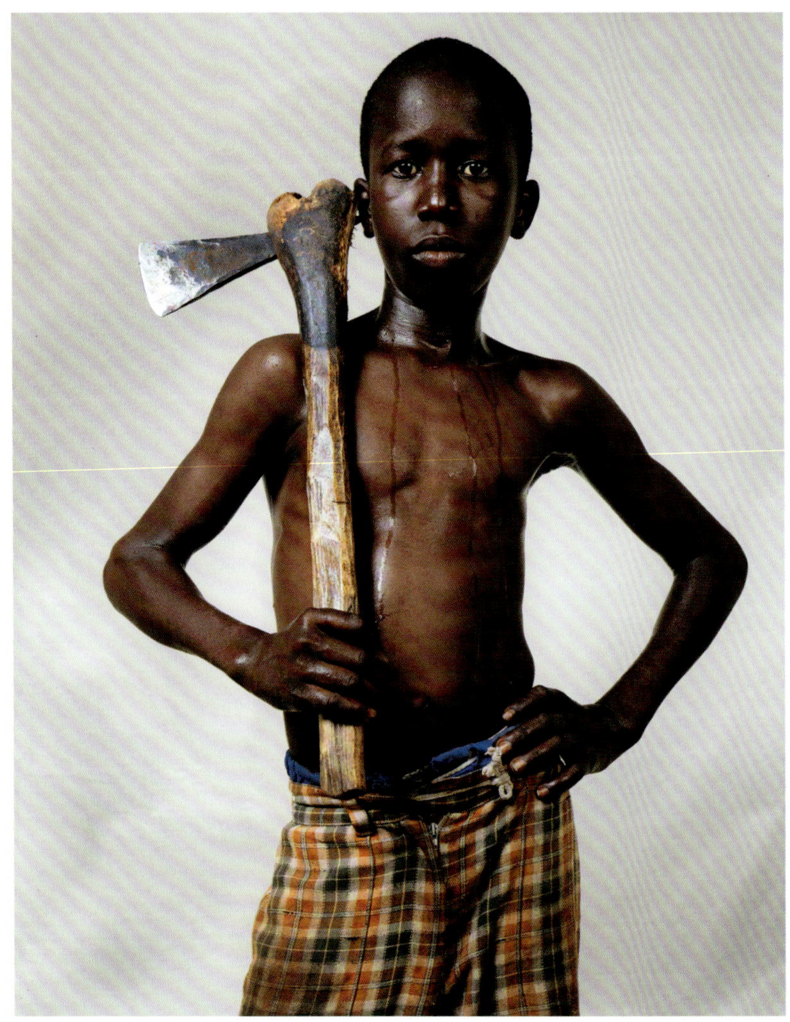

Lamine is twelve years old and lives in a village in Senegal, western Africa. He is a pupil at the village Koranic school, where no girls are allowed. He shares a room with several other boys from the school. The beds are very basic and uncomfortable, some supported by bricks for legs. At six o'clock every morning, the boys begin work on the school farm. Depending on the season of the year, they are taught digging, harvesting maize or how to plough the fields using donkeys. In the afternoon, they study the Koran, the holy book from which Islam is derived, learning to recite its verses from wooden tablets. They have the same teacher for all their lessons. Lamine enjoys school but finds the farming lessons hard work and very hot. In his free time, he likes to play football with his friends. When Lamine grows up he would like to be a teacher.

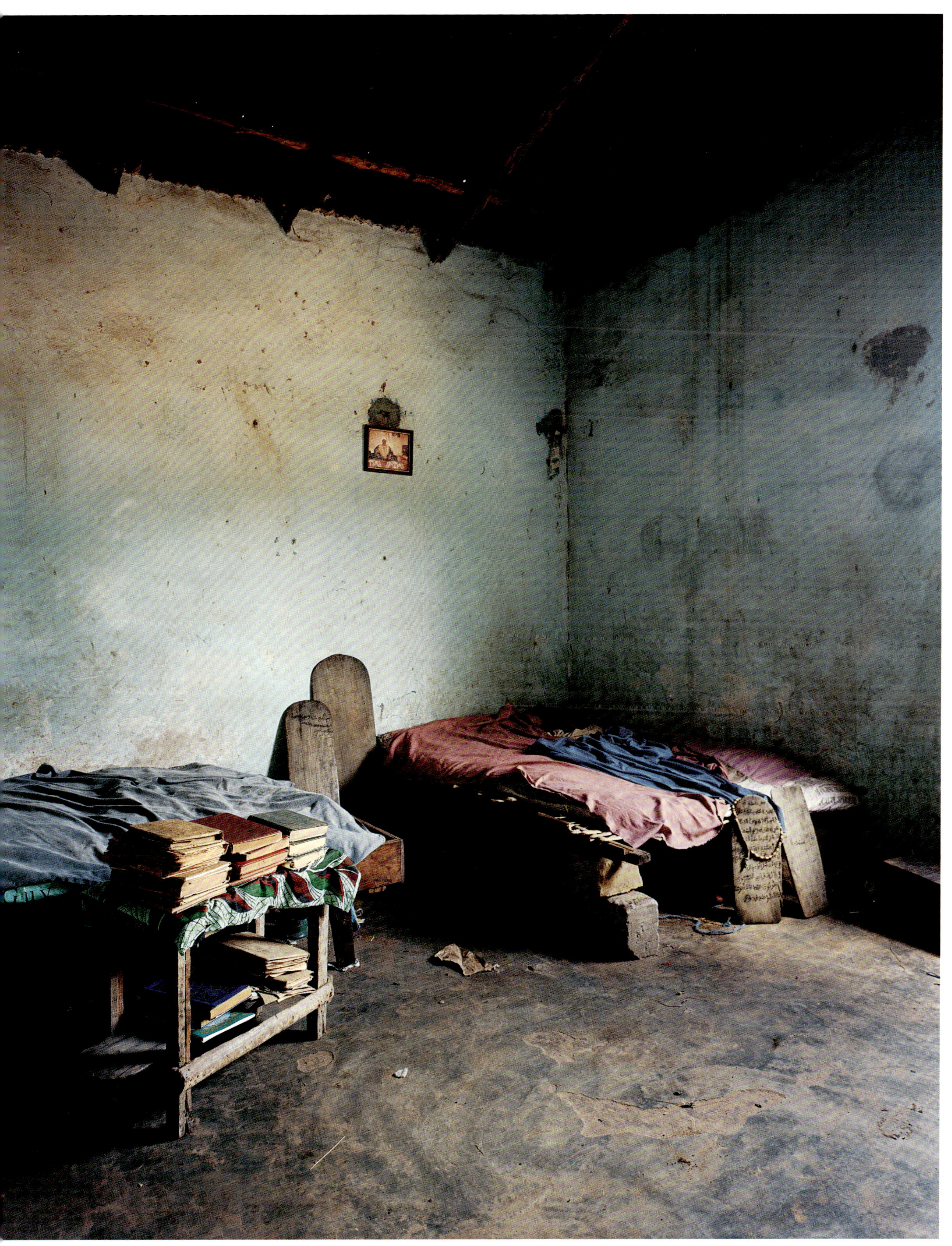

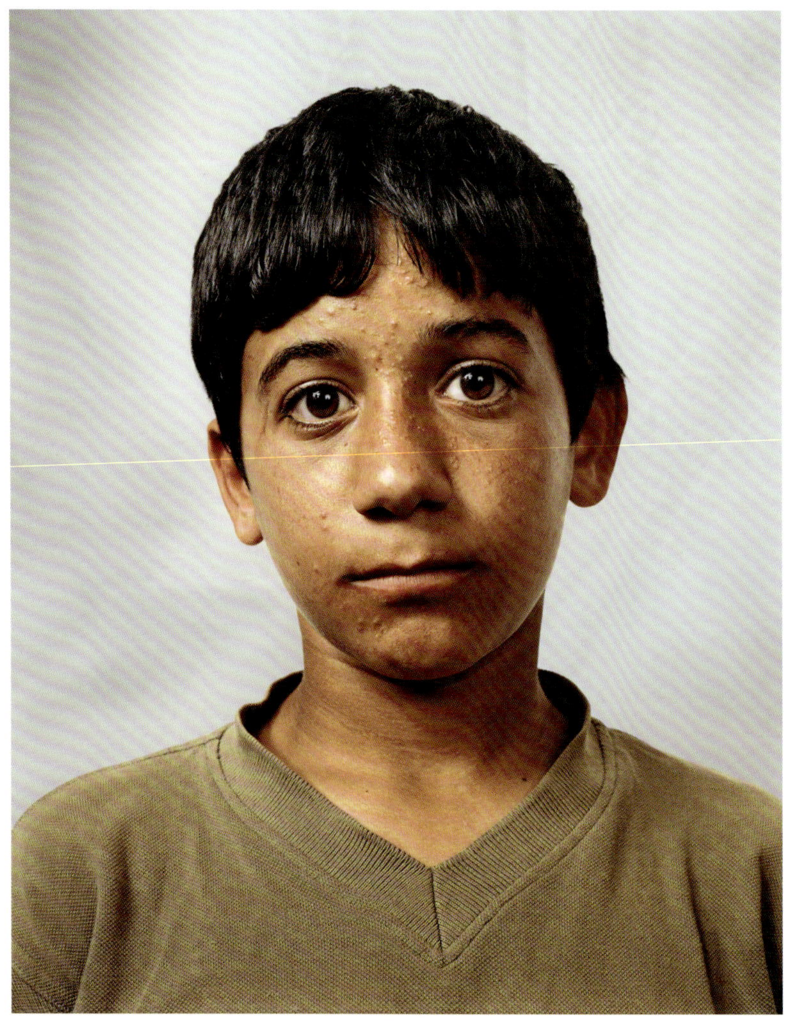

Hamdi lives in a block of flats with his parents and five siblings, in a Palestinian refugee camp on the edge of Bethlehem, West Bank. Their flat has a sitting area, a kitchen and three bedrooms. The camp was originally temporary, set up by the United Nations in 1948. More than sixty years later, it is still there, now housing three times as many inhabitants. It is overcrowded. Hamdi is thirteen years old and attends a boys' school where his father hopes he will study hard enough to gain a degree, to give him better opportunities than his father had. Hamdi has experienced violence on the streets of Bethlehem. His sixteen-year-old half-brother was killed by soldiers during a demonstration against Israeli occupation, and at the age of nine, Hamdi was shot in the foot for confronting Israeli soldiers in a tank. His injury has not deterred him from further confrontations.

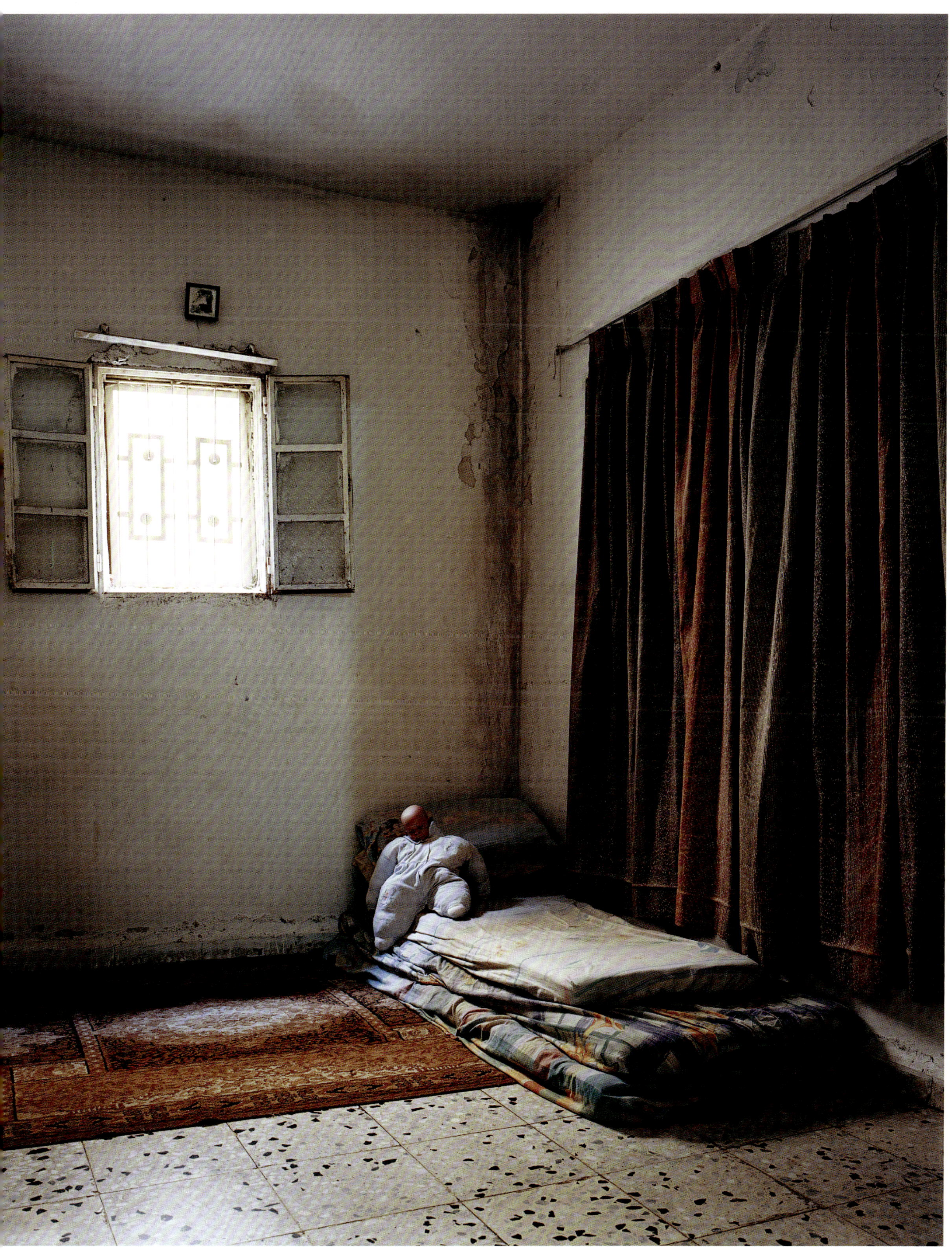

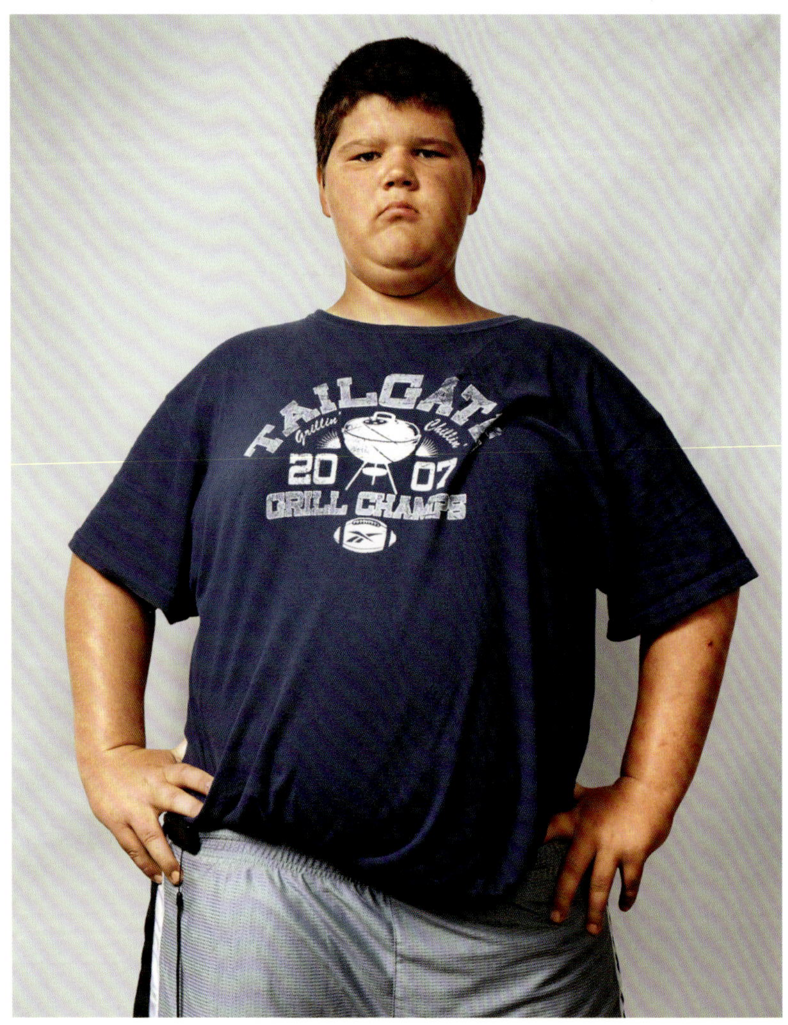

Ryan normally lives with his parents and two sisters in Pennsylvania, USA, but is currently staying at a school for obese children aged eleven to sixteen. Ryan is thirteen years old. When he was nine, he was found to have a brain tumour. As a result, he now suffers from 'Prader-Willi Syndrome', an inherited condition that causes Ryan to have an insatiable appetite. This led Ryan to gain a lot of weight, but since attending the school, he has lost nine kilos. He is determined to lose as much weight as possible so that he can play baseball with his friends again. Meal times are becoming easier for him because the school provides healthy versions of pizza and spaghetti alongside unlimited amounts of low-calorie foods such as soup, fruit and vegetables. This means he is not always as hungry as he used to be at home. All students have to take ten thousand steps per day. Ryan would like to be a doctor when he grows up, in gratitude to the medical profession for helping him through his illnesses.

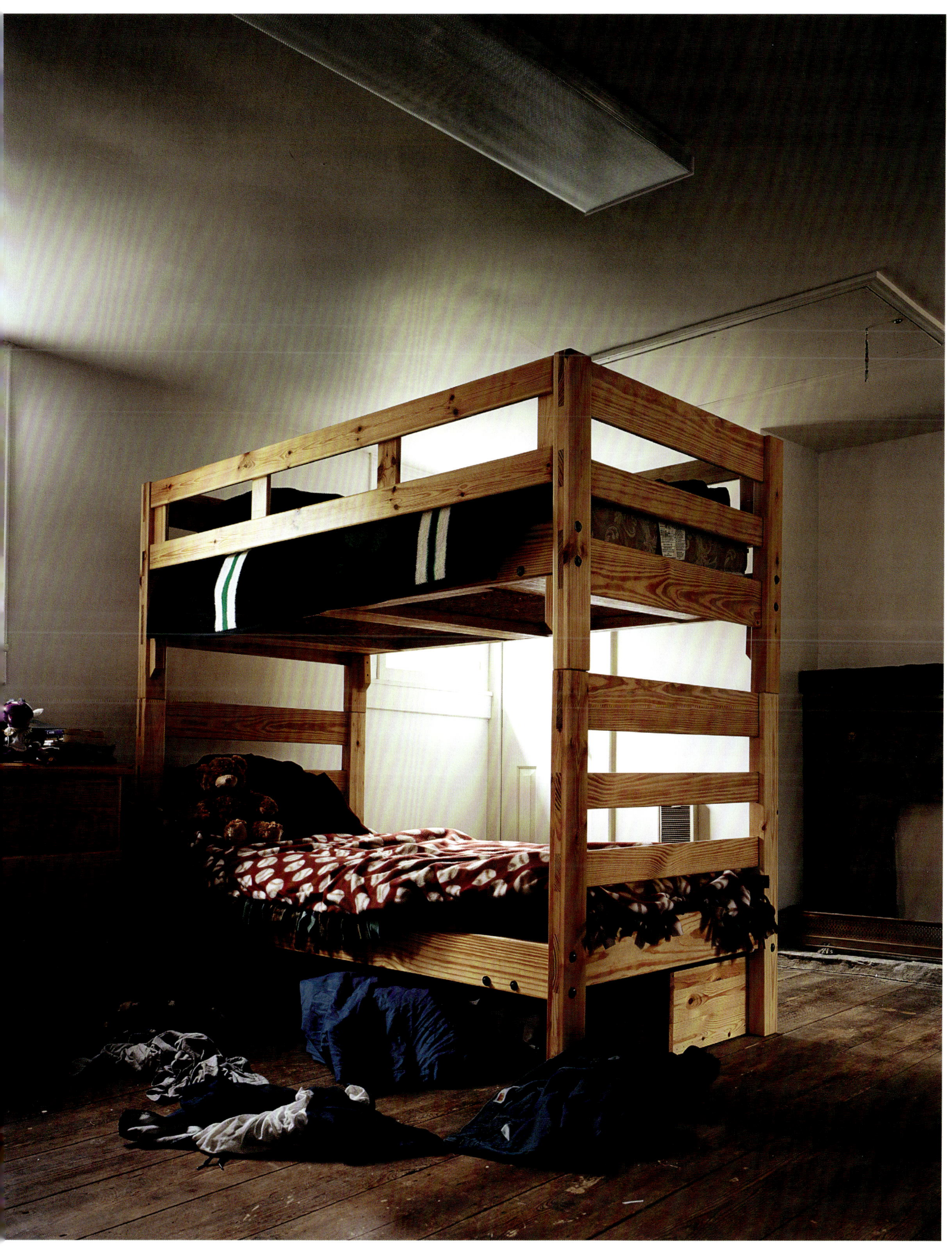

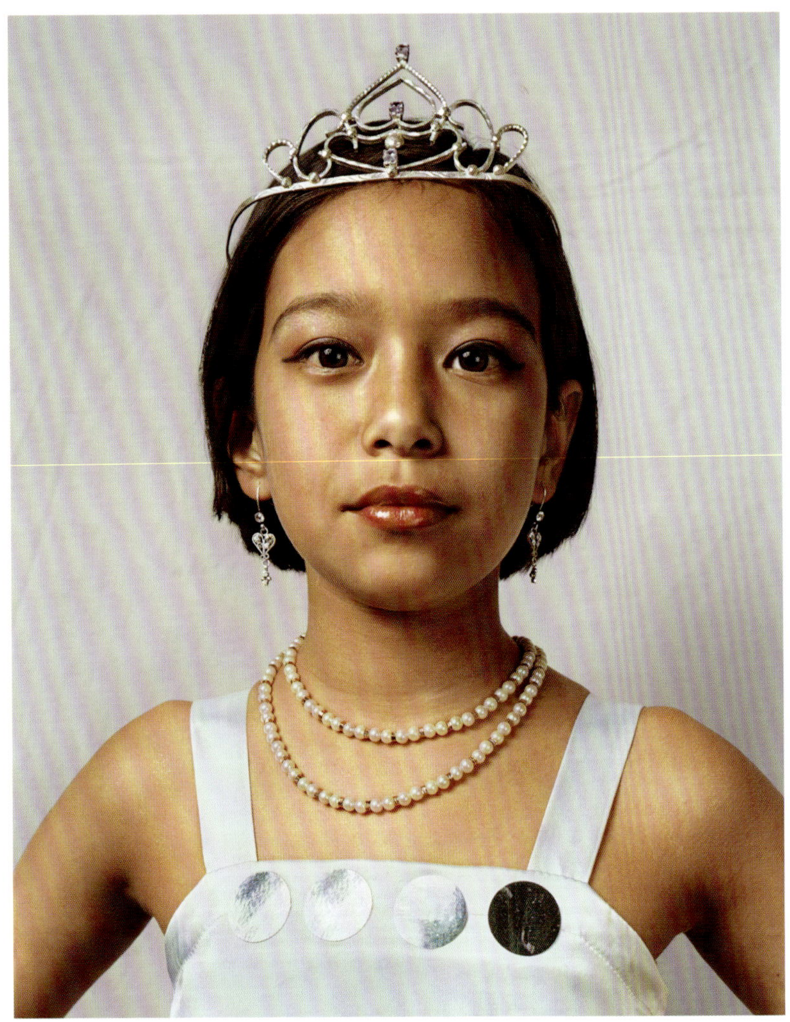

Anusha lives with her parents and older sister in a small house in Kathmandu, Nepal. She is thirteen years old. Her diet consists mostly of 'dhal bhat' (rice and lentil soup), 'roti' (flat bread) and rice, but she also likes fruit. Each day, she goes to school with her sister, just five minutes' walk away and one of the best in the city. Anusha likes to read about plants and science and would like to be a botanist when she is older. Her favourite pastime is dancing, especially to Bollywood songs. She entered a beauty contest in the hope of winning a crown. She recited a speech about child rights, which she memorized. She was the first runner-up and won the award of 'Miss Punctuality'. It took only fifteen minutes to get ready for the pageant, with three changes of outfit. Anusha says that she never wants to get married – she would like to live with her parents for ever.

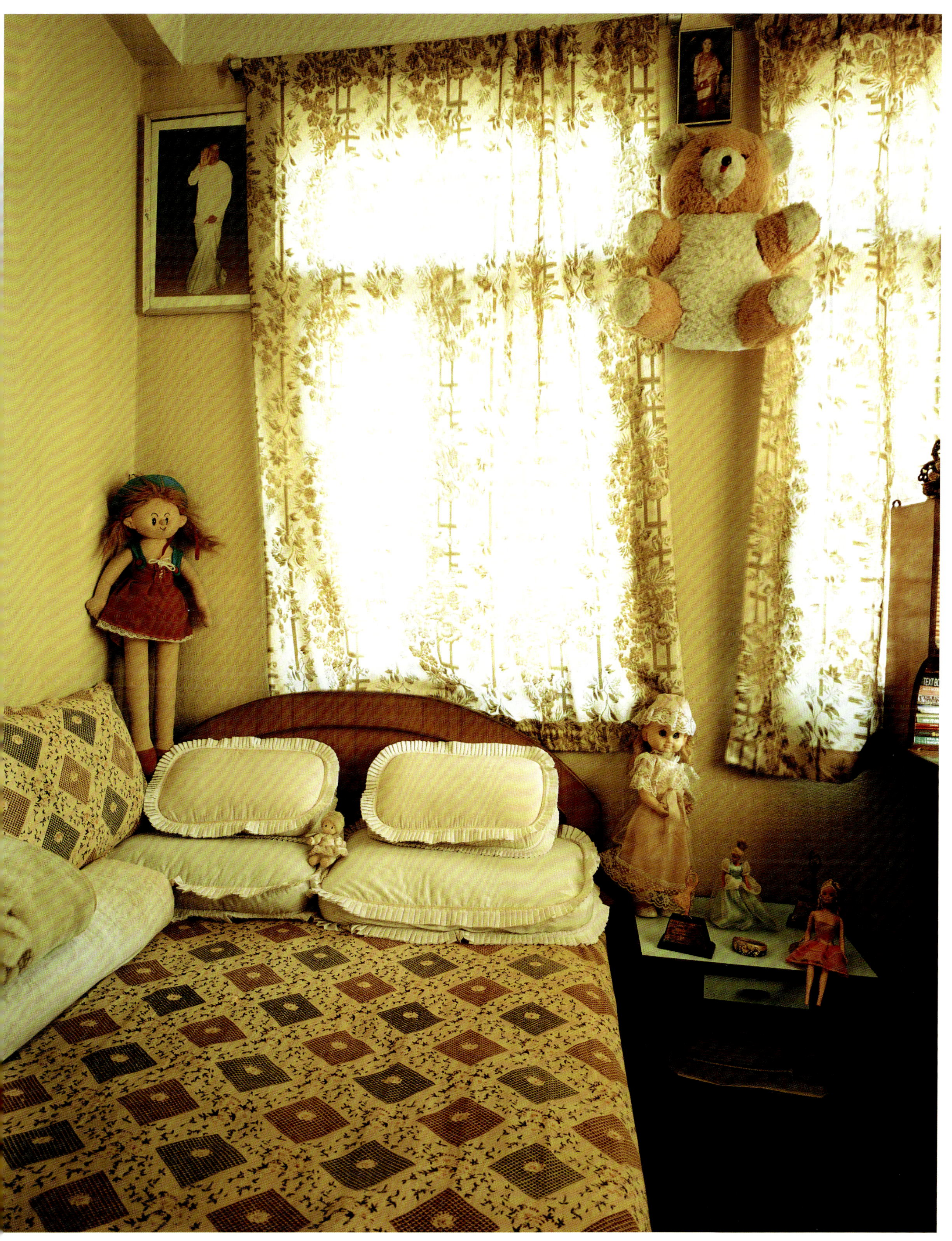

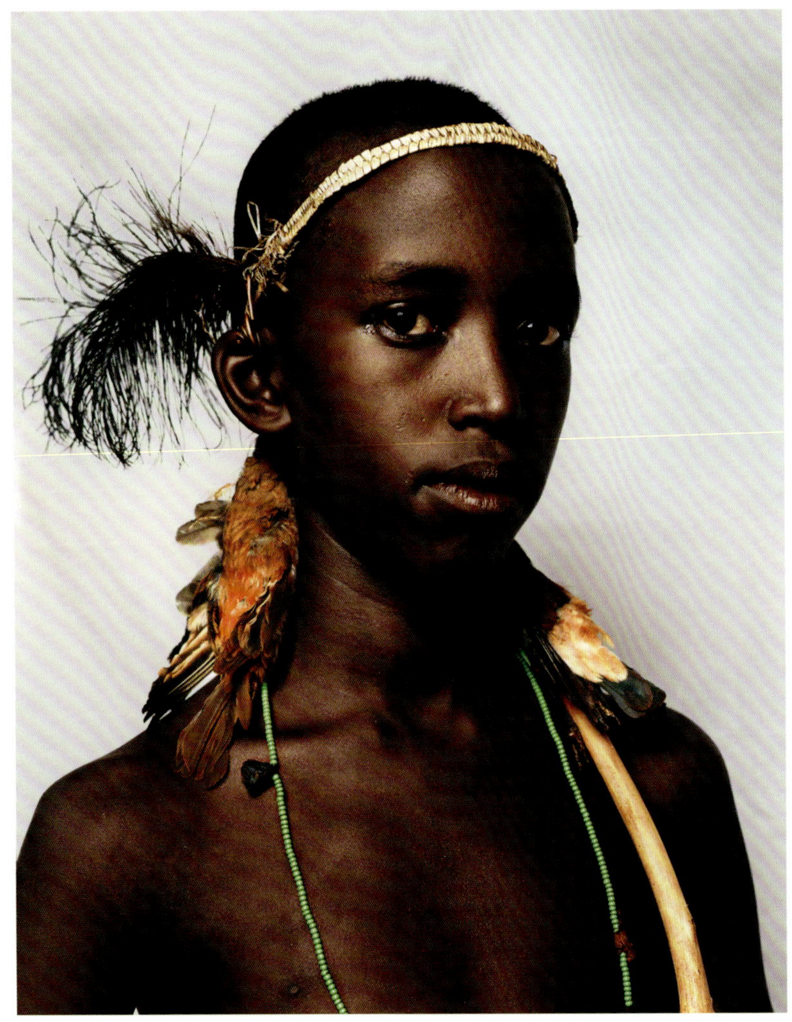

Irkena lives in Kenya with his mother, in a temporary homestead encircled by a strong thorn enclosure to protect the family's livestock. He belongs to the Rendille tribe, who live a semi-nomadic life in the harsh regions of the Kaisut Desert. Irkena is now fourteen years old and must be circumcised before leaving the community 'manyatta' (settlement). This ritual will mark the first stage of his initiation into adulthood. At the circumcision ceremony itself – which is held in public – he must not cry out or his family will be shamed. Irkena will then become a 'morani' (young warrior), and live in the bush with other warriors. He will have weapons for hunting and a wooden stool for a pillow. During the month before he is circumcised, Irkena kills as many birds as possible with his handmade catapult, and hangs the corpses round his head as a status symbol, signifying his maturity and skill at hunting.

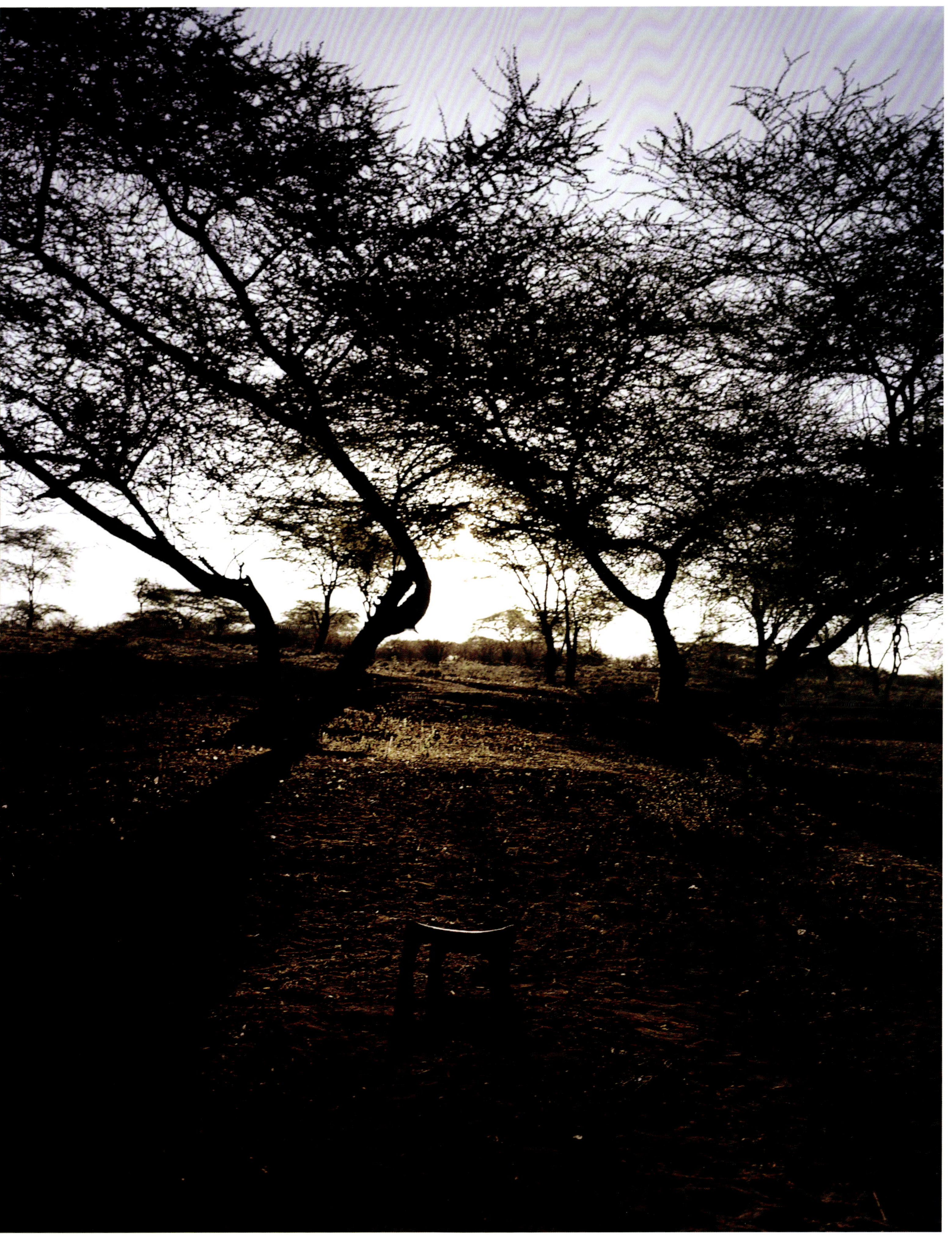

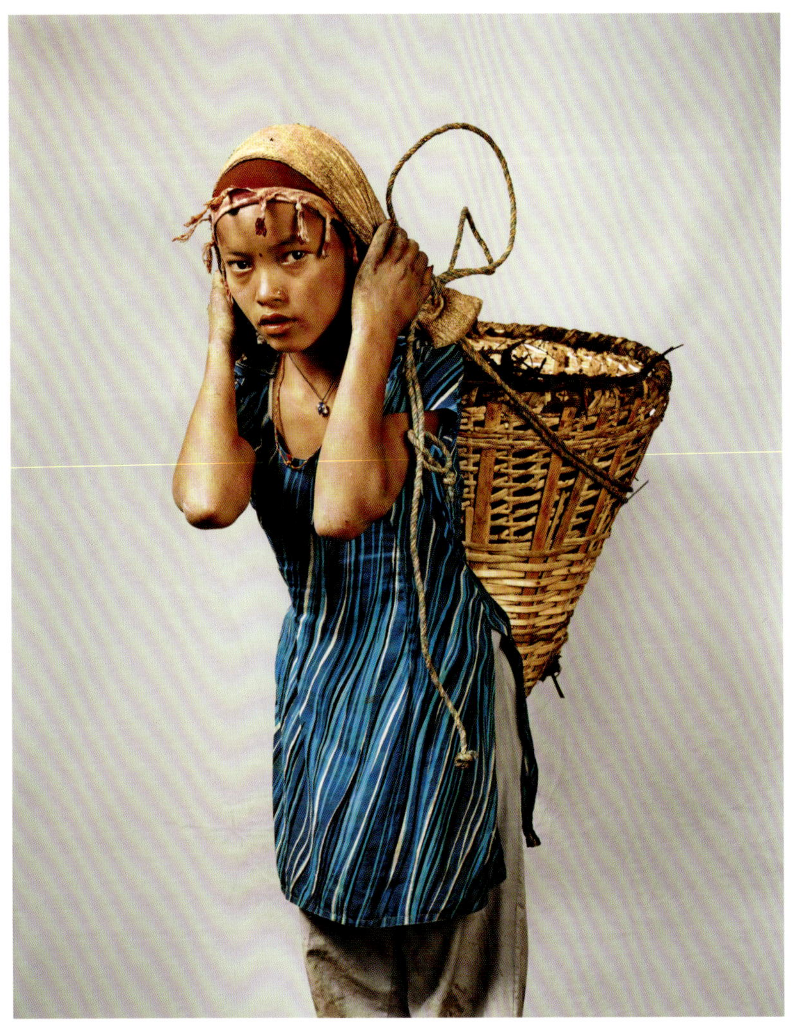

Jyoti lives in Makwanpur, Nepal. She is shown here with a basket of leaves she has collected for her grandfather's buffalo. She is fourteen years old but left school when she was younger, in order to be a domestic worker. Her employers had promised to send her back to school but, instead, treated her so badly that she had to run away. She is still trying to find employment as a domestic worker, looking for a salary of seven hundred Nepali rupees per month (about $9.50). Jyoti does not now want to return to school, because she feels she would be too old to rejoin the class. She has six sisters, four of whom are married. She lives with one of her sisters in the countryside, where she works in the fields. Her home is a wooden-framed structure with branches and twigs for a roof. There is a storeroom upstairs, where her grandfather sleeps. The rest of the family sleep on mats on the mud floor, with an open fire for cooking and warmth.

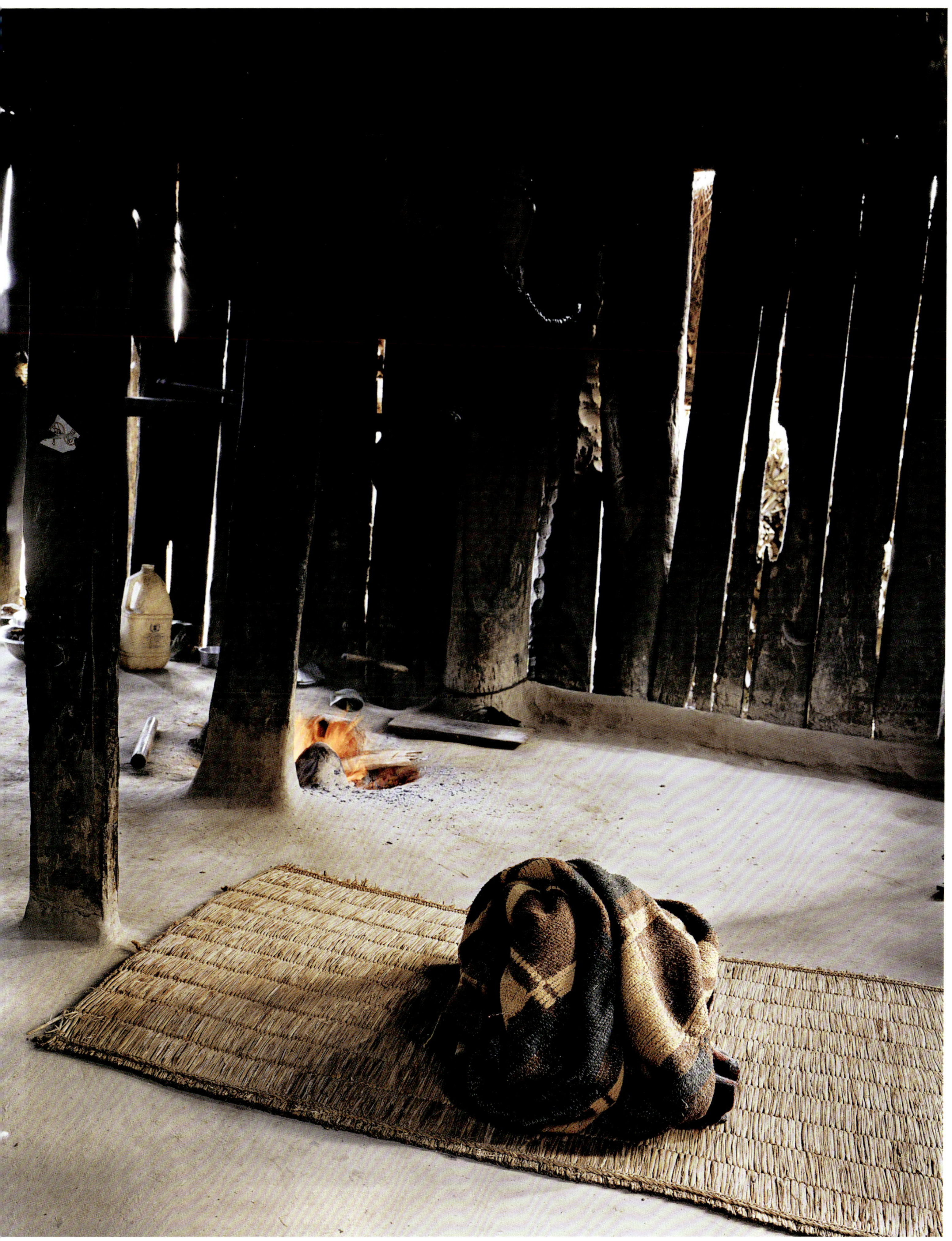

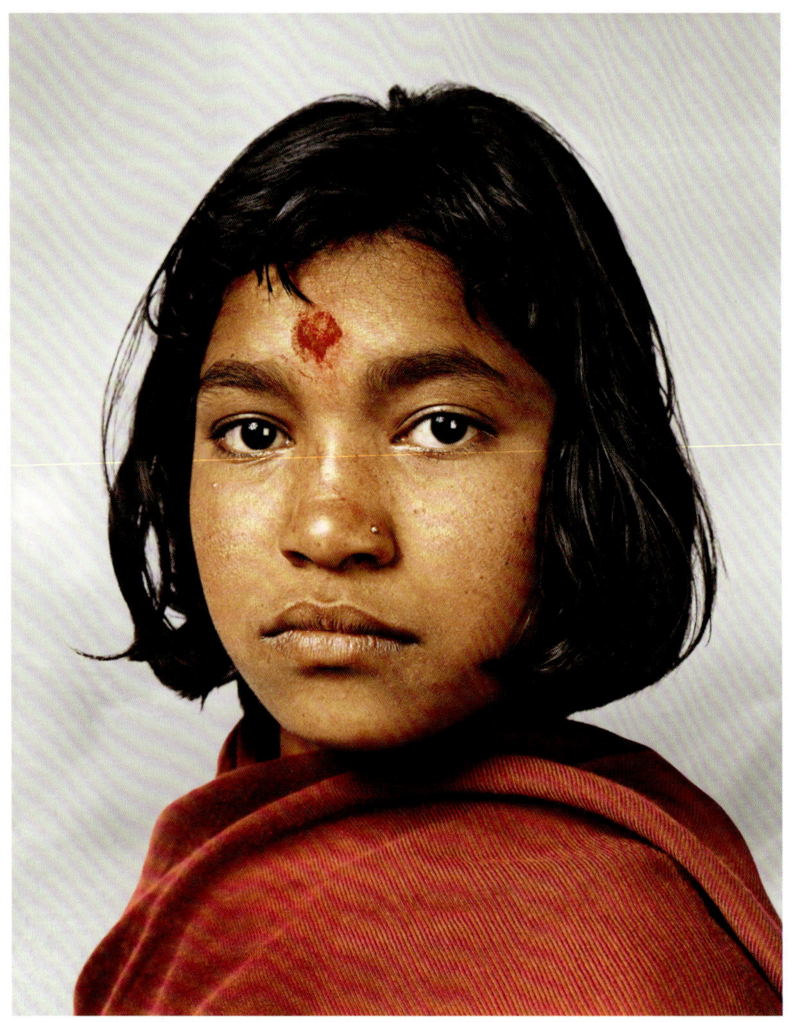

Prena lives in Kathmandu, Nepal. Her room is a tiny, cell-like space at the top of the house where she is employed as a domestic worker. Her diet is mainly rice and vegetables. She is fourteen years old and one of thousands of child domestic workers in the country. Prena carries out household chores such as sweeping, cleaning, cooking and washing. She starts work at five in the morning and finishes at six in the evening. For this, she earns five hundred Nepali rupees per month (about $6.50). She sends the money back to her parents, who have eight other children to support. Prena visits her family twice a year. She goes to school three times a week – which is the main highlight in her life. She admires her teacher, who has made it his mission to educate children like Prena. She would like to be a doctor when she is older.

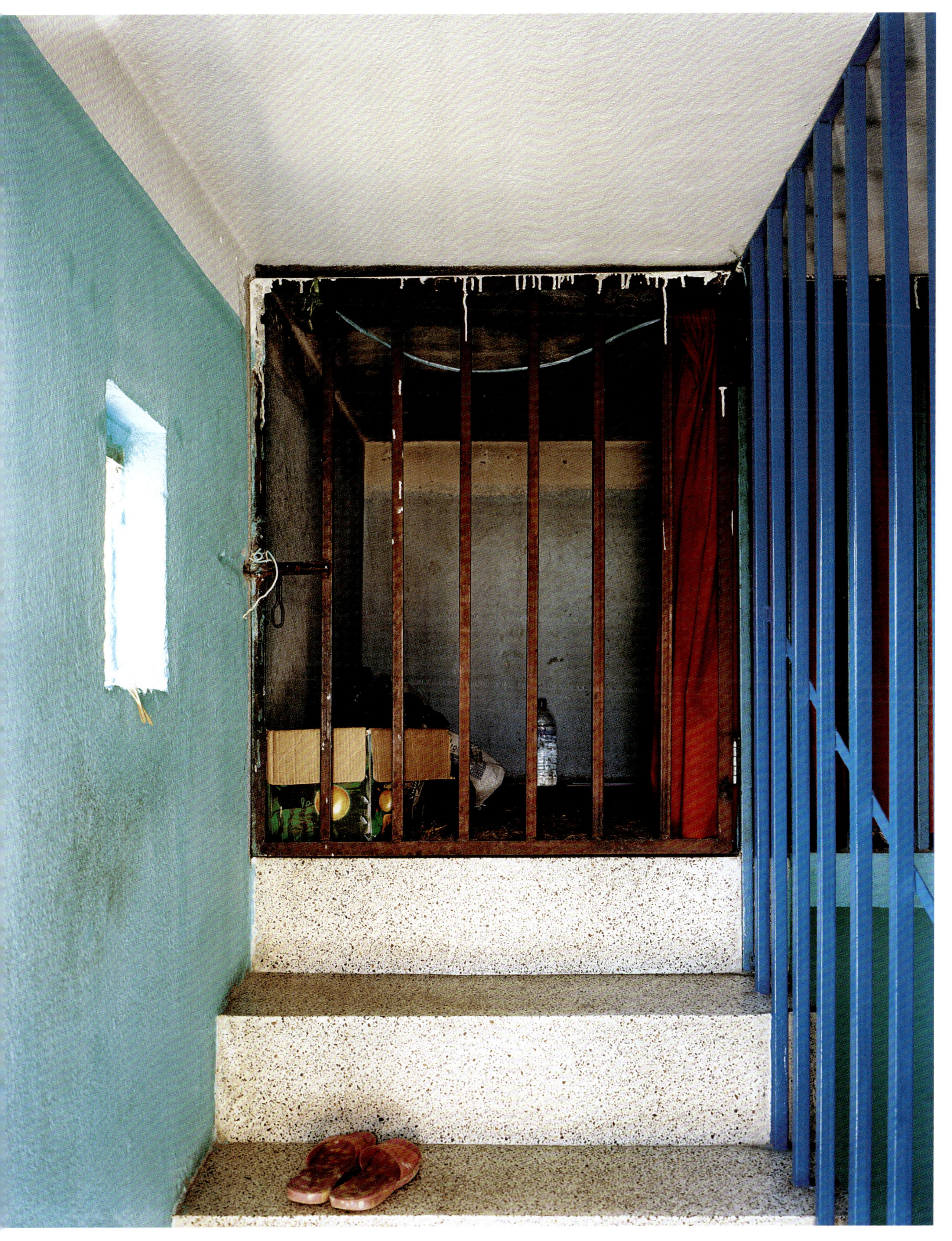

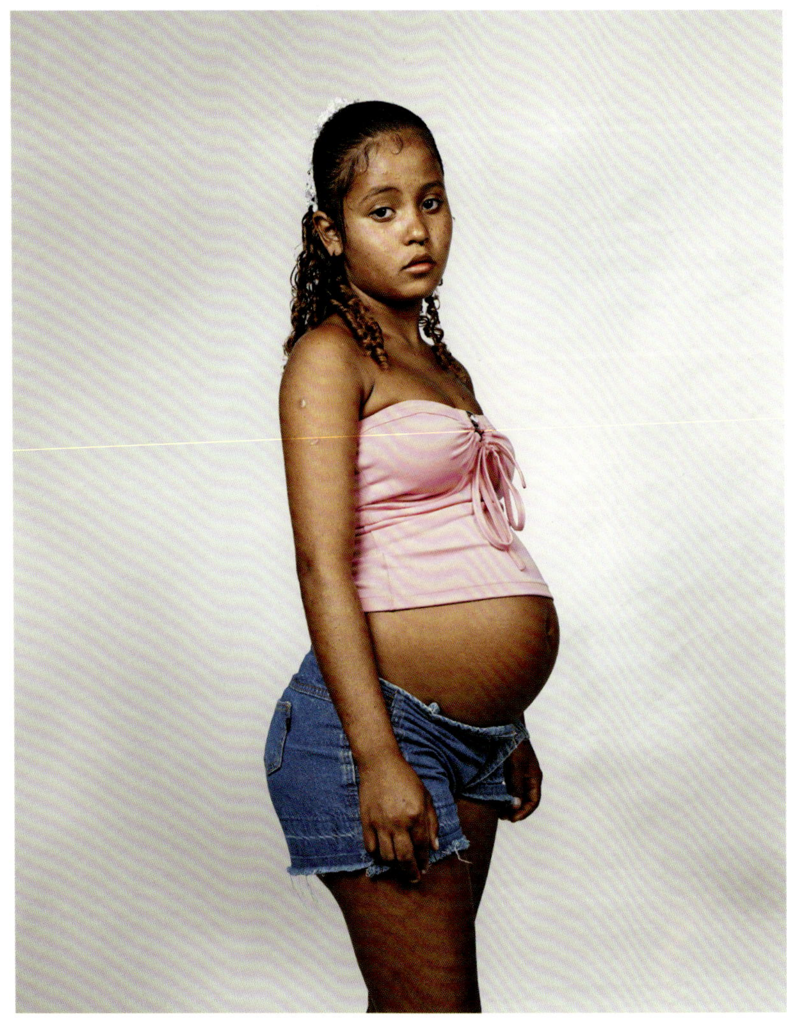

Erlen is fourteen years old and is pregnant for the third time. She lives in a 'favela' in Rio de Janeiro, Brazil. Her home is a small shack. She usually sleeps on the floor, but now that she is in the later stages of her pregnancy, her mother has swapped places and allowed her to sleep in the bed. Erlen was twelve when she first became pregnant, but her baby was stillborn. A year later, she lost a second baby soon after its birth. If her new baby survives, Erlen is unlikely to return to school as she will need to stay at home to look after it. She will be a single parent. The Brazilian government is concerned at the increase in teenage pregnancies despite its efforts to promote contraception. Abortion is illegal and can result in a three-year prison sentence. It is also very dangerous – one in five women die while having abortions in illegal back-street clinics. Erlen would like to be a vet when she is older, and to live somewhere else.

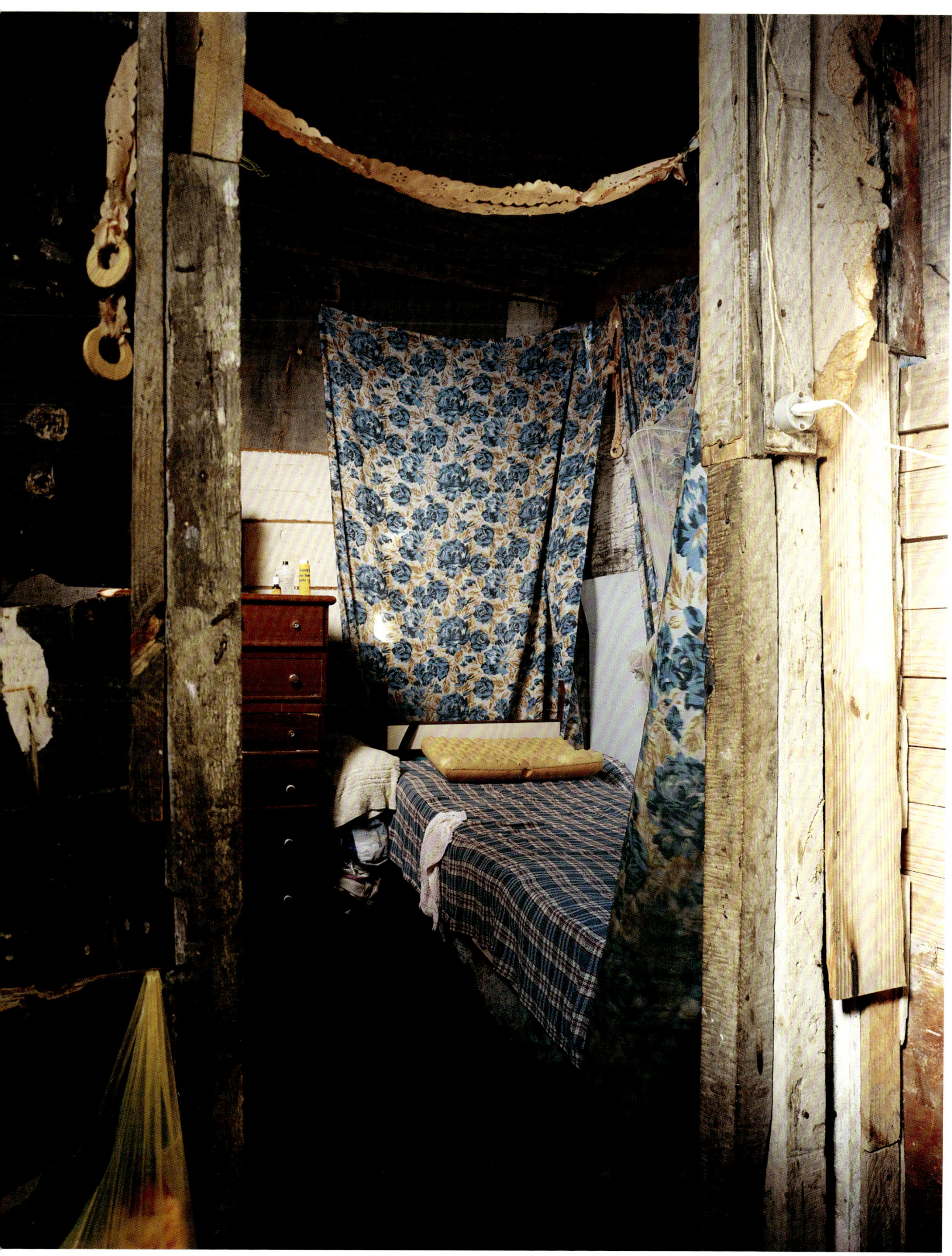

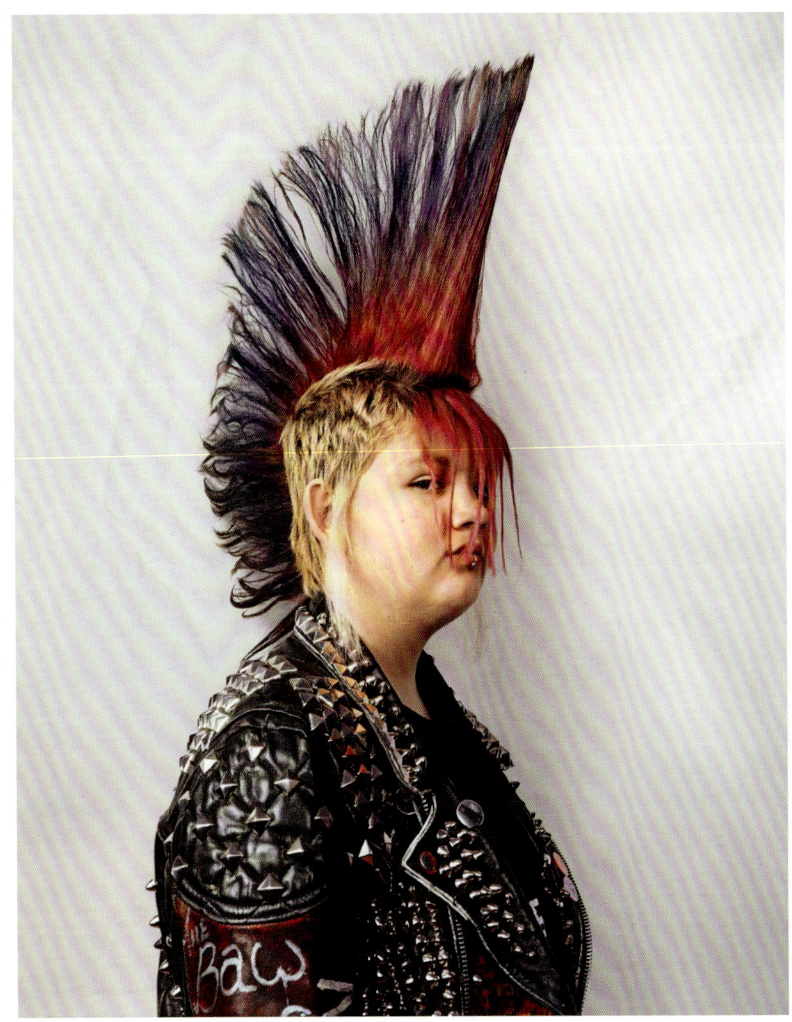

Rhiannon's home is a terraced house in Darvel, southern Scotland, a picturesque town which used to be famous for lace-making. She is fourteen years old and lives with her parents and brother. The area is now plagued by heroin addiction and gang violence. Her school is full of pupils who have been expelled from schools in nearby Glasgow. Rhiannon has had a mohawk haircut like her parents' ever since she was six. She and her family and friends are part of the punk subculture and have formed a community of support where they all look out for each other. They have become used to abusive behaviour from people in their neighbourhood. Rhiannon has suffered from bullying at school because of her appearance, but fought back and is now left alone. She plays guitar, drums and bass, and also sings. Her father has his own band.

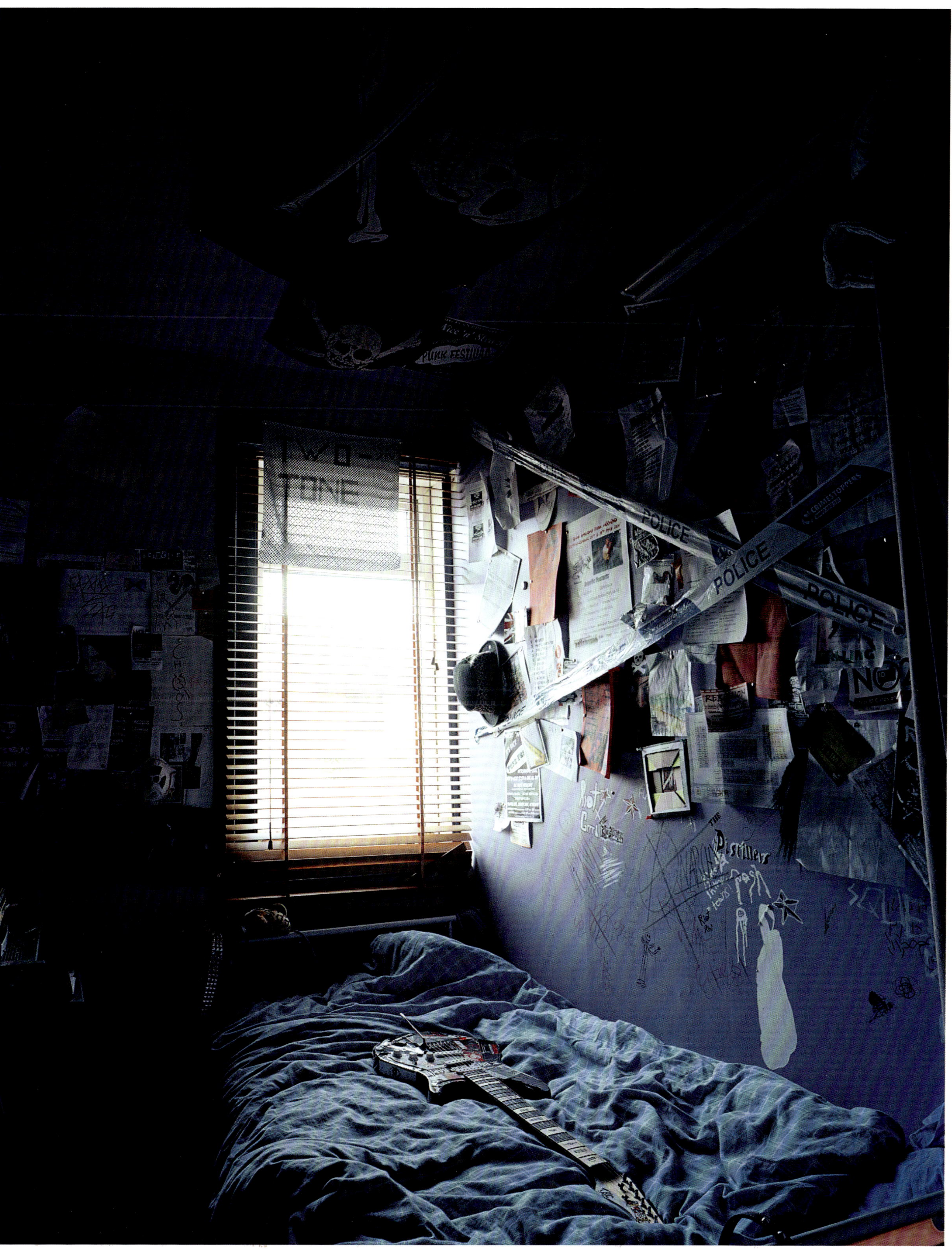
POLICE
POLICE
POLICE
CRIMESTOPPERS

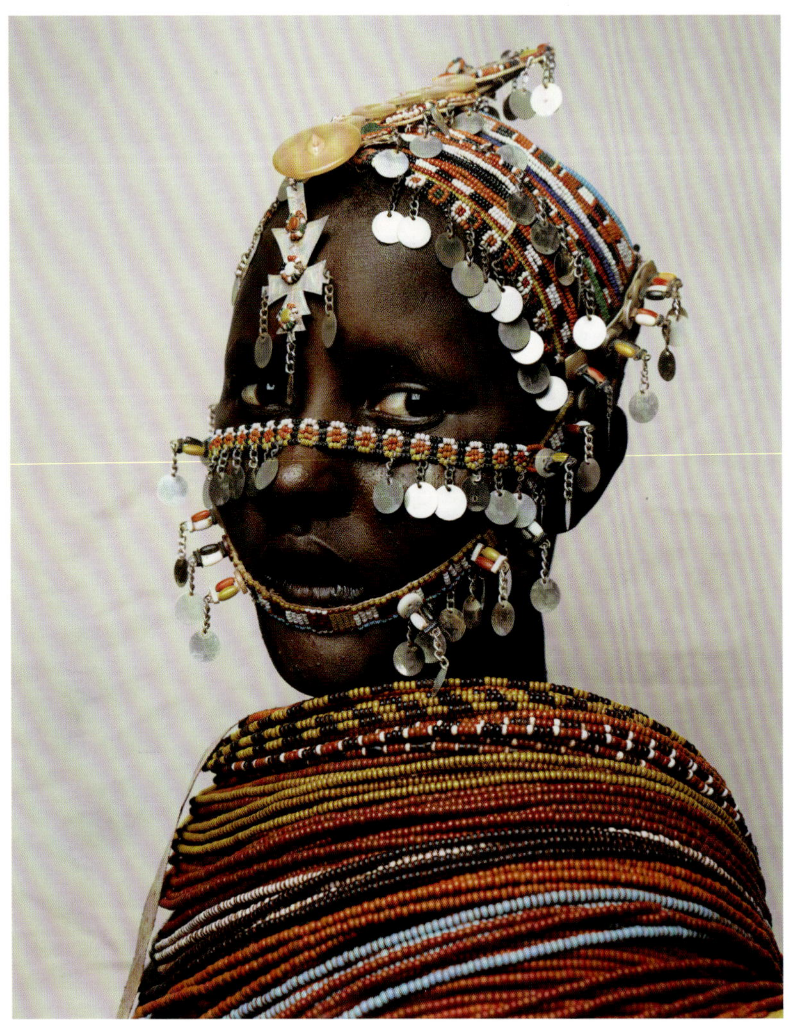

Nantio is fifteen years old and a member of the Rendille tribe in northern Kenya. She has two brothers and two sisters. Her home is a tent-like dome made from cattle hide and plastic, with little room to stand. There is a fire in the middle, around which the family sleep. Nantio's household chores include looking after the goats, chopping firewood and fetching water. She went to the village school for a few years but decided not to continue. Nantio is hoping a 'moran' (warrior) will select her for marriage. (She has a boyfriend now, but it is not unusual for a Rendille woman to have several boyfriends before marriage.) First, she will have to undergo circumcision, as is the custom. Nantio's status in life can be seen by the number of necklaces she wears and whether she also wears a white band, indicating that she has a boyfriend or that her menstrual cycles have begun.

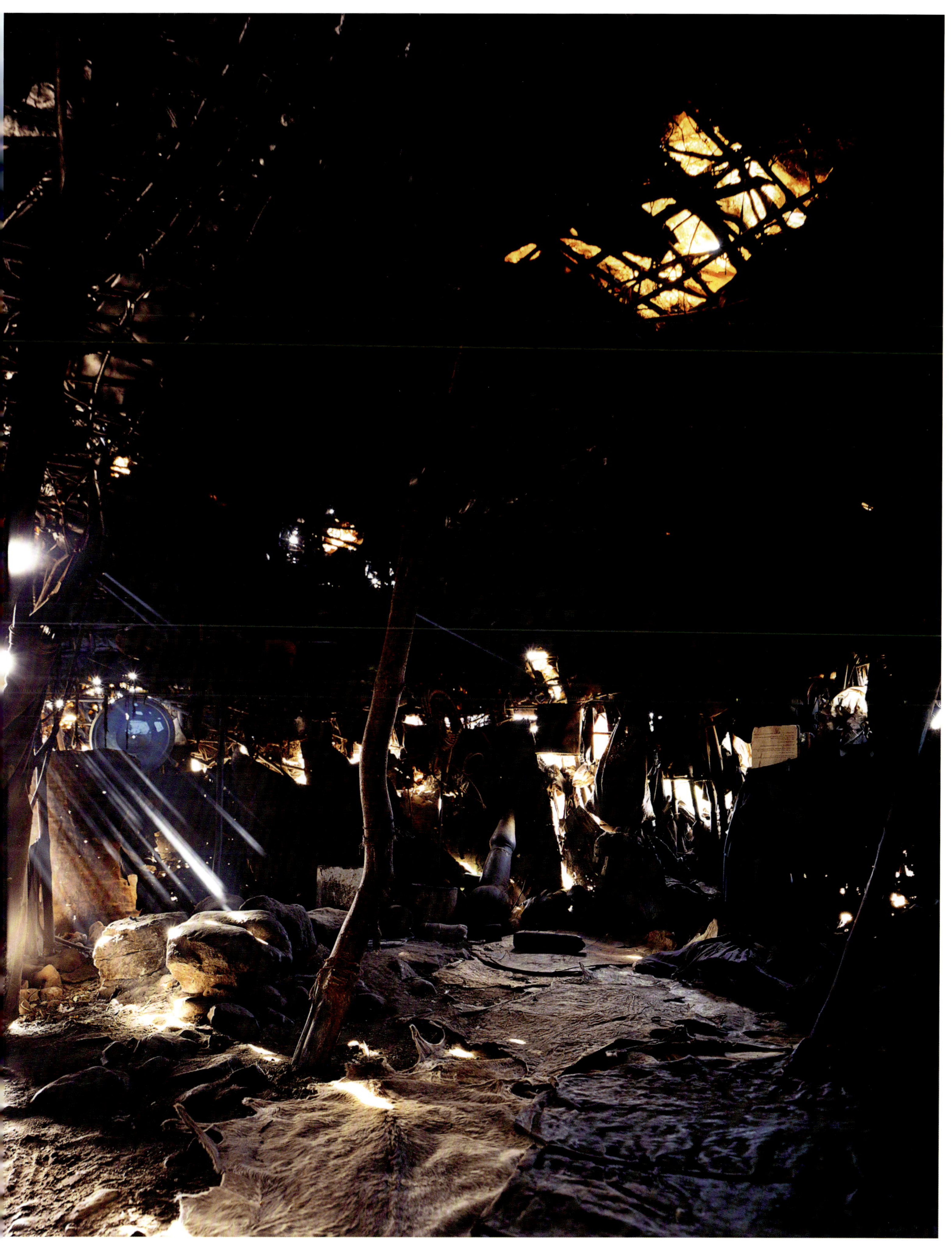

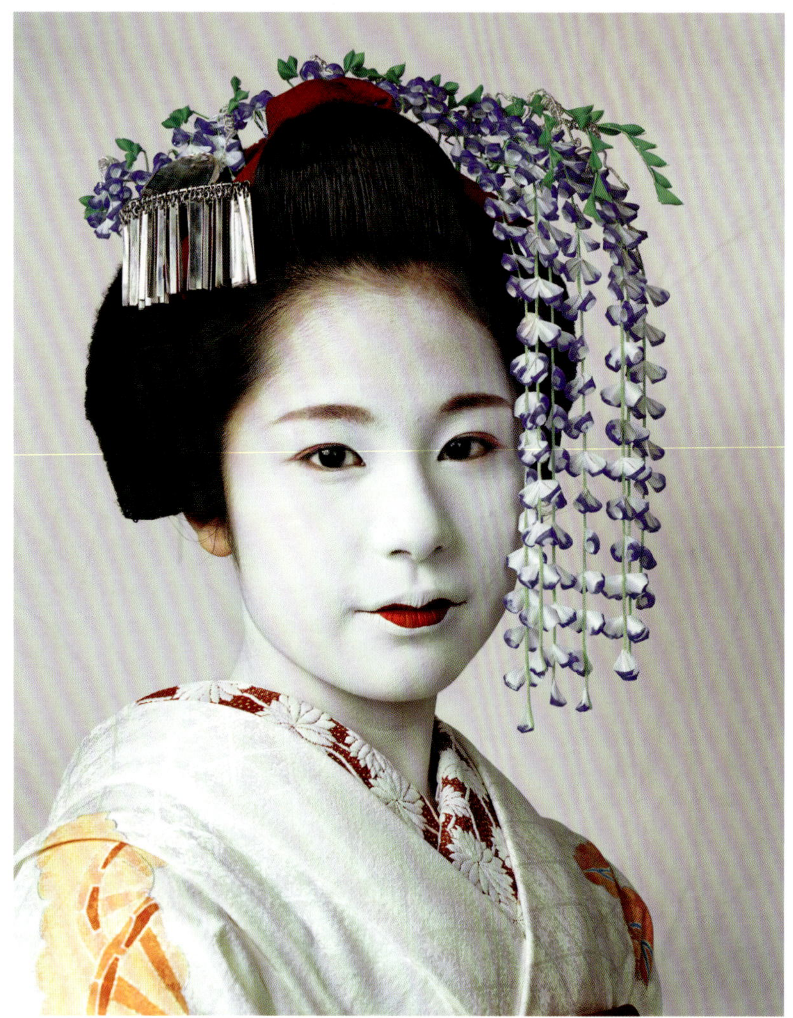

Risa is fifteen years old and lives with thirteen other women in a teahouse in Kyoto, Japan. She and five others sleep in a room that is also used as a dining room and tea room. She left her family in Tokyo a year ago after she saw a TV programme about geishas and decided she wanted to become one. Geishas are hostesses who entertain high-paying male guests by performing traditional Japanese arts. Risa is now a 'maiko' – a young girl who has passed the test to train as a geisha – and has been given a new name, Tomoyuki. She will have to train rigorously, with daily lessons in singing, dancing, playing Japanese drums, tea-making and mastering elegant Kyoto elocution. She spends two hours a day practising how to wrap her kimono, arrange her hair and apply make-up. She is the youngest maiko in Japan. Risa has two days' holiday each month and visits her family three times a year. She often gets homesick.

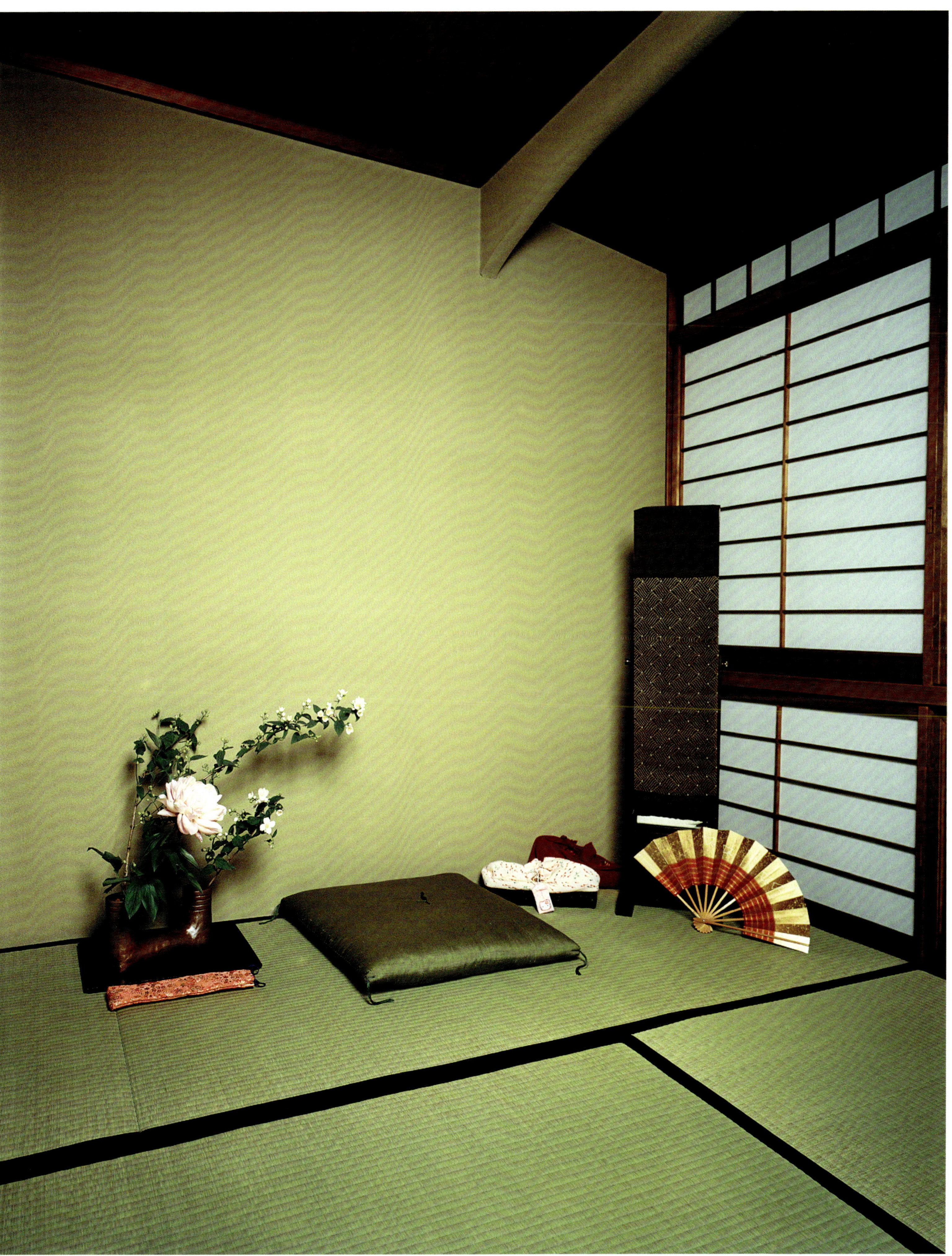

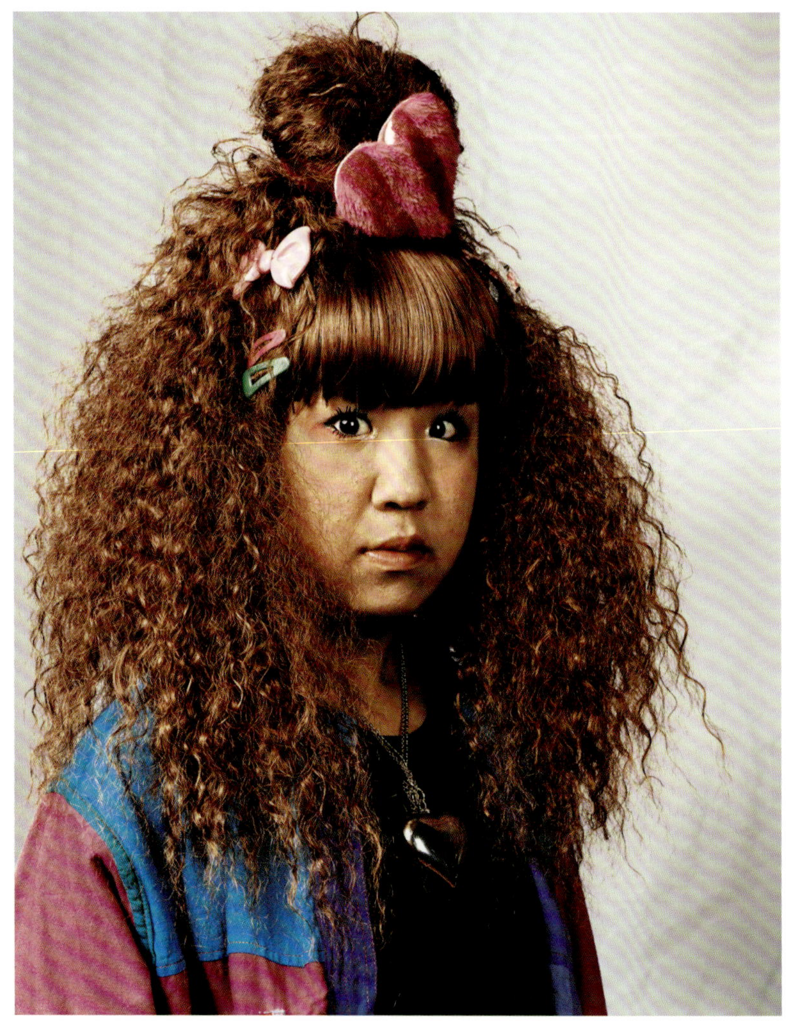

Kana lives in Tokyo, Japan, with four generations of her family – her sister, parents, grandmother and great-grandparents. She is sixteen years old and her passion is fashion. She loves to dress up and be noticed. It takes her an hour to put on her make-up, ready to go out to the trendy shopping district of Harajuku. She and her friends have formed a club whose aim is to look like dolls. Kana's mother does not approve of her style so Kana has taken a Saturday job in a factory to earn the money to buy her clothes and wigs. It takes her twenty minutes to cycle to school each morning, and once there, she has to contend with frequent teasing for the way she dresses and the wigs she wears. Kana is full of admiration for her mother for raising her. She hopes to have her own fashion boutique when she grows up, although she feels that her style is likely to become more traditional as she gets older.

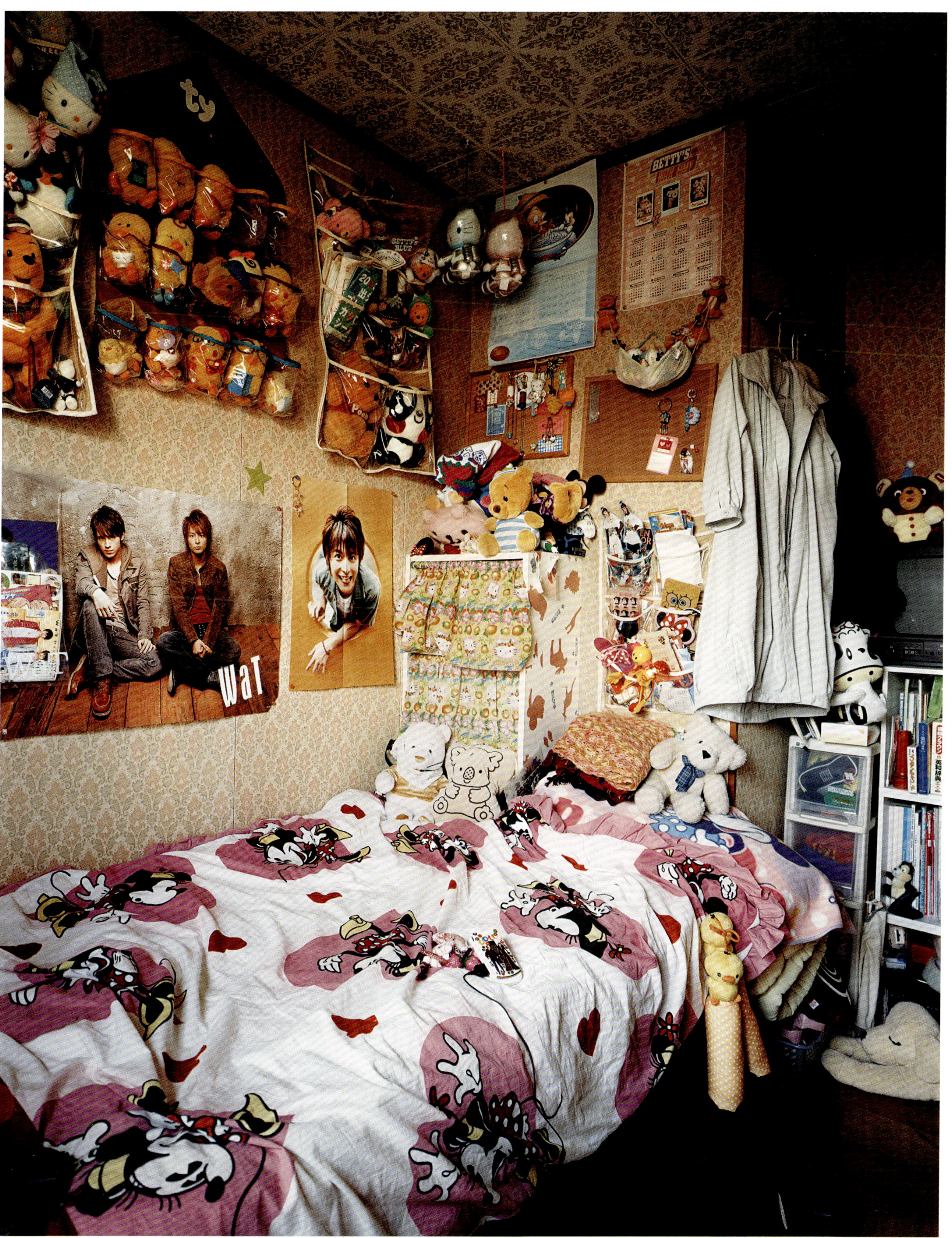
ty
BETTY'S
WaT

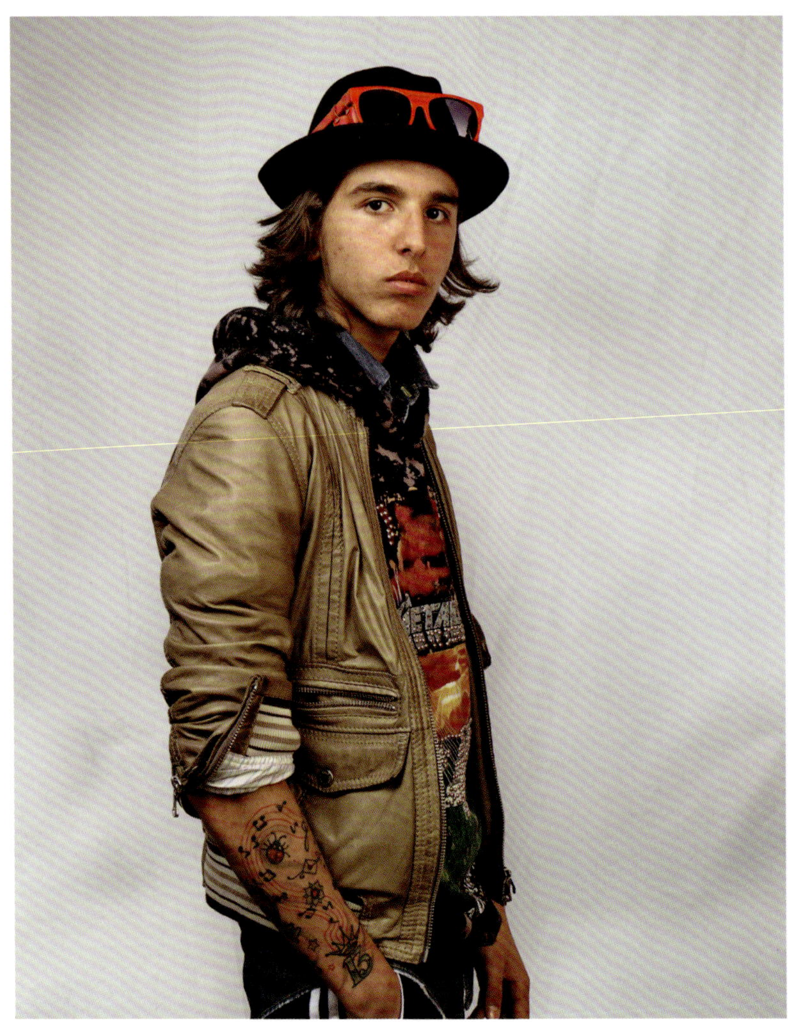

Antonio is seventeen years old and lives with his mother in an apartment block in Naples, Italy. He and his brother are called 'mammoni' ('mummy's boys') because they shared a bed with their mother for many years, following the death of their father in a car crash. Antonio did not move into his own bed until he was sixteen. He does not have to help with household chores. He is a keen body-builder and follows a strict diet to increase his stamina and gain weight. He goes to school on his moped, which his mother bought for him when he was fourteen, but he is not interested in school and can't wait for it to finish. He spends much of his spare time either on his computer, chatting to his 1,300 friends on Facebook, or doing public relations work for a band. He thinks he will probably marry his high school girlfriend, who – he expects – will take over the job of looking after him.

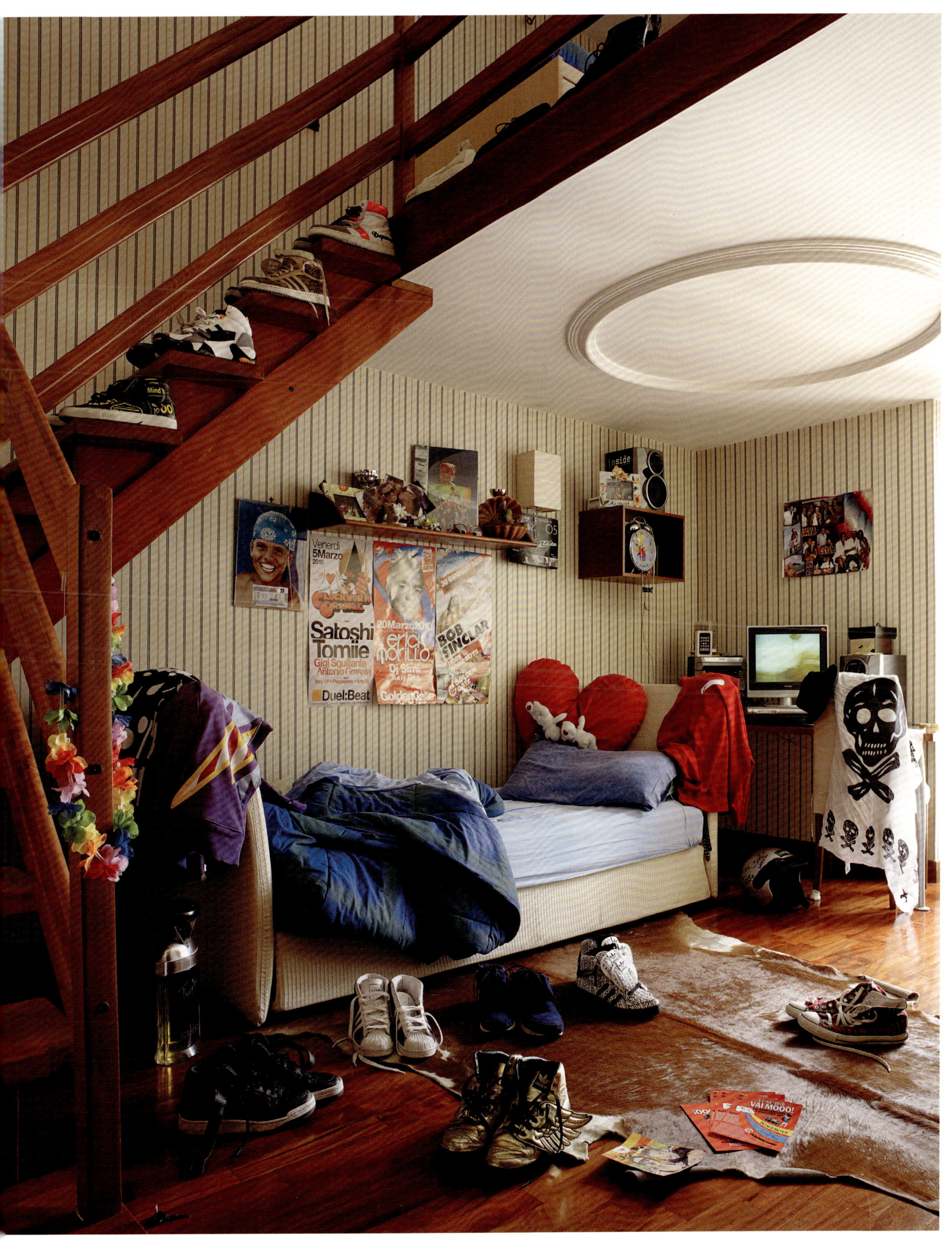

Venerdì
5Marzo
2010
Satoshi
Tomiie
Gigi Squillante
Antonio Grassia
Duel:Beat
20Marzo2010
eric morillo
BOB
SINCLAR
inside
VAI MOOO!

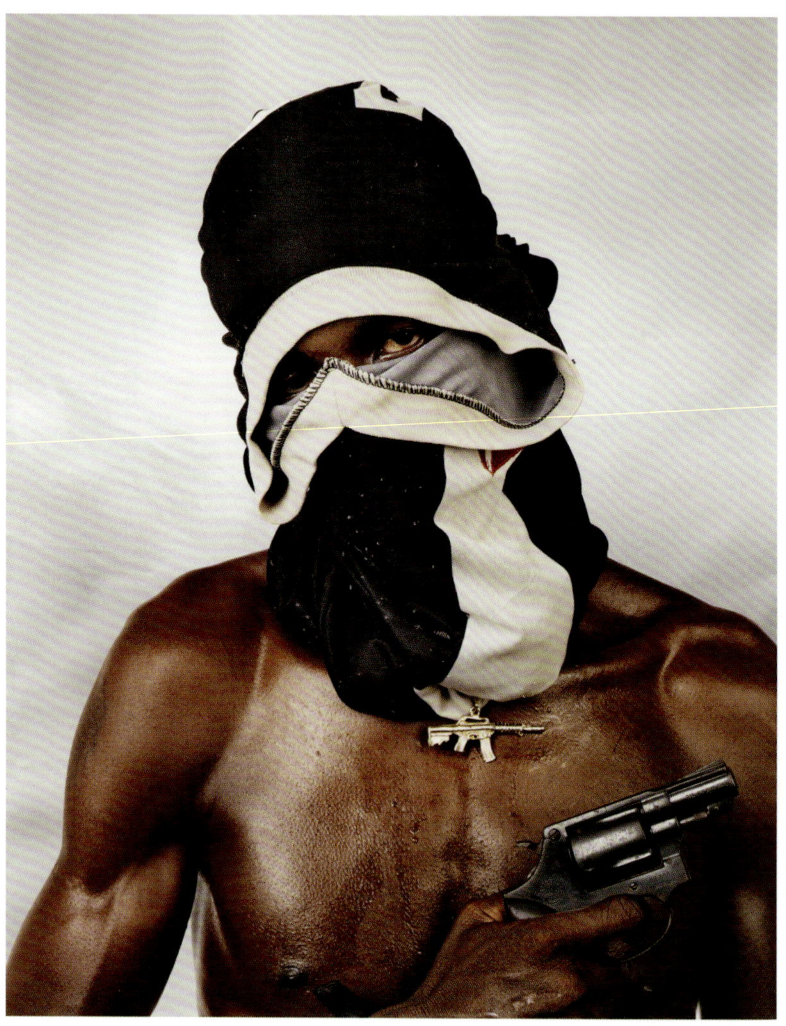

This seventeen-year-old teenager prefers to be known as 'X', after Malcolm X, the black activist. X lives in Complexo da Maré, a 'favela' near the airport in Rio de Janeiro, Brazil, where children from a very young age are coerced into declaring allegiance to one of the gangs in the area. Failure to do so can lead to violent recriminations, or even death. X works as a mid-ranking lieutenant in the Comando Vermelho ('Red Command'), a local drug-dealing gang. One of his duties is to look after 'soldiers' (young gang members) who are positioned around the favela, monitoring police movements. Soldiers set off fireworks to alert the gang if police enter the area. X carries a handgun for protection but also has the use of a powerful rifle, an AK-47, which he loves. His ambition is to be 'boss of the favela'. X has no fixed address. He moves around a lot, often sharing a room with other gang members.

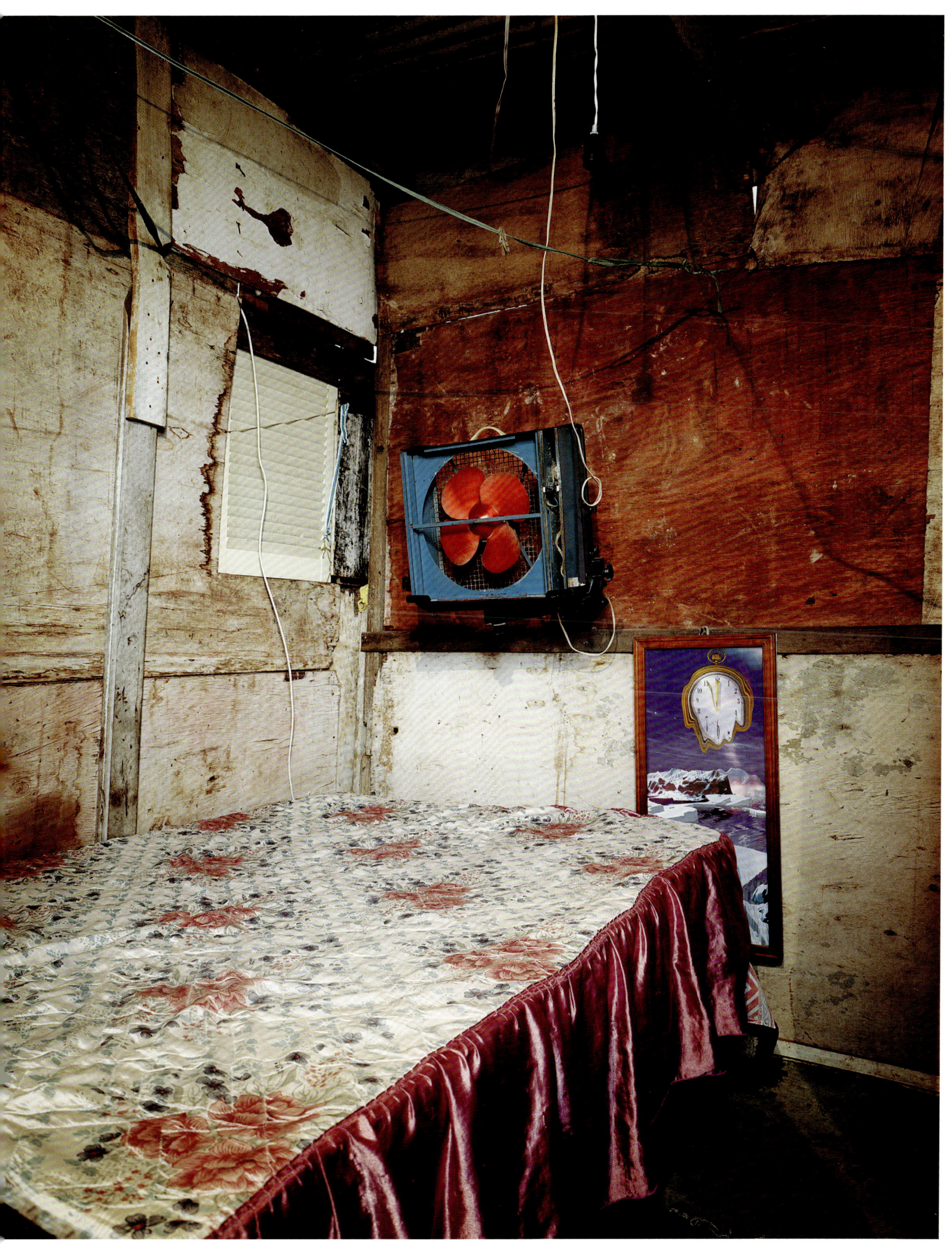

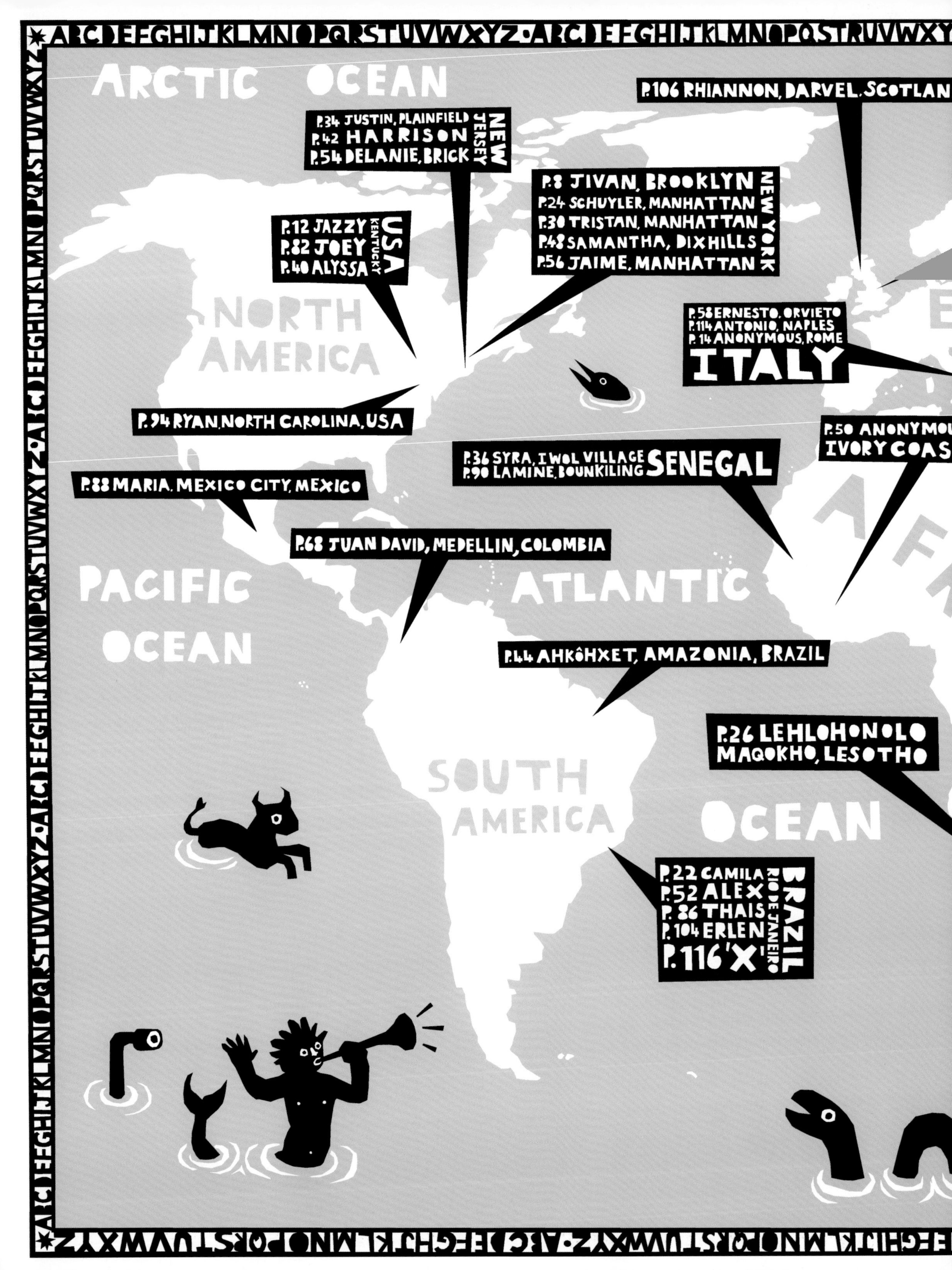
ABCDEFGHIJKLMNOPQRSTUVWXYZ
ARCTIC OCEAN
P.106 RHIANNON, DARVEL, SCOTLAN
P.34 JUSTIN, PLAINFIELD
P.42 HARRISON
P.54 DELANIE, BRICK
NEW JERSEY
P.8 JIVAN, BROOKLYN
P.24 SCHUYLER, MANHATTAN
P.30 TRISTAN, MANHATTAN
P.48 SAMANTHA, DIXHILLS
P.56 JAIME, MANHATTAN
NEW YORK
P.12 JAZZY
P.82 JOEY
P.40 ALYSSA
KENTUCKY
USA
NORTH AMERICA
P.58 ERNESTO, ORVIETO
P.114 ANTONIO, NAPLES
P.14 ANONYMOUS, ROME
ITALY
P.94 RYAN, NORTH CAROLINA, USA
P.50 ANONYMOU
IVORY COAST
P.36 SYRA, IWOL VILLAGE
P.90 LAMINE, BOUNKILING
SENEGAL
P.88 MARIA, MEXICO CITY, MEXICO
P.68 JUAN DAVID, MEDELLIN, COLOMBIA
PACIFIC OCEAN
ATLANTIC OCEAN
P.44 AHKÔHXET, AMAZONIA, BRAZIL
P.26 LEHLOHONOLO MAQOKHO, LESOTHO
SOUTH AMERICA
P.22 CAMILA
P.52 ALEX
P.86 THAIS
P.104 ERLEN
P.116 'X'
RIO DE JANEIRO
BRAZIL

ARCTIC OCEAN

P.70 LEWIS, BARNSLEY, ENGLAND

P.16 HANG
P.78 LI BEIJING, CHINA

P.20 BILAL
P.64 TZVIKA
P.66 DOUHA
P.74 YIFTACH
P.92 HAMDI
WEST BANK

EUROPE

ASIA

P.10 KAYA
P.76 RYUTA
P.112 KANA
JAPAN TOKYO

P.100 JYOTI
P.60 BIKRAM MAKWANPUR, NEPAL

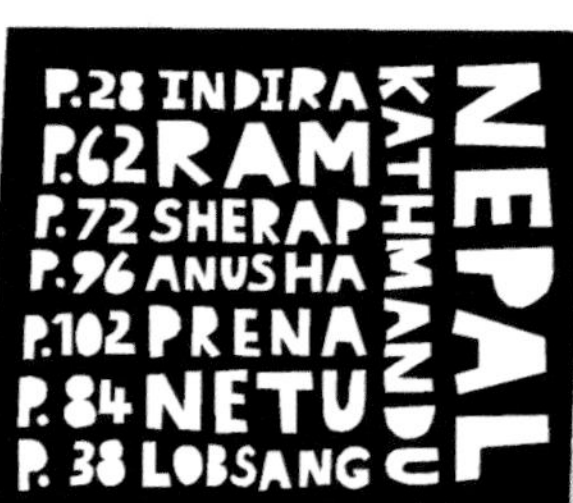

P.46 DONG
P.80 LEI
YUNNAN PROVINCE CHINA

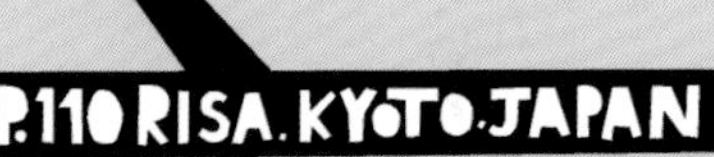

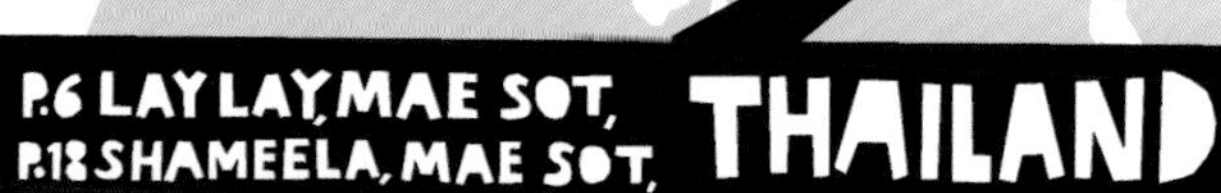

AFRICA

P.98 IRKENA
P.108 NANTIO
LAISAMIS, KENYA

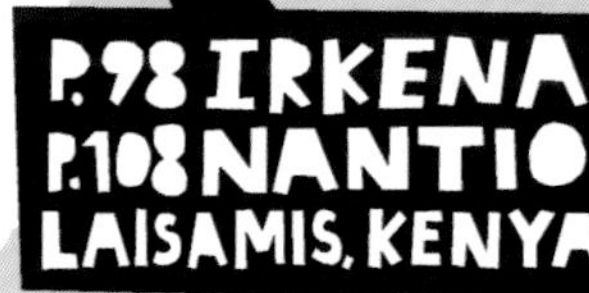

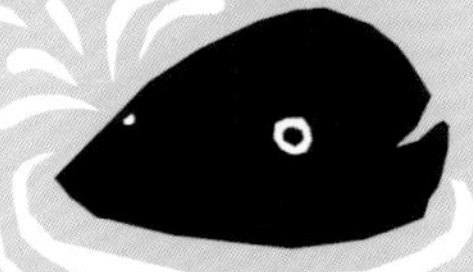

P.32 ROATHY
PHNOM PENH
CAMBODIA

INDIAN

OCEANIA

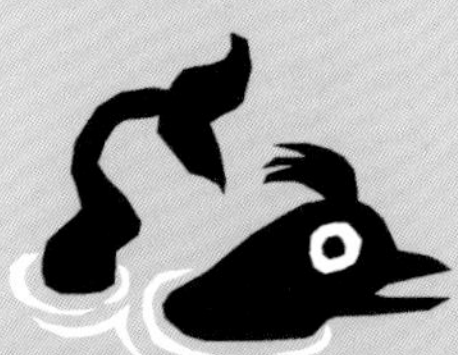

OCEAN

James Mollison was born in Kenya in 1973 and grew up in England. After studying art and design at Oxford Brookes, and later film and photography at Newport School of Art and Design, he moved to Italy to work at Benetton's creative lab, Fabrica. His work has been widely published throughout the world, including by Colors, the New York Times Magazine, the Guardian magazine, the Paris Review, the New Yorker and Le Monde, and his previous books published by Chris Boot include 'James and Other Apes' (2004), 'The Memory of Pablo Escobar' (2007) and 'The Disciples' (2008).

Acknowledgements

'Where Children Sleep' has been supported since its inception by Fabrica, Benetton's communication research centre, and the book's publication is accompanied by an exhibition produced by Fabrica.

Our special thanks are due to Luciano Benetton, Alessandro Benetton, Laura Pollini, Paolo Landi, Bernardo Lecci, Luciana Mattei and Filippo Parisi who have made this project possible.

We have relied on Mimmo Samele, Erik Ravelo, Enrico Bossan, Alfredo Ricca, Anna Dieksi, Stefano Beggiato, Valentino Sabialta, Lionello Boscardi, Carlos Mustienes, Giuliana Rando, Anna Frampton and Amy Flanagan for their help.

We are indebted to Save the Children for their support, their introductions to children in Nepal, China, The West Bank and Italy, and for the first-hand opportunity to understand the organization's work with some of the most neglected children around the world.

Meeting the children in this book was made possible with the help of: Batman Zavareze, Daymo Duncan and Tony Barros (Brazil); Noah Weinzweig, Ting Mai and Liu Chun Hua (China); Rainbow Nelson, Liana Martan, David Parra and Alejandro Lopez-Chicheri (Colombia); Ibrahim Faltas and Alon Farago (Israel & The West Bank); Salvatore Sparavigna (Italy); Rachel Pierre (Ivory Coast); Aya Kaburaki (Japan); Marcus Prior and Yves Niyiragira (Kenya); Manana Mashologu (Lesotho); Santiago Stelley and Claudia Alfaro (Mexico); Heather Sutliff, James Giambron and Suvani Singh Shrestha (Nepal); Mentor Diagne (Senegal); Kate Griffiths, Jennifer Venditti, Zan Ludlum, Ed Kim, and John & Pat Payne (USA).

We are grateful to all the families for showing such hospitality and kindly letting us into their homes.

This book is dedicated to our parents, who gave us wonderful childhoods.

James & Amber Mollison

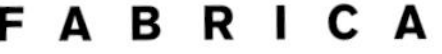

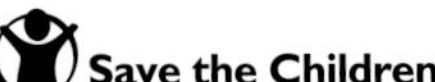